THE INTIMATE FRONTIER

THE INTIMATE FRONTIER

FRIENDSHIP AND CIVIL SOCIETY IN NORTHERN NEW SPAIN

Ignacio Martínez

THE UNIVERSITY OF ARIZONA PRESS

TUCSON

The University of Arizona Press
www.uapress.arizona.edu

We respectfully acknowledge the University of Arizona is on the land and territories of Indigenous peoples. Today, Arizona is home to twenty-two federally recognized tribes, with Tucson being home to the O'odham and the Yaqui. Committed to diversity and inclusion, the University strives to build sustainable relationships with sovereign Native Nations and Indigenous communities through education offerings, partnerships, and community service.

ISBN-13: 978-0-8165-3880-5 (cloth)
ISBN-13: 978-0-8165-5529-1 (paper)
ISBN-13: 978-0-8165-4064-8 (ebook)

Cover design by Carrie House, HOUSEdesign llc

Publication of this book is made possible in part by the proceeds of a permanent endowment created with the assistance of a Challenge Grant from the National Endowment for the Humanities, a federal agency.

Library of Congress Cataloging-in-Publication Data are available at the Library of Congress.

Printed in the United States of America
♾ This paper meets the requirements of ANSI/NISO Z39.48–1992 (Permanence of Paper).

CONTENTS

ACKNOWLEDGMENTS

THIS BOOK COULD NOT HAVE BEEN COMPLETED WITHOUT THE guidance, support, and encouragement of innumerable friends and colleagues. First and foremost my deepest appreciation goes out to my graduate advisors at The University of Arizona. Bert Barickman's insightful inquiries and suggestions about how to engage with a concept as flexible as friendship were instrumental in the writing of this book. Since his passing several years ago, I have thought a lot about what it means to be a mentor, a teacher, and a scholar, and I thank him for having inspired me to excel at all three. Martha Few was tremendously influential in strengthening my theoretical approach. Her insight and vast scholarly expertise always made me feel confident that I was headed in the right direction, even if I wasn't exactly sure what direction that was. Her openness and willingness to read individual chapters of my book will always be appreciated. Finally, my major advisor, Kevin Gosner, provided a sharp and critical eye. Under his guidance I learned how to write and think like a scholar. On several occasions when my spirits were down, Kevin always knew how to convince me that what I was doing was valuable and much needed work.

I cannot imagine a more collegial and intellectually rigorous atmosphere than the history department at the U of A. A special thanks goes out to all those who made my time there both special and formative. In particular, I would like to thank Alex Hidalgo whose friendship and advise was, and continues to be, a beacon along what at times has seemed like a rocky and uncertain road. At the Arizona State Museum, where I worked for many years, I would like to thank Dale Brenneman, Anton Daughters, Megan Sheehan, Lucero Radonic, Monica Young, Rebecca Crocker, Rodrigo Rentería-Valencia, and José Alvarez. Together we spent long hours in the Office of Ethnohistorical Research transcribing, translating, and annotating documents from the Spanish Borderlands. Many of the documents that I have used for this book came from that collective effort.

Only a few years after graduating from the U of A I was lucky enough to be invited to be a founding member of the Southwest Seminar. This Seminar has allowed me to remain current with the latest scholarship on colonial Latin America and has been a continued source of motivation and support in my own work. Here I would like to thank Ryan Kashanipour, Alex Hidalgo, Martha Few, Kevin Gosner, Mark Lentz, Dana Velasco Murillo, José Carlos de la Puente, and Joaquín Rivaya-Martínez. A special thanks is reserved for Jay Harrison who read a number of my chapters, always providing incredibly insightful and encouraging feedback.

At UTEP I'd like to thank my colleagues Ernesto Chávez and Charles and Cheryl Martin for their continued words of support. Cheryl's feedback on my Introduction was important in helping me to restructure my approach, which at the time was still a bit unclear. As department chairs, Sam Brunk and Yolanda Leyva were instrumental in making sure I was not overwhelmed with committee work and that I always had the resources I needed to complete my work. I would especially like to thank Jeff Shepherd for his friendship and for his keen ability to know when a few beers were exactly what I needed.

There are two very important people at UNM that I must also thank: Linda Hall and Charles Truxillo. Linda was formative in my journey toward the professoriate. Though I was only an undergraduate student, Linda allowed me to sign up for her graduate course on charismatic leaders in Latin America. I can honestly say that there wasn't a single class that went by that year when I didn't have my stomach in knots out of anxiety. But her gentle and encouraging demeanor convinced me that I could ultimately be successful in graduate school. Charles was a different sort of animal altogether. His lectures on Chicano and world history made me feel alive and empowered. With him I traveled the world and spent countless hours in bars and at bookstores discussing the most complex of ideas. The elite group of young Chicanos he succeeded in bringing together all possessed grand dreams and ambitions of changing the world. All of us earned professional degrees. In his own unique, yet somewhat destructive way, he inspired us to become great. To Roman, Dennis, Eloy, Eric, Antonio,

Alicia, Marcos, Xavier, Steve, and Mario I will be forever grateful. The friendships we formed during those seminal years, particularly while drinking and debating at the Copper Lounge, will remain one of the happiest and most invigorating times in my life.

A mis padres, Ignacio and Gregoria, gracias por todo su amor y ánimo. A ustedes les debo todo de lo que soy. Los quiero mucho. And lastly, I would like to say to my two daughters, Añieze and Zeñia, and to my wife, Daisy, I love you all more than words can express. Thank you for your support, your hugs, and most of all, your patience. I know this process has not been easy on you. Now that this first book is done, we can enjoy taking our dog Lilly to the park every evening without worrying about me having to get back to work.

THE INTIMATE FRONTIER

Introduction

An Arab who was about to die called his son to him and said: "Tell me my son, how many friends have you gained during my life?" "A hundred friends, I think I have gained." The father said: "A philosopher says that a man cannot count a man as a friend until he has proven his friendship. I am much older than you and I have with difficulty obtained only half of one man as a friend."[1]

THE ELEVENTH-CENTURY PARABLE ABOVE EXPRESSES A UNIVER-sally reoccurring motif, one in which a father about to succumb to the will of nature imparts his final words of wisdom to his son. The subject of his conversation is equally ageless. That the dying father chose to spend his final moments educating his son about the value of true friendship was not without precedent, for friendship has historically been a source of considerable reflection and represents one of the world's most enduring philosophical and literary themes. Over the centuries, friendship ideals have been articulated in innumerable ways, each generation delineating its guidelines and parameters and thus infusing it with a unique expression and significance. Today, friendship remains central to how people worldwide give meaning to their lives. Social media sites such as Facebook have allowed millions of users to count their friends (more accurately called Facebook friends) in the hundreds, sometimes even the thousands, and in so doing have taken side with the son.[2] But as the father so compellingly expressed, to count friends in the hundreds only diminishes the value of true friendship—friends have worth only when they have proven themselves, which can take more than a single lifetime, as evidenced by the fact that on his death-bed the father counted only half a friend.[3] To make his point, the father decided to test his son. He asked him to kill a calf, cut it into pieces, and place the bloodied fragments into a sack. Following this gory sequence, the son was to lay the sack before his "friends," telling them he had killed a man. To his utter surprise, the son discovered that none of them, not even his dearest companions, would help him. Instead, they callously shunned him, fearful of the social stigma their association with him would bring. The father, in not so tender a fashion, had proven his point.[4]

This cautionary apologue leaves us with two thought-provoking questions: How and why do friendship ideals change from generation to generation, century to century, and place to place? And what are the internal (psychological, physiological) and external (social, ecological, political, and economic) factors that shape the various intellectual and quotidian conceptions of friendship? These are questions especially suited to the historian's craft, for they ask us to trace a socially constructed concept across time and space. Friendship ideals in the eleventh-century Arab world, for instance, lacked the cosmic intensity of pre-Columbian Amerindian thought, the ethnic mélange of a place like colonial Mexico City, the political idealism of sixteenth-century Venice, the bonds of sensibility made fashionable among colonial Philadelphians, the fanatical camaraderie of men fighting in the trenches during the First World War, or the joy of immediacy introduced by the wireless revolution. These and countless other cultural and spatiotemporal factors have possessed a significant influence on the manner in which friendship ideals have been historically conceptualized and interpreted, allowing us to submit this rather elusive concept to historical scrutiny and analysis.

Analyzed more broadly, one also finds an exceptional stability and universality to its core tenets. Take just a few examples from the classical world. In the *Sigalovada Sutra*, written in the fourth century BCE, the Buddha provided sage advice to his followers on the nature of friendship. According to this influential guidebook, a true friend must be generous, speak kindly, provide care, be equal, and be truthful. The *Analects* of Confucius, written between the fourth and second centuries BCE, emphasized *xin* (fidelity, faithfulness, or trustworthiness) as the primary characteristic of friendship.[5] Books Eight and Nine of Aristotle's *Nicomachean Ethics*, written during roughly this same period, identified the highest form of friendship as being comprised of perfect virtue. And *Laelius de amiciata* (Laelius on friendship), one of the most influential treatises on friendship in the West, written by Marcus Tullius Cicero during the first century BCE, described ideal friendship as being between men of high status in which loyalty, virtue, reason, reciprocity, and shared interests determined its central worth.

Throughout Mesoamerica indigenous societies maintained friendship ideals that closely reflected those of the ancient world. Nahuatl lyric poetry, frequently sung at gatherings and accompanied by drums and flutes, represented one of its more common forms of transmission. The following poem titled "Friendship on Earth" addresses the notion of self-discovery through friendship by knowing "our faces." As it states, through words spoken in friendship a sincere fellowship will endure into death even though the spoken word remains confined to the world of the living.

> Let us have friends here!
> It is the time to know our faces.
> Only with flowers
> Can our song enrapture.
> We will have gone to His house,
> but our word
> shall live here on earth.
> We will go, leaving behind
> our grief, our song.
> For this will be known,
> the song shall remain real.
> We will have gone to His house,
> but our word
> shall live here on earth.[6]

The second line of this poem is reminiscent of a number of Old World scholars who believed that we could only come to know our true selves by means of a good friend, for true friends were always mirror images of ourselves. *Amicus quid? Alter ego* (What is a friend? Another self), sixteenth-century French humanist Michel de Montaigne famously stated, echoing what was by then an already age-old sentiment.[7]

Among other indigenous peoples of North America such as the Tohono O'odham of Sonora, friendships were cemented through the power of myth and ritual. Drinking, sport, dance, and hunting are commonly portrayed in their literature as social junctures where friendships were forged.[8] The Zuni of New Mexico formed and celebrated *Kihe* (friendship) through a days-long ritual that included a ceremonial dance and an elaborate exchange of gifts. For the Comanche, friendships were divided into *tūbitsinahaitsInūūs* (true friendships) and *haits* (formal friendships), effectively separating those they held in high regard from those who were valued solely as economic partners.[9] Among the Cherokee, *O li* (friendships) between humans and one's own spirit ancestors were central to maintaining balance and harmony in the world. It was in the council house, however, where formal friendships were most clearly expressed and performed.[10]

Central to the classical and indigenous literature on friendship has also been a near-universal consensus on the negative effects of false friendships. There are, wrote the prince Siddhartha, pretenders and false friends who commonly violate the core principles of friendship.[11] Thirteenth-century scholar Boncompagno da Signa (1165–1240) buttressed this assertion when he identified twenty-two versions of the "false friend."[12] Confucius, Cicero, Aelred of Rievaulx, Montaigne, and Kant, among many others, all reached similar conclusions on this point. It is somewhat telling, therefore, that despite minor stylistic and performative variations, societies across the globe and throughout time have embraced remarkably similar friendship ideals.[13] A third and fourth question then need to be asked: Are there, in addition to shifting regional and generational standards, also core or globally acknowledged features to the notion of ideal friendship? If so, what is responsible for this striking uniformity?[14]

Taken together, these four questions provide a working blueprint for how this book approaches the concept and performance of friendship as it relates generally to the far northern frontier of New Spain and specifically to the colonial province of Sonora. My main argument is that the ideals (chapters 1 and 3), logic (chapter 2), rhetoric (chapter 4), and emotions (chapter 5) of friendship played a foundational role in the regional development of an early yet remarkably nuanced, fragile, and sporadic form of civil society (*societas civilis*).[15] Civil society—or more generally speaking, civilized society—was highly touted and debated by scholars throughout much of Spain's American empire from the sixteenth through eighteenth centuries. It addressed two interrelated concepts, both of which were derived from and conversant with European religious and classical ideals.[16] First, civil society was founded on a platform of rational discourse, sociability, and the rule of law and order. Second, civil society postulated a moral imperative that set specific standards for the policing of proper and improper forms of behavior as it related to an organically structured social hierarchy. Undergirding these civic expectations was a rigorous adherence to a patriarchal form of government and to the idea of private property.

Throughout the Americas, civil society, in its Europeanized utterances, was frequently reconceptualized and retooled to fit local needs, but everywhere from the city to the countryside it came to represent "the essential preliminary to the permanent occupation of the land."[17] As a general outline for the colonization of northern New Spain, the idea of *societas civilis* fit squarely within the unique social and ideological contours of frontier society. Yet, because of its political, economic, and military isolation at the furthest reaches of the Spanish Empire, it was essential for Europeans to develop an ideologically relevant and socially acceptable form of friendship that could act as a functional substitute for civil law and governance. In this way, friendship, in its many forms, allowed for the limited implementation of civil society. Conceptualizing civil society within this unique intellectual framework creates an opening from which to incorporate otherwise marginal frontier communities into the larger discourse on empire. While modern definitions of civil society along the U.S.-Mexico borderlands have embraced a specific set of social and political standards, I argue that its ideological and behavioral beginnings rested firmly in the early colonial period, and that relationships of amity comprised its core. A targeted focus on friendship thus allows us to talk about northern New Spain's civic origins in a way that other studies have not.[18]

In both Spain and New Spain, it was the model of the Greek polis that informed the character and temperament of civil society.[19] Here, however, it represented "an agro-urban community based not on a 'covenant' among consenting individuals [as in Greece] but on a 'political' entity of functionally integrated groups."[20] Though Sonora remained sparsely populated for much of the colonial period, the process of colonization that largely began in the seventeenth century fundamentally upset and reoriented relations among members of that society, redefining their purpose of association while recasting hierarchies of power that separated people into functional categories.[21] Within this colonial superstructure rested the very seeds of civil society, for true friendship was possible, at least ideally, only among *gente de razón* (people of reason), and it was chiefly behavior that distinguished those who had reason from those who didn't.[22] Man, as the Thomists of the sixteenth century believed, is what man does. As I argue in this book, it was the conceptual value of friendship, which remained at the center of European interpretations of civilized society, that laid the initial foundations for the mental, emotional, and, to a lesser extent, physical construction of empire at the "rim of Christendom." But as these seeds blossomed into a series of intricate and highly sophisticated relationships between colonial subjects (mostly

Indians) and agents of empire (mostly Spaniards or mestizos), friendship, in its various manifestations, was pushed toward the periphery of colonial thought in order that it might embrace the full extent of acceptable nuance and pragmatism. As a number of recent studies have shown, nuance, universal along the edges of empire, frequently fed directly into irony since it was often the case that the Crown's most subjugated vassals were also its most loyal and ardent agents.

Spaniards were therefore not the only ones who participated in the gradual assemblage of empire. Indians also influenced and, in many cases, actively contributed to a variety of economic and political discourses—in which friendship emerged as a major component—also making them active participants in the promotion and maintenance of empire. "The classical image of the Indian as a victim continues to be true in many respects," writes Henry Kaman, "but it was only a section of the role played by the indigenous civilizations of America, where the Indian was no less a creator than a victim."[23] Martin Austin Nesvig goes a step further, arguing that in many cases the "Indigenous peoples of Mexico operated less as oppressed and conquered victims and more as shrewd and self-interested operatives involved in a complex process of mitigation."[24] Private and public relationships of amity between Natives and Spaniards thus redefined the parameters of power and authority in colonial Sonora, adumbrating, figuratively and materially, what Cynthia Radding has described as "landscapes of power."[25] These symbiotic relationships flourished despite early missionary efforts to segregate Indian neophytes (often forcefully) into mission communities, away from what they saw as the corrupt and corrupting influences of secular Spaniards. In fact, the level of interaction, mainly between elite Indians and Spaniards, remained significant throughout much of this period. It wasn't until the 1750s that political and administrative leaders such as Viceroy Revillagigedo (1738–99) and José de Gálvez (1720–87) began to advocate for a renewed call to "civilize" *all* Natives by integrating indigenous and Spanish communities (perhaps with the added goal of more effectively exploiting Indian labor) in the belief that through their commercial dealings with Spaniards, Indians would more readily embrace the rudimentary trappings of civilization.[26]

Working within a similar frame of mind, a good number of Franciscans, who by 1768 had taken over the northern missions from the recently expelled Jesuits, also promoted and formally encouraged greater interethnic cooperation and friendships. Thus, the idea of "civilizing" indigenous peoples, which initially began with early Jesuit missionaries who saw Natives as mere seedlings in dire need of spiritual watering, culminated in the combined administrative effort to fully integrate them economically. This point of view was by no means universal, however. Influential Mexican-born criollos such as José Antonio de Alzate y Ramírez (1737–99) and Francisco Javier Clavijero (1731–87) continued to adhere to the belief that if some Indians were vice ridden and "uncivilized" in their behavior, it was because of their dealings with immoral Spaniards, for it was well understood by many that "the shadow of a Spaniard kills the Indian."[27] Overall, throughout much of the eighteenth century significant efforts were made by Bourbon reformers to streamline the economic, ethnic, and cultural ethos of the Spanish borderlands.[28] But it remained the sophisticated and highly nuanced temperament of amity, guided as it was by ideology and emotion and braced by relationships of power and pragmatism, that laid the initial foundation for the later implementation and measured success of Bourbon policies.

The quality and character of these early colonial friendships were subject to an ongoing and highly contentious interethnic dialogue (verbal as well as performative) over what it meant to behave and act as a friend. As I show, defining the parameters of friendship and then creating associations based on those parameters was essential to the colonial project because it legitimized its own purpose while setting the stage for the future development in the nineteenth and twentieth centuries of fully developed political associations and economic institutions—and, ultimately, the creation of a national identity. Put plainly, in the absence of a strong centralized state, violence and friendship framed the contours of Sonoran society. Both extremes shifted back and forth in a seesaw of ambiguities and contradictions that Raphael Brewster Folsom has referred to as the "ironies of Empire."[29] Within this calculating and often Machiavellian social environment in which power and influence were in a constant state of flux, friendship became more than an idealized standard by which to judge and police indigenous behavioral norms; it also developed into a strategic ideological and cultural expedient through which Natives challenged colonialism and negotiated the limits of power. The tenuous origins of civil society developed within this highly contentious social laboratory in which friendships set the social and ideological parameters for conflict and, conversely, cooperation. Far from the coffee houses of Restoration London or the lecture halls of the Republic of Letters, civil society in Sonora stumbled forward amid the ambiguities and contradictions of colonialism and the obstacles posed by the isolation and violence of the Sonoran Desert.

To gain a clearer perspective on the connection between amity and civil society as it existed on the northern fringes of the Spanish Empire, I analyze criminal proceedings, Jesuit letters and treatises, travel journals, and bureaucratic reports. Though I also make use of Native poetry, myths, and stories, the bulk of my sources, many of which have been previously published and translated, come from seventeenth- and eighteenth-century clerics, soldiers, and civil magistrates. Yet, while "there are two sides to every friendship, and often only one subject who testifies," as Vanessa Smith has written in her work on friendship in Tahiti, there remains plenty of testimony from indigenous informants and declarants in the documentary record to make credible and convincing arguments about their friendship practices.[30] But it remains limited, and in most cases the Indian voice can only be inferred though Spanish scribes and interrogators. Keeping in mind the importance of rectifying such a conceptual imbalance, I provide in the chapters to follow important intimations of the ways in which indigenous peoples used friendship for their own strategic purposes.[31] So, while their unfiltered voice may be sporadic, their presence is without exception seen and felt everywhere.

The feminine voice is another issue altogether. Due partly to my targeted interest in the study of masculinity, and largely because of the male-oriented content of my sources, the feminine voice is virtually absent save for a few select instances. That is not to suggest that women do not constitute a viable venue through which to study friendship. Indeed, focusing on the nature of female friendships—Inquisitional records, for instance, frequently point to *malas amistades* (bad friendships) among women living along the frontier—or perhaps juxtaposing male and female relationships, as Cassandra Good has recently done, could prove extremely illuminating for borderland scholars.[32] Laura Alejandra Buentura, Ana María Atondo Rodríguez, Amanda Herbert, and Marilyn Yalom have already produced important works that speak directly to this subject matter.[33]

Despite any conceptual shortcomings produced by the current study, centering on this relatively remote and isolated region of the Spanish Empire allows us to identify many of the characteristics and qualities of friendship that were culturally and intellectually specific while simultaneously highlighting its unchanged and unchanging qualities that linked northern New Spain to a habitus of universal traits and dispositions. Throughout the chapters that follow, I position friendship alongside a continuum of other factors such as marriage, violence, sexuality, religion, land rights, and ideology that acted as sites of power through which residents of Sonora navigated the frequently hostile and subversive social landscape.

This book is heavily indebted to the likes of Herbert Eugene Bolton, John Francis Bannon, Edward Spicer, Ernest Burrus, José Luis Mirafuentes Galván, Charles Polzer, Peter Dunne, David Weber, John Kessell, Susan Deeds, and Cynthia Radding for having laid much of the groundwork for the study of the Sonoran frontier.[34] Nevertheless, I chose to focus my attention on the colonial province of Sonora from the seventeenth and eighteenth centuries because I believe scholars have yet to fully explore and research the immensely complex web of interpersonal relationships and layers of emotional intelligence inherent in this region of the Spanish borderlands. Understanding this emotional ingenuity as expressed through friendship is essential if we are to achieve a fuller understanding of frontier peoples and of their strategies for survival and power. I therefore focus on four principal questions: (1) How did relationships of amity, both authentic (emotional) and feigned (strategic), foster the negotiation for space and power at the edges of empire? (2) To what extent did indigenous peoples manipulate their friendships with Europeans and mixed-race peoples in an effort to derail the negative effects of colonialism, and how in turn was this deception understood and dealt with? (3) To what end did Europeans, Natives, and mixed-race peoples utilize the rhetoric and emotional properties of friendship in their attempts to colonize and foster a nascent form of civil society? And lastly, (4) what were the rules of friendship at the edges of empire, and how were these rules conceived of and ultimately enforced?

In an effort to ascertain answers to these complex questions, I build on the insights of Albert Hurtado, who has emphasized that colonial frontiers in North America represented "intimate spaces" where the cultural categories of power were constantly being negotiated and rearticulated by its multiethnic inhabitants.[35] By focusing specifically on friendship, I advance the scope and utility of Hurtado's argument by positioning it along the social continuum of intimacy and power. I also build on Folsom's notion of "ironies of Empire," emphasizing what I consider to be the most ironic of all colonial relationships: friendship between previous and sometimes current enemies. In colonial Sonora, the language of friendship was commonly evoked despite the persistence of adverse and often hostile relations. Folsom's acute attention to the inherent complexities and contradictions in colonial relationships of power is therefore useful for understanding life on this colonial frontier.[36] The present book not only recognizes the ubiquity of these colonial ironies and contradictions, it goes a step further, arguing that they formed a vital and necessary part of the highly sophisticated logic that structured colonial behavior. In other words, the ironies and contradictions present in colonial society facilitated—for those most attuned to the nuances of frontier life—the navigation and manipulation of social space and power. Ambiguity of this sort, while valuable under the right conditions, also made life on the frontier unstable and highly unpredictable.

This book is an attempt to tell, through the purview of a regional study, a universal story about the ways in which colonial actors used and performed amity in colonial settings, thereby adding to the recent effort to understand frontiers and borderlands within a comparative and global framework.[37] In doing this, *The Intimate Frontier* builds on the most recent scholarship on frontiers and borderlands, which aims to expose the complexities, nuances, and contradictions inherent in the various public and private dialogues that Europeans, Natives, and mixed-race people had with one another. By addressing friendship as my central category of analysis, I aim to redirect the study of the frontier away from being perceived solely as a site of incessant violence and despair (commonplace topics in the historiography) toward a place where bouts of hostility went hand in hand with authentic and oftentimes feigned relationships of amity and goodwill. Although violence, as Miguel León-Portilla, Ana María Alonso, James Brooks, Thomas Sheridan, Ned Blackhawk, Pekka Hämäläinen, Lance Blyth, and David Yetman have argued, shaped the mental world of frontier settlers, friendship, I maintain, structured the social mechanisms of livability.[38] I am not simply saying that there were periods of war and periods of peace—that fact seems self-evident and has been outlined by a number of scholars. Rather, I maintain that throughout these oscillating periods of violence and tranquility, friendship remained a constant strategic variable in the way people navigated their social landscapes. The brand of friendship that was forged along the far northern provinces of the Spanish Empire, while ideologically influenced by a number of New and Old World intellectuals, religious thinkers, Native leaders, and administrators and settlers, was specifically tailored to accommodate the harsh realities of frontier life—namely, its isolation and distance from colonial centers, the constant violence and uncertainty inherent in everyday life, and the harsh climatological and ecological conditions of the Sonoran Desert.

Defining Friendship

The study of friendship is haunted by the problem of definition. It can, and often does, have multiple meanings and can refer to anything from an economic or political association to an emotional comradeship. Friendships can be inherited or they can be acquired; they can be highly ritualistic or they can be casual.[39] In Spanish America, friendships held diverse meanings and responsibilities and were used for a number of purposes from forging local alliances between Indians and Spaniards to cementing emotional and spiritual ties between the monarch and his American vassals.[40] This definitional quandary, write Amit Desai and Evan Killick, has compelled scholars to "stabilize the category" by constructing workable frameworks and typologies.[41] "Is friendship," they write, "a relationship characterized by autonomy, sentiment, individualism, lack of ritual and lack of instrumentality? Or are these requirements peculiarly Western expressions of friendship imposed on other places and times?"[42] Richard Godbeer and Dale Kent astutely remind us that our modern conception of what friendship is or ought to be oftentimes clouds our ability to gage the ways in which it was understood and practiced in earlier centuries.[43] Similarly, write Desai and Kilick, "the way in which friendship acts to express fixity and fluidity in diverse social worlds, is as exciting and problematic for the people that practice friendship, as for the social scientists that study it."[44] Therefore, according to these four scholars, greater significance and explanatory potential reside within the ideologies, spaces, and rhetoric that shape particular expressions of friendship than in any single definitional standard. Like them, I shy away from isolating a fixed and unbending definition; rather, I hope to identify the various colonial disguises friendship wore, the crevasses under which it lurked, the manner in which it made itself public, the timing of these appearances, and most importantly, the conflictive process by which it acquired meaning. It is precisely this social process of hide-and-seek—of submission and contestation—that makes the study of friendship equal parts elusive and fascinating.

Nonetheless, there remain a number of interesting commonalities across time and space that allow us to place friendship within a social framework that can help us locate a suitable starting point for our discussion. There are two main areas from which scholars have already made significant headway in outlining the parameters of friendship for colonial New Spain: friendship as a vector for and of socialization (as in relations of *compadrazgo* [godparentage], marriage, or other nonkin or fictive kinship-based associations)[45] and intimate friendships (mostly male but often female as well) and their connection to gender and/or sexuality. Allow me to provide some context for these approaches. In New Spain friendships were formed through a multitude of social networks. Friendships forged at taverns, work sites, markets, universities, seminaries, missions, and in the barracks represented important conduits for the transmission of knowledge about social norms and behavioral expectations.[46] As such, these friendships became important pathways for socialization—although the temperament of a friendship fostered in a tavern was of a plainly distinct quality than a friendship established at a seminary or a café. In this way, the particular behavioral codes and ethics of a friendship oftentimes reflected the social conditions under which it originated. It is important, however, to acknowledge that a person could, over the course of a single lifetime, experience and perform numerous friendship styles (often simultaneously), thus highlighting the incredible versatility with which people, then as now, engage with the world around them.

Take as a more modern example the *palomillas* of south Texas, in which young Mexican-American/Chicano men formed friendship associations that facilitated their entrance into civil society.[47] Formed during the 1960s, these associations consisted of men who "while away the hours telling stories, discussing one another's amorous adventures, drinking, arranging such social events as dances and barbecues, and in discussions of problems in which they share concern. It is in the *palomilla*, rather than in his family, that a boy becomes a man and learns to express himself as such."[48] This pattern of friendship is remarkably similar to the "middle ground of sociability," which Sarah Chambers has argued was highly structured by gendered space, though in the particular case of the *palomillas*, it was an exclusively male space.[49] According to anthropologist Arthur Rubel, these friendship associations were especially important because they created the necessary conditions whereby men could act out in a manner not suitable at home; it was an accepted way to circumvent familial structures without abandoning or destroying them.[50] In the process, these men, linked through ties of friendship, learned the moral codes and behavioral expectations of their specific social environment.

Anthropologists such as Eric Wolf and George Foster have also been interested in addressing how specific forms of friendship were reflected in societal structures.[51] Writing at about the same time as Rubel, Foster interpreted friendship as an atomistic social system whereby amicable connections were often formed outside the sanctity of the home (a theme we will revisit later in the book) and based on a contractual relationship that he called a "dyadic contract."[52] These contracts represented the origins of reciprocity. They were informal and, in most cases, lacked a ritual or legal foundation. "The dyadic contract," notes Foster, "as expressed within the formal systems of the family, *compadrazgo*, and neighborhood-friendship, provides the institutional framework for organizing most interpersonal relations within the community. Each of these systems provides norms that define the ideal behavior appropriate to the settings in which people find themselves."[53] Friendship among neighborhood residents, for instance, embodied a different set of behavioral ideals, patterns, and expectations than among families or *compadres* (godparents).

Embracing a similar framework but using a different set of methodological tools, sociologists have long maintained that people associated by way of close friendships have tended to adopt similar perspectives on a wide range of issues, such as occupation, dress, religion, race, sex, ethnic language, political views, and behaviors and mannerisms.[54] Homophily of this sort has been a long-held convention stretching back for millennia. Ancient Greek scholars such as Polybius (200–118 BCE) were fond of reminding their reading audience that friends should share the love of similar things (self, family, country) and have a common hatred of other things, while Plutarch (CE 46–120) noted that "friendships seek to effect a thorough-going likeness in character, feeling, language, pursuits, and dispositions."[55] Modern sociologists, in addition to feminists and queer activists, have refocused much of this early attention toward homophily onto the voluntary nature of friendship, challenging in the process the earlier anthropological and sociological scholarship that emphasized formal and contractual systems of responsibility associated with the family and *compadrazgo*. For scholars like Gloria Anzaldúa and Ray Pahl, friendship (same-sex or otherwise) has served as an important relational structure, liberating many gays and lesbians from the oppressive constraints of biology and familial obligation. For these scholars, then, friendships represented "families of choice" free from the rigid demands of "communities of fate."[56]

Over the last two decades, studies into the history of emotions have further elaborated the role of friendship in society.[57] The study of emotions, which began at the turn of the twentieth century with the scholarly works of Johan Huizinga, Norbert Elias, and Lucien Febvre,[58] has been at the center of a number of scholarly fields from political science (determining voting behavior or the psychological traits of Republicans or Democrats)[59] and behavioral economics (determining buying behavior) to anthropology, sociology, history, and even neuroscience. A number of scholars believe, for instance, that as science progresses a physiological, evolutionary, or chemical analysis of the role of neurons, neurotransmitters, and hormones could possibly provide us with a sharper image of how emotion generally and friendship specifically functions at the cellular level. Such studies, controversial as they might be, could give us greater insight into how human societies across the globe have engaged with and structured their particular emotional and behavioral standards. Anthropologist Daniel Hruschka has made significant headway in this endeavor, but, he maintains, it will take time for scholars of the humanities to embrace science or biology as tools of analysis. "The fact that there are so few observations about the physiological underpinnings of friendship," he writes, "says more about the relatively short time period in which they have been studied than about the relative importance in the functioning of friendship."[60]

All this is not to say that there are predetermined laws in nature or biology for how friendship is or should be practiced. Suppositions of this sort, which stretch back millennia to ancient thinkers who believed that the laws that governed the natural world also governed human action, have been largely laid to rest. Jon Elster, a prominent rational choice theorist, challenged this theory when in 1989 he argued that the social sciences were "light years away from the stage at which it will be possible to formulate general-law-like regularities about human behavior."[61] Octavio Paz made this exact claim decades earlier when he wrote in an essay from *El orgo philantrópico* (The Philanthropic Ogre) that "los hechos históricos no están gobernados por leyes o, al menos, esas leyes no has sido descubiertas" (historical events are not governed by laws, at least those laws have yet to be discovered).[62] During much of the colonial period, however, Europeans and criollos adhered somewhat faithfully to an understanding of society, especially of indigenous society, that focused on the very existence of such universal laws.[63]

While it may seem convenient to assume that similarities in race, ethnicity, class, sex, *calidad* (social race),[64] and perhaps even gender and birthplace functioned as stabilizing forces in the formation and development of friendships in colonial Spanish America, Douglas Cope aptly reminds us that throughout its tumultuous history such social constructs have never been entirely secure.[65] We should not so easily assume, he argues, that people simply followed the socially prescribed dictates regarding their "proper" roles in society. These social identities were evoked situationally and were constantly being leveraged, abandoned, manipulated, and redefined—obviously to the extent that it was possible to do so in colonial society. Therefore, while friendships lubricated the transmission and adoption of certain ideas, behaviors, and emotional styles, they always proceeded in lockstep with larger structural changes in society that occurred at the local, regional, and empire-wide levels. Those most adroit at reading and interpreting changes in the social climate adapted accordingly. But, as is universally the case, the level of skill in evaluating social change varied greatly from individual to individual, which perforce meant that friendships were almost always messy and very often unpredictable and counterintuitive.

Frameworks for the study of friendship have also rested on the manner in which scholars have read and interpreted the performance of friendship, especially in relation to gender and sexuality.[66] How, for instance, do we judge friendships in which the individuals involved caressed, kissed, held hands, and verbally expressed love for one another? Were these associations homosexual? Possibly. But as Godbeer and Daniel Yaconove note, for premodern men living in colonial America, intimacy of this sort was not necessarily an indication of homosexuality since, in the first place, such a social identity did not exist.[67] "Instead of imposing our own assumption onto the evidence and then concluding that such men must have been in denial about the true nature of their feelings for one another—in other words, assuming that they were closeted gay men," writes Godbeer, "premodern American men embraced a range of possibilities for relating to other men that included intensely physical yet non-sexual relationships."[68] We must get away from assuming that passionate friendships, as evidenced by sentimental letters of love and affection, were clear-cut indicators of homosexuality.

A rather insightful example comes from the work of anthropologist Ruben Reina, whose 1960s case study of friendship patterns in Santa Cruz de Chinautla, Guatemala, outlined two distinct models of intimacy among teenage boys.[69] Reina's research illustrates that among heterosexual male friends from this community, kissing, holding hands, and joking about marrying one another were considered perfectly commonplace. Though some scholars may find this behavior suspect, Reina concluded nothing of the sort. Everyone in Santa Cruz, he wrote, understood intimacy of this kind as entirely within the range of acceptable male behavior. Godbeer found a similar acceptance of intimacy among devout New Englanders: "Declarations of love by one man to another would not automatically have suggested to relatives or neighbors that sexual relations might be taking place. Most Anglo-Americans living in the colonial and revolutionary periods," he argued, "treated emotional ties between male friends as quite distinct from sexual desire."[70] Even during the medieval period, notes Stephen Jaeger, there existed an identifiable difference between the homoerotic and the homosocial with the latter being the dominant model for much of that time.[71]

We cannot, therefore, unambiguously accept that young men who loved each other, and expressed that love through physical closeness or in letters, necessarily wanted to have sexual relations. Yet we also cannot discount the fact that in colonial Mexico, as several scholars have acknowledged, close friendships could in certain instances be indicative of homosexual relationships or, as in the case of celibate monks, of a sublimated sexuality.[72] This was certainly the case among fifth-century (BCE) Athenian pederasts.[73] George Mosse has quite rightly reasoned that "the history of sexuality cannot be separated from the history of personal relationships, and especially that of friendship."[74] Though I would add that the history of friendship need not necessarily be tied to the history of sexuality as the Rubel and Reina case studies clearly show. While the potential for a closeted same-sex relationship always remains an intriguing possibility, arriving at such a conclusion should be achieved cautiously and with a healthy level of skepticism.[75] It is quite likely that a sizable percentage of sentimental friendships, which have been read as homosexual, were simply influenced by the language of sentimentality that was prevalent throughout the Atlantic World during the seventeenth and eighteenth centuries.

Rebecca Earle has isolated this linguistic "inflation," precisely in the manner in which the language of love was used during the eighteenth century. Writes Earle, "The increase in affectionate language within the family more broadly, which has been observed in eighteenth-century correspondence elsewhere in Europe, suggests that a language of sensibility had penetrated the Hispanic world."[76] David Weber has similarly acknowledged that during the late eighteenth century "*love* and *kindness* became fashionable watchwords in the missions and Indian parishes of Spanish America," which reflected a new discourse of "enlightened sensibility towards Indians."[77] As evidenced by Reina's Guatemalan case study, this same language continued to thrive in some communities well into the twentieth century. It is in the very study of the language of sentimentality and its transatlantic circulation and implementation to which, I believe, scholars should direct more of their attention. "The culture of sentimental friendship," writes Godbeer,

was a transatlantic phenomenon, by no means unique to early American society. But it would acquire a particular and explicitly political significance for North Americans during the revolutionary period, when the encouragement of intense and loving male friendships came to be seen as crucial to the nation-building project and the creation of worthy republican citizens. . . . Drawing on the ideas of moral philosophers who stressed the importance of sympathetic friendship in nurturing social benevolence, republican thinkers crafted a blueprint for nationhood that shifted attention away from patriarchal authority toward fraternal collaboration and called for the active encouragement of brotherly love between friends.[78]

In northern New Spain, there was no real conception of a national identity prior to the nineteenth century. According to Stuart Voss, it wasn't until the late eighteenth century that a "distinct, lasting, regional society took shape."[79] Up to that point, the language of amity, as I assert in this book, was utilized as a way of gaining advantage within the colonial superstructure and as a means of cementing bonds of loyalty in an effort to negotiate power, thus setting the stage for civilized society.

Locating Friendship in the Archives

The archival sources for northern New Spain occasionally provide insightful glimpses into friendship rituals. They cast silhouettes that, however faintly, outline the makeup of personal friendships. And quite regularly they divide Native peoples into categories of friendly and unfriendly Indians. Many scholars have confidently affirmed that allusions to *indios amigos* (Indian friends or, perhaps more accurately, friendly Indians) found in colonial documents represented little more than references to either cooperative Indians or military allies.[80] While accurate in many cases, colonial documents also distinguish between the two, commonly making reference to certain groups and individuals as being both friends and/or allies.[81] In other instances, frontier Indians were expected to live "with friendship and quiet" in addition to properly carrying out their function as allies.[82] Similarly, legal documents from this period make the distinction between emotional ties of amity and strategic ones.[83] The conflation of allies with friends was also quite common among Middle Republic Romans who spoke of Rome's allies as also being their friends, but took care to make important distinctions between the two.[84] Thus it makes a great deal of scholarly sense to look at friendship as both a generic catch-all phrase for labeling nonhostile Indians and as a personal and potentially emotional relationship. As Graham Smith astutely suggests, "Without friendship—without the bonds between person and person—no recognizable human world is possible."[85] The story behind indios amigos and *indios enemigos* (unfriendly or hostile Indians), specifically, and friendship, generally, is therefore far more interesting and convoluted than scholars have previously acknowledged. As I argue in this book, the generalized language of friendship, widely utilized along the edges of the Spanish Empire, belonged to a larger system of representative authority that reinforced the colonial state's attempt to exert hegemonic control upon its denizens and over their emotional and moral states of being.

Colonial Sonorans used the language of friendship to convey sentiment, to promote social and political agendas, and to advocate for a structured hierarchy of behavior. They also used friendship as a principle of social organization, whereby the dual categories of enemies and friends defined the mental parameters of frontier life, thus constituting the conceptual simplicity that was representative of the Spanish medieval mind. As Ann Stoler has written, "Colonial state projects . . . attended minutely to the distribution of appropriate affect (what sentiments could be shown toward, and shared with, whom), to the relations in which carnal desires could be safely directed, and to prescriptions for comportment that could distinguish colonizer from colonized."[86] Others such as political scientist James C. Scott have reasoned that while the state constantly seeks to find ways to control the psychological, emotional, and physical manner in which people live their lives, subaltern groups maintain their own strategies and logic for subverting social control.[87]

It is precisely this type of emotional manipulation through language and state efforts at normalizing acceptable behavior—which I have isolated in the available sources for colonial Sonora—that I see functioning in the core concept of friendship.[88] A central feature of this book looks at how the state, through its agents (conquistadores, missionaries, administrators, and soldiers), sought to foster the language of amity with the aim, on the one hand, of creating a simplified social structure and, on the other, of regulating subaltern behaviors and emotion.[89] The process of regulating affect was partly accomplished through the long-held ideal of "civilizing" and Christianizing Natives. But, as I highlight in chapters 2, 4, and 5, two could play at that game. As frontier society grew in complexity, indigenous and mixed-race people (who in many cases were also agents of empire) skillfully utilized the language of friendship and the performance of emotion to their respective purposes, becoming in the process masters of manipulation and deception. According to Barbara Rosenwein, people frequently vacillate among different "emotional communities," adjusting their emotional behaviors accordingly.[90] Sonora was no exception. This subtle (and often not so subtle) back-and-forth drama became a chief characteristic of life on the frontier, continually redefining the way in which ethnic groups on all sides saw and understood their connections to one another. Given that the potential for exploitation was so great, why then were friendships so important for colonial Sonorans? One of the main goals driving this book is to show that despite the potential for manipulation and exploitation, the benefits of friendship typically outweighed its drawbacks.

In most social circumstances, as in the ones highlighted in this book, it paid to be a friend so long as it paid to be a friend. In colonial Sonora, friendships were sincere and authentic when they had to be and cunningly malleable when the circumstances demanded it. Susan Deeds has labeled this kind of complex social maneuvering "mediated opportunism," the highly nuanced process by which Natives "formulate mixed strategies and exercise choices in adapting to changing cultural and ecological circumstances."[91] This constant give-and-take required Sonorans of all ethnic backgrounds to become acute students of their social surroundings. Just like twenty-first-century Mexicans, colonial Sonorans were highly attuned calculating machines, always juxtaposing risk and reward. Would aiding Captain So-and-So on his campaign against indios enemigos help me or perhaps members of my indigenous community to gain access to chocolate, reduced labor demands, Spanish weapons, horses, loot, or perhaps some much-needed social status? What are the chances, given our enemy's significant resources and size, that I will win military accolades, thus enhancing my perceived masculinity and by extension my chances of acquiring a high-quality mate(s)?[92] Is this reward worth the risk of death? Such calculations, which were computed and negotiated on a constant basis across a multitude of scenarios, were as essential to the high-stakes game of survival then as they are today.

Unfortunately, despite its widespread practice throughout the globe and its deep and long-lasting literary footprint, friendship in Spanish America has received little attention as a historical topic. While scholars like Richard White, David Weber, James Brooks, Juliana Barr, and Pekka Hämäläinen have analyzed the variegated nature of diplomacy between Indians and Europeans along frontier zones, none has looked systematically at friendship as the foundation or culmination of such diplomacy.[93] There are, I believe, two main reasons for this reluctance. In the first place, the study of friendship is commonly fraught with predetermined modern assumptions of what friendship is or ought to be, making it difficult to isolate in time and space.[94] If a modern social media site such as Facebook allows you to tag someone you just met at an airport as a friend; if you can call your wife of thirty years a friend (oftentimes your "best friend" or, if you lived in seventeenth-century England, your "bosom friend");[95] if you can address a business associate or colleague with whom you have drinks once a month as a friend; if you can relate to your dog or your pet hamster as a friend; and if a state can carry on a diplomatic relationship with another state whom it identifies as a friend, what then is a friend?[96] This alone presents an existential problem of meaning that scholars have throughout the ages taken to defining in their pages. Yet when a modern person calls someone who is more than a mere acquaintance a friend, there is—as there was for Aristotle and Cicero or for sixteenth-century Jesuit missionary Andrés Pérez de Ribas and Native *capitán general* (captain general) of the Pimería Alta Luis Oacpicagigua—an implied understanding of rudimentary expectations that gives the idea of friendship measurable meaning.

To complicate matters further, friendships often function in interesting, odd, and sometimes counterintuitive ways. How, for instance, do we interpret the relationship between two individuals who indiscriminately hawk insults at each other? Take, as an example, a Wandeki man from the highlands of Papua New Guinea who yells out at an old acquaintance *Den neie* (I should like to eat your intestines), only to have his acquaintance respond *A! Ene den neie!* (Yes, I too should like to eat your intestines)? Is this affirmation toward cannibalism a sign of deep antagonism and hatred or one of close friendship?[97] What of an O'odham man who challenges his *nawoj* (friend) to a dangerous game of chance in which one or both may lose their lives? Or a Spanish soldier who constantly mocks his close associate's masculinity, accusing him of being a cuckold?[98] Film critic and philosopher Slavoj Žižek has claimed that insults of this sort are a pivotal part of establishing authentic friendships because they produce a proximity that is otherwise inhibited by polite discourse.[99] In other words, insults help break down psychological barriers, which in turn allow for a more personal and sincere association. Are these insulting—and some might say violent and barbaric—behaviors thus reflective of friendship across cultures? Furthermore, do such callused comments possess the same qualitative significance for male friends as they do for female friends? Given that Sonoran society was largely oriented around war and violence, did male friendships elicit a unique value in society?[100] Conversely, because indigenous women were often used to broker alliances with Spaniards and other indigenous tribes, as Juliana Barr reminds us, how exactly did friendship factor into their unique form of gendered diplomacy?[101] These are important questions that have yet to be fully resolved but remain key if we are to acquire a more holistic and accurate understanding of borderland communities.

In the second instance, the relatively limited number of colonial sources that speak directly to friendship has, I believe, dissuaded scholars from digging too deeply into unyielding archives. While references to friendship are not uncommon in the documentary record, direct references to the practice and performance of friendship are uncommon, particularly for the northern frontier. The sources that I have analyzed for this project rarely address friendship in its more intimate and personal expressions—though one would expect to find such sources in larger cities where diaries and personal letters were more common— nor do they wax philosophically about its more noble truths.[102] What I discovered as I conducted research for this project, however, was that even though intimate associations were present everywhere on the frontier—and despite a relative dearth of diaries and intimate personal letters, there is sufficient evidence to suggest this—if one looks carefully enough, the documentary record also reveals a more conniving, manipulative, and intricate web of associations cleverly masquerading as friendships. In this multiethnic colonial borderland where cross-cultural alliances and friendships were essential to survival, sincere and feigned friendships often functioned side by side, making it exceedingly difficult to judge personal sincerity.

So while anthropologist J. Carrier has stressed that it is impossible to speak of friendship without accepting its inseparable bond to sentimentality (love, affection, loyalty), and Victor Manuel Macías-González has written that "nineteenth-century Mexicans understood *amistad* (friendship), like its older form, *amistanza*, as a reciprocal relationship of love, benevolence, and trust between individual *amigos* (friends) who cared deeply for each other and who through the relationship found completion and achieved wholeness," I argue that in northern New Spain sentimental friendships were neither as essential nor as important as these two scholars proclaim for their respective regions and time periods.[103] As I show, though idealized conceptions of friendship remained widely held for much of the colonial period, not all friendships were built around love, affection, or even virtue. In fact, most were not; instead, they were manipulative, secretive, exploitative, and strategic. These calculated associations were central to the development of an early form of civil society because they facilitated social interaction by concealing a person's true feelings or intentions, creating in the process a sort of modus vivendi among the various sectors of frontier society.

Indigenous peoples, who were often empowered to act as Spanish functionaries, frequently participated in this sort of charade, acting out their social role as friends to perfection while veiling their inner animosity. Certain Native leaders, and in some cases entire communities, were conceived of as friends by the Spanish; Indians referred to their Spanish associates in like manner. Secretly, and outside of the public eye, both groups often spoke differently about each other, often harboring ulterior motives. Although Luis Oacpicagigua (chapter 5) publicly asserted his admiration for and friendship with Diego Ortiz Parrilla, Spanish governor of Sonora, one source suggests that he secretly spoke to his kinsmen of his desire to kill him. In 1751, Oacpicagigua organized one of colonial Sonora's most devastating Indian revolts. Yet despite such overt defiance, Ortiz Parrilla continued to refer to Oacpicagigua as a dear friend and companion. The same can be said of Joseph Romo (chapter 4), nicknamed El Canito, who publicly declared himself to be a "sincere friend of the Spanish" while simultaneously planning an uprising against them that ultimately ended in failure. Or what of the numerous indigenous communities who welcomed Spaniards with "signs" of friendship and hospitality (chapter 2) only to later ambush them or misdirect them away from their communities and toward hostile and dangerous territory? These are only a few of the various examples throughout this book where indigenous peoples utilized the language and performance of friendship to hide and advance their individual and sometimes communal agendas.

Framework and Outline of Book

This book begins by outlining the intellectual development and construction of friendship, tracing it from medieval Europe through central Mexico and finally to the northern frontier. It looks at how classical and religious representations of amity were interpreted and reinterpreted within each new social setting, eventually engaging with indigenous variations of friendship that belonged to a very different intellectual and social tradition. Chapters 2 through 5 then highlight the numerous ways in which friendship was conceived, practiced, performed, and manipulated by a wide range of social actors across multiple scenarios, all of which helped foster a unique version of civil society. Taken together, I highlight the highly versatile nature of friendship as well as the ways in which it can act as a cultural lens through which to view the hidden, yet deeply rooted sophistication inherent along New Spain's colonial frontier. In this way, this work provides historical breadth, though lamentably not an exhaustive investigation of friendship.

I focus chiefly on male friendships from two main vantage points: as individual relationships between men from various socioeconomic and racial backgrounds and as a referent for identifying and influencing individual and group (usually indigenous) behavior. Unlike eighteenth-century men from the North American colonies—whom Godbeer asserts were influenced and conditioned by a host of sources such as articles about friendship written in newspapers, letter-writing manuals, epistolary novels, new editions of classical works, and religious sermons—men on the Spanish frontier took their cues about friendship from a distinctly medieval literary and scholastic world, embodied within and refracted through a small group of missionaries, administrators, and soldiers.[104] This European worldview clashed, and in many cases melded, with indigenous modes of practice, the desert environment, and the social realities of life on the frontier.

In chapter 1 I look at how in the years that followed the military conquest of the New World, Spanish intellectuals and legal jurists set in motion a series of vigorous intellectual debates surrounding the appropriate space for Indians within the new social hierarchy.[105] Through this colonial discourse, early American thinkers attempted to reconstruct Indian bodies while degrading their attendant behavioral expressions.[106] This colonial reconstruction process was undergirded and advanced by a strong tradition in religious and classical literature. Idealized European interpretations of friendship taken from classical philosophers, early modern religious thinkers, and humanist writers were reformulated in New Spain during the seventeenth and eighteenth centuries to become an integral part of the new sociopolitical layout. Spanish scholars used these idealized interpretations of friendship as ideological instruments from which to systematically exclude, dehumanize, and set in place behavioral standards on Indians and other non-Europeans.

By recasting friendship as an essential element of high culture, Spanish and Creole thinkers effectively placed themselves at the pinnacle of civilization while at the same time exploiting non-Europeans, who, by virtue of their "barbaric" status, were supposedly incapable of understanding notions of ideal friendship and thus of contributing to the formation of civil society. By incorporating nonviolent Indians into their emotional hierarchy of friendship, Spaniards had skillfully colonized the very notion, turning it into a subtle form of subjugation, while creating specific behavioral expectations founded on Old World rules of amity. Both forms of friendship (the practical and the ideal) functioned side by side. Along the northern frontier, friendship in its dual manifestations elevated one behavioral aspect above others. If the empire was to be successful, it needed its residents to be loyal. Spaniards required loyalty to them as individuals and, secondly, as subjects of the Crown. It was the former (friendship among individuals or among small groups) that set the stage for the latter (friendship with the Crown). Throughout the colonial period loyalty remained a highly touted yet ambiguous concept, making life on the frontier unpredictable, hostile, and highly nuanced. Colonial philosophies of friendship, which occupied a prominent place within the social tapestry of New Spain, thereby dehumanized those deemed racially inferior precisely by defining their inadequacy as friends.

But, as I argue in chapter 2, this perspective changed over the course of the colonial period, especially on the northern frontier as Spaniards, realizing the necessity of Indian cooperation, readjusted their hardline ideological stance. As time wore on, Spanish explorers, missionaries, and administrators realized a workable arrangement between archetype and practice, making inevitable concessions to their indigenous charges while influencing and in some cases adopting Native friendship practices, all in an effort to justify and facilitate the development of civil society. Spaniards along the northern frontier utilized two forms of friendship to their advantage: the first centered on the practicality of friendship, giving credence to the value of Indian knowledge about the environment, local dangers, access to food and water, assistance in fighting "hostile" Indian tribes, and labor; the second focused on the idealized usage of Western ideals of friendship as a tool for establishing specific standards of behavior and civility.

Once the intellectual foundation for the proper practice of friendship had been outlined, Spaniards also began to mentally and spatially map friendship. The mapping of the frontier occurred in two interrelated ways: through the commission of physical maps like those drawn by Father Eusebio Francisco Kino, Juan Matheo Manje, and Juan de Salvatierra, who divided the landscape into physical spaces featuring indios amigos and indios enemigos; and through travel logs, missionary letters, and soldiers' accounts, which created mental maps by means of the written word. Unlike the material images created by maps, this mental process produced perceptual images of the physical qualities, behaviors, and expectations of friendly Indians, creating idealized archetypes that would in turn allow settlers to envision what civil society might look like if people behaved accordingly.

In chapter 3 I address the manner in which idealized interpretations of friendship among New World Europeans intersected with the political jockeying that occurred at all levels of colonial society. By looking at the associations between Jesuit missionary Eusebio Francisco Kino (1645–1711), Don Carlos de Sigüenza y Góngora (1645–1700), and Francisco Xavier de Mora, I show how transatlantic conceptions of friendship and civil society converged and frequently clashed with local realities, leading to heated conflict over proper ethical behavior among friends. Through the purview of amity and betrayal, I expose the unique set of behavioral codes, ethics, and expectations that structured these interactions, making friendships at once pleasurable and potentially contentious. In this way, I reveal the complex process by which friendships were culturally and intellectually constructed by New World intellectuals. As this chapter highlights, in the colonial world friendships could be as much an essential component of civilized life as they were a burden.

Advancing on the idea of a civilized frontier, in chapter 4 I look at a criminal investigation from 1686 to show how the language of amity was strategically used to construct moral order among frontier residents. Aside from serving a basic communicative function, the language of friendship represented a moralizing mechanism for influencing, molding, and in some instances controlling indigenous behavior and their attitudes toward frontier settlers. It was left up to agents of the state to monitor and influence such morality. By juxtaposing criminal or potentially criminal activity against idealized patterns of friendship, these agents attempted to normalize proper behavioral standards, using morality as a tool of colonialism.[107] The frequent literary usage of friendship during the seventeenth and eighteenth centuries, skillfully crafted to promote civilized thought and behavior, formed an important and consistent part of the colonial language for the northern frontier. Though Spaniards and indigenous peoples both utilized this same language to advance their respective interests, if misunderstood or overplayed, such linguistic expressions of friendship often led to conflict.

Because civilizing the frontier could not have succeeded without Native allies and friends, chapter 5 addresses the various ways in which cross-cultural friendships were at once strategic, manipulative, and potentially emotional. It details the unlikely and "unequal" friendship between Luis Oacpicagigua, Indian governor of Sáric and *capitán general* of the Pimas Altos, and Diego Ortiz Parrilla, Spanish governor and military captain of Sonora. As I argue, this friendship grew out of two interrelated factors: war and humiliation. Both men became friends through repeated military engagements with indios enemigos and by way of their mutual disdain of several Jesuit missionaries who challenged their power and status within the Pimería Alta. Oacpicagigua's charismatic persona, his authoritative influence over his kinsmen, and the respect he had earned from both Indians and Spaniards over the course of several years made the idea of friendship a smart and logical move for the governor. Through Oacpicagigua, Ortiz Parrilla was able to effectively govern and maintain order and obedience throughout the Pimería. Conversely, Oacpicagigua earned a high degree of social status, respect, and access to Spanish goods and services from his association with the governor. While their friendship served both of their practical needs, it also produced an emotional connection. Founded on the practicality of events, this friendship provides an important example of the presence of cross-class, cross-cultural, and socially unequal friendships that were central to the formation of frontier society.

As a largely ill-defined geographical and political space where social categories often blurred and where power relations were hotly negotiated, the frontier is a particularly appropriate place to study friendship. Examining the idiosyncrasies of friendship along the northern frontier offers scholars a unique framework for better understanding how colonial elites, indigenous peoples, and lower-class populations all participated in the construction of their social realities. In this vast, arid, and capricious landscape, friendship functioned as an effective medium through which missionaries, settlers, soldiers, and Indians could navigate social space, developing in the process the germs of a fully functioning society. These socially constructed bonds of amity, which were highly situational and dependent on a variety of political, ecological, and economic factors, functioned at distinct levels of purpose and intensity. Some friendships were rooted in convenience and practicality; others adopted a more subversive and manipulative character; and still others maintained deep and authentic sentimental qualities. Taken together, the following chapters provide us with a glimpse into the highly convoluted, nuanced, sophisticated, and intimate world of the frontier.

CHAPTER ONE

An Ideal Friendship

Classical Interpretations and Everyday Reality

Friendship is a single soul dwelling in two bodies.
—Aristotle, *Nicomachean Ethics*

My lady, you made no mistake. This too is Alexander.
—Alexander of Macedon, in *Anabasis of Alexander*, by Arrian

An eloquent man, a great orator, created civil society by the power of persuasion.
—Cicero, *De inventione*

FRIENDSHIP AS A SOCIAL INSTITUTION, AN INTELLECTUAL IDEAL, and an intimate spiritual bond has been celebrated by virtually every known human society across the globe, representing what one scholar has described as "the highest ideal of ethical, political, and social development."[1] In New Spain, friendships developed and found expression within a particular set of social, economic, and political realities. These unique colonial structures imposed specific demands and limitations on its practice and representation, ensuring that friendship in Spanish America would be different in character and purpose than in either the English or French colonies.[2] Intellectually, conceptions of amity throughout the New World were the product of a European and indigenous tradition that stretched back for millennia. From the urbane and sophisticated poetry of the Mexica and the highly nuanced Cherokee friendship dance to idealized European literary representations of heroic pairs and the "ultimate" friendship between the divine and the community of believers, friendship throughout the Americas represented a confluence of Old and New World philosophical viewpoints. What emerged from these varied perspectives was a complex intellectual patchwork through which colonial society was envisaged and subsequently organized.

Friendship in Ancient Literature

The *Epic of Gilgamesh* (ca. 2150–2000 BCE), discovered by British archeologists during the mid-nineteenth century, remains one of the world's most iconic and cherished friendship narratives. Quite possibly the first "imaginative master-piece" in world history, this epic poem embodied many of the central literary tenets universally found in relationships of amity.[3] Originating from a series of Sumerian legends, this story celebrated the friendship between two men of preternatural ability: the mythological hero-king Gilgamesh and his faithful and loyal companion Enkidu. Savvy to the emotive gradations of human nature, its author(s) tunneled through the deepest recesses of the human psyche in order to unlock our most basic fears and desires. Death, immortality, adventure, ambition, tragedy, and friendship all reverberate with significance throughout the tale. The inspired use of such timeless and universal motifs created a com-posite claim on idealized human relationships, allowing for this ancient piece of literature to remain as relevant to us today as it was so many millennia ago.

As the discerning storytellers of this epic recorded, Enkidu and Gilgamesh became friends—the best of friends, akin to the closest of brothers—in the troughs of hand-to-hand combat. Their initial clash, which took place in the "great walled city of Uruk," shook the earth, both literally and figuratively, con-vincing Gilgamesh that this "natural man," being his equal in both strength and purpose, represented his second self.[4] Though Enkidu was created by the gods to be Gilgamesh's equal, and therefore to act as a counterbalance and moral com-pass to his overaggressive temperament, there remained a clearly identifiable hierarchy. The hero of the story was Gilgamesh; Enkidu was his loyal friend who, though like him in almost every way, was second to him in social standing. Despite their inequality, the deep love they held for one another afforded them the impression of "sameness" necessary in the maintenance of their friendship.

Their bond grew by means of the youthful and reckless search for fame and glory. Together they vanquished Humbaba, the guardian of the Cedar Forest, thereby engraving their names in the annals of history. Then they brazenly killed the Bull of Heaven, cutting off one of its thighs only to arrogantly sling it at the heavens as an affront to the goddess Ishtar. Their acts of valor were genuinely heroic and, in the case of the Bull of Heaven, they saved many lives, but they also angered the gods who, in no mood to entertain such impertinence, struck down Enkidu with a mysterious illness. Typical of so many friendship accounts handed down to us over the ages, the loss of a close friend evoked an almost unbearable pain:

> All day and all night have I wept over him
> And would not have him buried—
> My friend yet might rise up at my (loud) cries,
> for seven days and nights—
> until a maggot dropped from his nose.
> Since he is gone, I can no comfort find,
> Keep roaming like a hunter in the plains.[5]

Yet no matter how long or hard Gilgamesh wept, no matter how much hair he pulled from his kingly scalp, no matter how forcefully he beat the walls of the palace complex, the gods would never return to him his beloved friend and brother. Having experienced the joy of friendship, Gilgamesh was now destined to live without it.

The sorrow and despair that followed Enkidu's death was highly stylized and acted as a pathway through which the poem's author(s) guided Gilgamesh in an eternal search for answers about life and death. Grief-stricken, the legendary hero-king set out in search of immortality—an unsuccessful journey that ultimately ended in utter defeat, for as the gods had so arrogantly decreed, Gilgamesh was fated to be king, but everlasting life was not his destiny. In all, this deceptively simple story was meant to convey a moral lesson about the impetuousness of youth, the grandeur of friendship, the agonies of loss and failure, and the inevitability of death. Many of the characteristics found in this early story of friendship—love, compassion, adventure, devotion, loyalty, and sacrifice—have remained cherished ideals throughout the Western world.

Centuries later, as *philia* (friendship) came to occupy a prominent place within Homeric Age literature (ca. 1200–800 BCE), Greek storytellers introduced as a normative ideal the friendship between Achilles, the legendary hero of Troy, and Patroclus, his longtime companion.[6] This friendship, which originated in childhood and became fortified amid the glory and agony of warfare, reached its zenith when Hector, prince of the Trojans, killed Patroclus in battle.

Though Patroclus was Achilles's "squire," and therefore his social subordinate, he seamlessly transformed himself into Achilles's equal the moment he donned the Greek hero's immortal armor, which, despite the fact that he was smaller in stature, fit him perfectly, as if he were another Achilles.

The wrath and yearning for revenge awakened within Achilles after the death of his close companion was clear testament to the powerful quality of their fellowship. Following Patroclus's death, which was partly Achilles's own fault given that the legendary hero was sulking in his tent at the time his friend rode out to fight Hector, Achilles made an offering of twelve of Troy's fairest youths so as to lay them at his companion's tomb. Following this dramatic event, he cut off two of his best locks of hair and placed them in the hands of his resting friend. In elevated agony, Achilles reiterated their sameness: "Dear comrade . . . the man I loved beyond all other comrades, / loved as my own life."[7] Then, before all of Troy, he met Hector and vanquished him only to then exult over him as he dropped the prince's corpse at his chariot wheels. That night as Achilles slept, "the spirit of Patroclus prevailed in the strength of friendship to burst the barriers of Hades and stood by his sleeping friend."[8]

Centuries later, Francisco López de Gómara (1511–66) christened Hernán Cortés (1485–1547) the Achilles of the New World.[9] A century after that, Gaspar Pérez de Villagrá (1555–1620) did the same for the founder of New Mexico, Juan de Oñate (1550–1626). Guided by the ethos of the Italian Renaissance and trained in the humanist tradition in Alcalá and Salamanca, respectively, both scholars utilized this comparison as a way of justifying the "glory" of conquest. For, as Gómara had so zealously pontificated, had not Cortés brought to the New World the accoutrements of civilization—that is, just laws, the concept of private property, freedom from tyranny, and Latin letters—thus relieving the Indians of their "barbarity"?[10]

The poetic relationships between Gilgamesh and Enkidu and Achilles and Patroclus, to name but two, portrayed a literary ideal founded on love, loyalty, and the willingness to die for one other. These idealized friendships were difficult to attain and therefore not readily available to average men. But alas this was not their purpose—at least not according to American mythologist Joseph Campbell, who believed that these ancient stories were meant to say something deeper and more meaningful about who we are and, more importantly, about who we want to be; they were designed to reflect the most universal of all human tropes: the hero's journey.[11] Aristotle would later place these particular types of idealized friendships at the pinnacle of his philosophical tripos on friendship.

For him they were the most authentic, heroic, virtuous, meaningful, and long-lasting, and therefore worthy of the greatest veneration. They were also exclusively male. As Ivy Schweitzer writes, these stories, centered as they were on the heroic and the noble, highlighted two inescapably masculine components: reason and virtue. Virtue in particular, "one of the defining requirements of ideal friendship" in the Old World, was synonymous with this male-centered orientation "since its Latin root *vir* translates as 'man.'"[12]

It remains true to say—at least in the West—that many of our most cherished thoughts on friendship have their philosophical roots in the Greek world.[13] But while most educated Greeks idealized the heroic friendship between Hercules and Hylas, Apollo and Hyacinth, Damon and Phintias, Achilles and Patroclus, and Alexander and Hephaestion, among others, most forms of friendships—such as *xenia* (guest-friendships) among fellow travelers and advantageous friendships among business associates, soldiers, political clubs, and workers—represented more common types of everyday associations.[14] Homeric era quotidian friendships, as David Konstan argues, represented a "system of calculated cooperation, not necessarily accompanied by any feeling of affection," because in the Greek world friendship "served as a matrix for relations that in modern society are governed by autonomous economic and legal practices." These ancient societies, he maintains, "didn't have an economy as we understand it, so they were embedded in a complex web of social relations that included personal bonds."[15] In economically developing regions such as the Greek polis, therefore—and, I would add, the missions and mining communities of northern New Spain where there was not yet a formal economy or national identity to speak of—friendship carried a socially unique importance as a commonly recognized bonding agent.

For H. E. Yuanguo, however, the importance of friendship in the ancient Mediterranean world was far more basic, resting less on an economic drive as proposed by Konstan and more on the desire for protection from rivals and thieves. In this unpredictably hostile environment, "where piracy was an honorable profession and every stranger was a potential enemy, it was essential for people to know on whom they could rely."[16] To this demand spoke no better wellspring than the family, which represented the primary source of daily interaction and trust. Accordingly, quotidian friendships between male associates were largely conceptualized as an extension of this primal bond, representing what amounted to a fictitious blood-relationship.[17] These types of selective fellowships were solidified through a highly ritualized ceremony that took place in the privacy of one's home in which a meal, shared before the host's sacred hearth, bound both men in timeless union. During this "friendship ceremony" both men were sworn to render mutual aid and hospitality to one another, contractually cementing what amounted to a lifelong bond. Combining both of the aforementioned perspectives, historian and Arabist Shelomo Goitein stresses the instinctive desire for protection with the complexities of economic promotion, asserting that while formal friendships were indeed common throughout the Mediterranean and Indian Ocean, they were particularly strong among merchants who utilized the institution of friendship to advance their commercial interests. "Any respectable trader," writes Goitein, "has a *sāhib*, or friend, on the other side of the sea who acted for him not merely as a legal and business representative, but as his confidant in every respect."[18]

For indigenous societies throughout the Americas, the ritualization of friendship carried equivalent value. Among the Zuni of New Mexico, for instance, *kihe* (friendship) represented an important social designation highly esteemed by members of that society. Conducting anthropological fieldwork among the Zuni at the turn of the twentieth century, Elsie Clews Parsons sketched out what she considered to be authentic Zuni friendship customs.[19] Emphasizing historical continuity from generations past, Parsons detailed the process by which a middle-aged man named Kumma became friends with a much younger boy, Jim. In order for them to become friends, Kumma, because he was much older than Jim, required the permission of Jim's father.[20] Once permission had been granted, Kumma and Jim engaged in an elaborate and highly structured friendship ritual that lasted several days. First, during a public ceremonial dance, Kumma gifted Jim a pair of moccasins, cloth, and a silk kerchief, "such as the men wear around their heads." The following day Kumma's aunt took Jim to their house where she "washed his head in yucca suds." This type of traditional hair washing was a common friendship practice among the Zuni, stretching back several centuries. Jim was then given "the bowl he had been washed in, two other bowls, one big Navajo rug, and one blanket."[21] During the "return ceremony" Jim's grandfather used the fraternity *mili* (the decorated ear of corn and feathers every friend received) to say a prayer, rub Kumma with meal, and wash his hair and face, "the chief purport of it being that now they would be one and belong to the same family."[22] Before leaving, Kumma was gifted a blanket, beads, a pan, two bowls, and the bowl he was washed in. Both *kihe* were now recognized by the community as lifelong friends and brothers.

Due to the burdensome financial obligations represented by the ceremonial act of gift giving, however, most members of the Zuni community could only ever afford to have one *kihe*—this was also the case among Mayan friends, as highlighted by Ruben Reina. In fact, Reina's anthropological research among twentieth-century Mayan adolescent friends revealed a similar pattern of community involvement in the acknowledgment and sanctioning of male friendships.[23] Parsons also found that while women were known to engage in similar friendship ceremonies, they were much rarer and seemingly less prized. Noted Parsons of an indigenous man she interviewed, he "had never known a pair of women *kihe*; another man knew of only one such instance."[24] Friendships between men and women, while possible, were also uncommon, though, as she discovered, not as rare as between two women.[25]

The practice of friendship making through ritual gift giving has been widely documented across the globe. Among the indigenous peoples of New Guinea, for instance, boys born on the same day were made friends through a similar process of ritual exchange. In this particular scenario, the friendship ceremony was enacted by the boys' fathers, possibly as a way of consenting on their behalf to a lifelong committed partnership. "Such fast friends—*eriam* is the New Guinea term—are expected to lend one another fishing-nets, garden produce, wives. They hunt and do irrigation work together. They 'entertain' one another; and before going to war or on returning from communal hunts they feast together. They wail for one another at death and help dig the grave."[26] The friendship between Jonathan, the son of King Saul, and David equally exemplifies the centrality of this practice. In order for Jonathan to secure David's friendship (whom he loved as his own self), Jonathan gifted him his robe, armor, belt, and sword—in effect his most prized possessions. By donning these intimate items, David "became" Jonathan, just as Patroclus had become Achilles centuries earlier. "And it came to pass . . . that the soul of Jonathan was knit with the soul of David, and Jonathan loved him as his own soul."[27]

This well-known biblical story bears a striking resemblance to the Cherokee friendship dance, in which, similar to the Zuni gifting ritual, young men who wished to become friends were required to publicly proclaim their intentions before the community by means of an elaborate ceremonial performance. During the event each dancer slowly removed his clothes and replaced them with his companion's, echoing in many ways the Old World literary ideal of "twinning" or "doubling."[28] Thus "each of them publicly received the other as himself and became pledged to regard and treat him as himself while he lived."[29] Variations of this "twinning" archetype, aside from the more representational forms I have already alluded to, are found across a number of societies. Thirteenth-century Persian poet Rūmī, for instance, was known for concluding his poems with the name of his master, in essence paying due homage to his second self; Israeli prophets initiated their novices by cloaking them with their own mantles, symbolically transferring their wisdom to what they saw as a future them.[30] The modern-day practice of hooding a student at graduation could be seen as representing the continuation of this ancient practice.

In the West, the idea of a friend representing a second self has its philosophical musings in the writings of Socrates (469–399 BCE), Plato (429–347 BCE), Aristotle (384–322 BCE), and Cicero (106–43 BCE).[31] These men were arguably the greatest luminaries of their age, and their formulations on friendship continue to represent some of the most influential ideas on the topic. For them, friendship was "the germ of whatever is divine in the heart of man, the spark that, if fostered and fed, transfigured the whole being."[32] It was also, as Aristotle had proposed in his *Politics*, at the very nucleus of what it meant to live in a polis and therefore an essential component of civil society.[33] For Socrates, the most self-effacing of the aforementioned Greek thinkers, friendship had a much simpler and direct purpose: the attainment of wisdom. Wise men, he believed, entered into relationships of amity with other wise men solely to enhance their own, and since only the truly wise understood the purpose of friendship, it stood to reason that only they could attain its benefits. Therefore, only those of high moral standing could become true friends because only they, being the wisest, understood the difference between right and wrong.[34] From this philosophical vantage point it followed that criminals, being immoral (a product of their lack of wisdom), could not form true friendships. This limited ethical outlook, however, proved far too simplistic for many of his students.

Plato, in particular, Socrates's greatest pupil, modified his teacher's narrow application of friendship by creating inferior and superior forms, opening the door onto a broader analysis. To exemplify the centrality of his thesis, Plato utilized a class-based perspective whereby he argued that associations between the poor and the wealthy, while technically considered friendships, were inherently inferior. This was because it was impossible for the poor not to be envious of the rich, ensuring that they would always be driven toward self-indulgent and nefarious ends. Such friendships were "terrible and savage, and seldom mutual among us."[35] So, while a friendship between a wealthy man and a poor man could theoretically exist, it would not be beneficial nor worthwhile for the rich man to engage in such a fellowship. Simply put, unequal class-based friendships could never foster the type of sincerity and disinterested admiration representative of loftier forms. For Plato then, the only friendships that possessed the ability to manifest themselves into superior forms founded on goodwill, and thus devoid of jealousy and intrigue, were those that embraced the notion of "like is friend to like." Still, Plato's formulations on friendship, focused as they were on sameness, left little room for social hierarchies or asymmetric levels of influence, leaving much to be desired. The task of developing a more complete analysis was then taken up by Aristotle.

Outlined in the eighth and ninth books of his *Nicomachean Ethics*, friendship represented a natural and universal inclination in which goodwill and sociability motivated men into actively entering into lasting fellowships with other men. Like Plato, Aristotle believed that not all friendships were equal. Even though they rested firmly under the canopy of *philia*, they ranged widely in quality, significance, and purpose. But unlike his former teacher, Aristotle tried to make sense of such variability by proposing that there existed three basic forms: the useful, the pleasant, and the good. The most common of these, the useful, were utilitarian associations based solely on necessity. This type of friendship had two basic variants. The first emphasized natural obligation, as in the friendship between a mother and her son. This was, simply put, altruistic *philia*. The second focused exclusively on the possible material benefits that either party took away from their fellowship. This latter form, which Aristotle promoted as transparently egocentric and ephemeral, was easily dissolved once either party felt it was no longer worth their while. Those who engaged in friendships based on the second form of utility did so out of complete self-interest.[36] Because of this, these friendships suffered from an absence of love and virtue. Despite its lack of intrinsic sincerity, Sibyl Schwarzenbach maintains that utility-friendship retained the fundamental aspect of "wishing the other well." Any association that did not at the very least do that, she believes, was not characterized as *philia* by Greek citizens.[37] While advantageous under the right circumstances, this species of friendship represented the lowest rung in Aristotle's friendship schematic.

The second tier of friendship was based on pleasure and existed purely for the enjoyment it produced. Much like its utilitarian counterpart, it lacked an authentic sense of goodness and purity, making it dispensable and easily replicable. Writes Aristotle, "For it is not being the man he is that the loved person is loved, but as providing some good or pleasure. Such friendships, then, are easily dissolved if the parties do not remain like themselves; for if the one party is no longer pleasant or useful, then the other ceases to love him."[38] Such, he argued, were the friendships of children, as they were quick to dissolve when the quality of pleasure changed.

The final and highest subdivision in Aristotle's friendship pyramid was occupied exclusively by men of virtue and honor. Here is where Aristotle believed rested "ideal," or "perfect," friendship. These men, he advanced, entered into relationships of amity because of the love they had for themselves and for one another and not because of the pleasure or potential monetary or emotional benefits that such a friendship might provide. Though pleasure and personal benefit were not absent from these associations, they came unsought and were not its primary goal. These friendships represented the organic outgrowth of authentic feelings of love, and because of this they required a sense of sameness—namely, that a "friend be a second self" (*philos allos autos*). Aristotle made this proposition clear in his *Magna Moralia* when he stated that "whenever we wish to know our own character and personalities, we can recognize them by looking upon a friend."[39]

Though "perfect" friendships were infused with love and admiration, they were not, as Aristotle saw it, emasculating to the men who practiced them because they, being creatures of reason, were entirely capable of controlling their emotions. The severity of preconditions behind "ideal" friendships made them extremely rare—only men of elite ranking and high moral integrity had ready access to them—and as a consequence they were highly esteemed. Not only did these types of friendships make individual men better versions of themselves, they also brought them true joy—not the type of joy experienced by those who practiced it for pleasure, but rather, the joy of reason. It was this final form of friendship that helped sustain the polis because, as Aristotle believed, in any just society it was up to its citizens to want to wish one another well, do things for one another, share similar values and goals, and through civil discourse find a unifying sense of justice. It was this political and civic ideal, as represented by the Greek polis, that later served as the organizational blueprint for residents of the Hispanic world.[40]

The spread of Hellenism during the fourth century BCE ensured that the Roman Empire would fully adopt Greece's intellectual legacy and deep admiration for idealized friendships.[41] The most influential Roman treatise on friendship that comes to us from this time is Cicero's *De Amicitia* (On Friendship). Written in 44 BCE, *De Amicitia*'s philosophical influence shaped the discourse on friendship in the West for several centuries thereafter. As a work of fiction that placed Greek philosophical principles squarely within the Roman literary genre, *De Amicitia* highlighted the friendship between Gaius Laelius, Cicero's father-in-law, who was also a statesman and general, and Scipio Africanus the younger, his lifelong friend. In this work, Cicero delimited the "rules" of friendship, defining "true" friendship as *omnium divinarum humanarumque rerum cum benevolentia et caritate consensio* (a relationship based on agreement about all human and divine matters, together with goodwill and affection).[42]

Echoing a deep admiration for the heroic friendships of classical literature, Cicero's narrative on friendship reached its apex at the death of Scipio. Distraught by the death of his friend, Laelius echoed his love for him: "For my part, of all the advantages that either nature or fortune has bestowed upon me, there is none that can compare with that of having had Scipio for my friend." For Laelius, the love he felt for his friend was equivalent to the love he had for himself because it was only through a "perfect friend" like Scipio (his second self) that he was able to truly understand himself: *omnium divinarum humanarumque rerum cum*—"both in our public and private lives he and I shared all the same interests. Our tastes and aims and views were identical and that is where the essence of a friendship must always lie."[43] Herein lies Cicero's longtime admiration of heroic pairs, for while "ordinary commonplace friendships, delightful and valuable though they may be," were adequate for most people, they were incapable of acting as true mirrors onto ourselves and were therefore inherently inferior and of little value.[44] He proposed that only *viri boni* (good men) of high moral character and virtue could engage in the types of heroic friendships he admired because only they understood the obligations of reciprocity and equality central to their development.

Seneca (4 BCE–CE 65), Stoic philosopher, statesman, and dramatist, followed closely in Cicero's intellectual footsteps when he too made the claim that ideal friendship represented an indispensable avenue through which the individual could perfect himself. By maintaining a friend of similar moral, social, and spiritual standing, as had existed between Scipio and Laelius, men could enhance one another's virtue on the way to achieving individual excellence, or as the Greeks called it, *arête*.[45] In a similar manner, first-century Persian philosopher and historian Ibn Miskawayh's book *The Refinement of Character* expressed the desire for homogeneous friendships in this way: "Man is by nature a social being, consequently his intrinsic and highest destination, spiritual perfection, can be reached only through association with a congenial friend."[46] The extent to which Cicero, Seneca, and Ibn Miskawayh were influenced by Plato and Aristotle's reflections on friendship remains undeniable.

While classical conceptions of amity retained a dominant place within the philosophical and literary canon of the Hellenistic and Middle Ages, by the third century CE Christian theologians had begun to redraw the boundaries of ideal friendship. Men like St. Ambrose (337–97), St. Augustine (354–430), and St. Jerome (374–420) redefined the classical conception of ideal friendship, which was exclusively male and elitist, by moralizing and augmenting it with spiritual qualities, refocusing its anthropocentric character onto the interiority of the human spirit. In particular, this new association centered on the fellowship of the faithful (subsequently described as a universal brotherhood) and on the privileged relationship between the divine and the community of believers.[47] Because this Christological interpretation of friendship was universal in scope, it included for the first time women and slaves. For Jesus stated, "My command is this: Love one another as I have loved you. Greater love has no one than this: to lay down one's life for one's friends. You are my friends if you do what I command. I no longer call you servants, because a servant does not know his master's business. Instead, I have called you friends, for everything that I learned from my Father I have made known to you."[48] Fully spiritual and embodied in the love of Christ, this transformed conceptualization of friendship was embraced by Christian communities throughout the Old World.[49]

Examples abound. Twelfth-century cleric Bernard of Clairvaux (1090–1153) superimposed Cicero's conceptualization of true friendship as it existed among men onto the archetype of *amicita perfecta* (perfect friendship) in terms of man's relationship with God.[50] English Cistercian monk Aelred of Rievaulx (1110–67) similarly relied on Cicero's *De Amicitia* when in his *De Spiritali Amicitia* (On Spiritual Friendship) he reconfigured ideal human friendships as being religiously inspired. For him, these types of friendships were nothing less than a heavenly gift.[51] Much like Aristotle, Aelred of Rievaulx divided friendship into three basic types: carnal, worldly, and spiritual. Of the three, the spiritual represented its purest, most ideal form. French theologian Peter of Blois (1130–1211) composed a treatise titled *De amicitia christiana et de dilectione dei et proximi* (About Christian Friendship and the Love of God and Neighbor) in which he too draped Ciceronian notions of friendship onto an Augustinian perspective in an effort to systematize principles of how one could combine the love of one's neighbor with the love of God.[52] Boncompagno da Signa's (1165–1240) *The Book on Friendship* (ca. 1205) identified twenty-six different types of friendships, only four of which were truly worthy of the label friend—the friend for friendship's sake, the faithful friend, the equal friend, and the substantial (*realis*) friend. The remaining twenty-two types were different versions of the "false friend."[53] But it was Thomas Aquinas (1225–74) who, laboring to reconcile faith with reason, had the most significant influence on the moral thinking of medieval European theologians. Aristotle had presented a conundrum for scholastic-minded men like Aquinas: Because Aristotle had arrived at his universal truths solely through reason, where was faith to reside? Aquinas dealt with this theological problem, particularly in his *Summa Theologica*, by granting that there were some truths that could be acquired by reason and others that could be arrived at *only* through faith, but the two were never in conflict. Later Hispanic scholars came to know many of Aristotle and Plato's most important ideas through the diagnostic mind of Aquinas.

While the Christian notion of ideal friendship between the community of believers and the divine grew in influence across much of the West, it did not entirely eclipse the classical representation of heroic pairs. New pairs emerged with all the daring and majesty of centuries past: Charlemagne and Alcuin, Philip of France and Richard the Lionheart, the fictional friendship between Tristan and King Mark in Gottfried von Strassburg's twelfth-century rendition of *Tristan*, and the friendship between Engelhard and Dieterich in Conrad von Würzburg's thirteenth-century novel, *Engerhlard*.[54] As Albert Classen writes, during this period "the vast corpus of literary experiments with the theme of two friends who are willing to give their life for the other in time of need quickly assumed even hagiographical character."[55]

The literary trend of devoted friends willing to die for each other continued on into the early modern period when we begin to see the formalization of friendship into cultlike status. This proclivity for the heroic and the formal also undergirded the development of increasingly elaborate greetings in formal letters. Letter-writing manuals such as Antonio de Nebrija's *Gramática de la lengua castellana* (1492), Gaspar de Tejados's *Cosa nueva: Estilo de escribir cartas mensajeras cortesanamente* (1549), and Antonio de Torquemada's *Manual de escribientes* (1552), among others, sought to codify a more formal and rigid friendship language. The overriding emphasis on language and rhetoric as a central ingredient in the formation of civil society was largely a by-product of Cicero's *De inventione*, which was initially conceived of as a handbook for orators.[56] The extent to which these manuals had an actual effect on how people conceptualized their relationships with loved ones and friends, especially for those living in

New Spain, is, as Rebecca Earle asserts, highly debatable.[57] Overall, while classical and medieval writers developed a general outline for what comprised ideal friendship, they remained unable to agree on whether it existed solely among pairs of friends, among a group or community, or among unrelated individuals.[58] As the following chapters in this book suggest, friendship in its more practical expressions existed and flourished among all three.

Friendship in the Early Spanish World

Spanish interest in idealized forms of friendship can be traced back to at least the thirteenth-century reign of Alfonso X (1221–84). In his *Siete Partidas*, written between 1256 and 1265 and given this name because of the number of sections it was divided into, Alfonso presented medieval Europe with its most comprehensive law code. This highly influential document established a uniform body of normative rules for the kingdom while providing a practical framework for the appropriate application and performance of friendship.[59] Its divisions treated the following subjects:

Partida 1: The church and religious life

Partida 2: Public law and government

Partida 3: The administration of justice

Partida 4: Marriage

Partida 5: Commerce

Partida 6: Wills and inheritance

Partida 7: Crimes and punishment

The fourth partida on marriage made friendship one of its central themes. Title twenty-seven, for example, had the rubric, "*Del debdo qe han los homes entre si por razon de amistad*" (Of the obligation which men have to each other because of friendship).[60] A significant portion of this section, which could also be found in Aristotle's *Nichomachean Ethics*, characterized friendship as the strongest of bonds uniting men, reinforcing the widely held belief that friendship ties were often stronger than familial affiliations. In a somewhat representative passage about the treatment of prisoners. Alfonso noted that the greatest sorrow among many of these men was the separation they experienced, not from their families, but from their friends.[61]

Law 3 of the fourth partida titled "*Cómo se debe home aprovechar des consejo del amigo, et qual home debe seer escogido por esto*" (how a man should utilize a friend's advice, and what type of man should be selected for this purpose) offered advice on how to select a friend for the purpose of providing counsel. Here the author(s), speaking through the experienced voice of Cicero (referred to in this text by his middle name, Tullio), advanced the claim that "there was nothing as sweet as having a friend to whom one could confide as if he were speaking to himself."[62]

Law 4 titled "*Quántas maneras son las amistad*" (how many are the forms of friendship) promoted friendship as a virtuous way for *los figosdalgo* (the nobility) to settle duels and disputes with one another, thereby keeping them civil and honorable. In this way, the moral and ethical obligations of friendship, which the nobility, according to Alfonso, innately embraced, would help civilize their otherwise violent nature as men. Much like a modern-day college fraternity, *los figosdalgo* also created friendship pacts through which they vowed to protect one another while simultaneously striving to enhance one another's economic and political interests. In a similar fashion, they also benefited from friendships with undistinguished men. Within the legal parameters of thirteenth-century Castile, a lowborn friend was permitted to stand in for a nobleman in judicial cases of treason. But to be considered the friend of a nobleman, one first had to meet a number of preconditions: the non-noble person should have "performed the marriage of the person [who was to appear before the king] or the marriage of his children, or he [the nobleman] had to have made him a knight or an heir, or [the non-noble friend must have] helped him [the nobleman] recover lost property, or saved him from death, dishonor or great harm, or rescued him from captivity."[63] Put succinctly, in this particular legal scenario, given the disparity in status between an aristocrat and an untitled man, a friend was legally defined for the purposes of maintaining the integrity and honor of the former. The untitled friend was, in a manner of speaking, the "second self" of the nobleman, but because he was not of equal social standing as his aristocratic friend, he was expected to approximate his stature through grand demonstrations of virtue and loyalty.

Law 5 of the fourth partida titled "*Como debe seet guardada la amistad entre los amigos*" (how friends should preserve their friendship) set forth three rules for how to maintain and keep a friend. As this section explicitly clarified, friends should, first and foremost, be absolutely loyal to one another, since fidelity of this sort represented the most important trait in maintaining a strong and vigorous friendship. Second, friends should never speak ill of one another because defaming a friend's character could easily destroy the relationship. Additionally, secrets—which, if treated properly, represented an important element of sincerity and loyalty—should be closely guarded and never revealed to anyone outside the partnership. Third, law 5 stipulated that both friends should actively work toward maintaining a basic level of equality. Men of equal social and economic status, as a number of classical writers had previously given notice, made the best types of friends because jealously was not an integral part of their relationship. Preserving a likeness of character and disposition was important because once it changed—once one individual gained more prestige, wealth, or status than the other—the friendship entered turbulent waters because not only was jealousy now a factor but so was resentment. Friendship, it was clear to Alfonso, was wont to flounder amid such conditions of inequality.

In a general sense, Alfonso believed that friendship, in its various intellectual and emotional expressions, maintained the social and moral stability of Iberian society, making Castilians, Leonese, and Galicians "fulfill what justice demands."[64] In this respect, laws directed at enforcing specific friendship styles codified moral practice, thereby serving as the foundation of civil society—an idea that, as I argue in this book, was reproduced, though in a more unstructured and instinctual way, along the isolated and dangerous frontiers of northern New Spain. As we have already seen, the connection between friendship and civil society was at the core of Aristotle's conceptualization of the polis. In fact, throughout the entirety of the fourth partida, Alfonso cited Aristotle no fewer than seven times and Cicero (Tullio) four. But while Aristotle had privileged the idealism of perfect friendship, the *Siete Partidas* addressed a more practical everyday usage. According to Anthony Pagden, this type of simplicity and practicality was more appealing to a medieval public "who had hitherto shown little interest in complex ethical systems" and who instead desired a "practical handbook on how to run their affairs."[65] It wasn't until a more streamlined and simplified translation of Aristotle's *Ethics* appeared in the fifteenth century, free from its earlier versions that were "liberally scattered with untranslated Greek terms," that Aristotle began to draw in university men, independent scholars, churchmen, and the aristocracy.[66] By the sixteenth century, most conquistadores were cognizant of at least the most basic decrees outlined in the *Siete Partidas*. This medieval legal oeuvre maintained a strong influence throughout Latin America well into the nineteenth century, constituting "the premise on which the Spanish patrimonial state in the Indies was constructed."[67]

In late medieval Spain, both Aristotle and Cicero were required reading during a student's initiation into the art of composition and rhetoric.[68] Prior to the fifteenth century, however, it was mostly Cicero's *De amicitia* that acted as a model for imitation. His *De militia*, which in like manner extolled the values of friendship, was also required reading for young men. But because Aristotle's *Nichomachean Ethics* was not as easily accessible to young readers, it was not introduced until students took advanced courses in moral philosophy, generally at the university level. Aristotle's ideas tended to be complex, they did not lend themselves to the "scissors and paste treatment," and most importantly, "they were not easily divorced from their context which lacked the obvious simplicity of the Roman moralists."[69] For these reasons, Aristotle himself had suggested that the young should avoid engaging with his moral philosophy until they achieved intellectual maturity.[70] By the mid-fifteenth century Aristotle's ideas began to reach a much wider audience. From 1474 to 1509 nine vernacular versions of his moral works were printed in Spain; Seneca was reproduced in seven editions, and Cicero in one.[71] By all accounts this was a prodigious number of translations. Because Aristotle, Cicero, and Seneca so thoroughly permeated Iberian society, even those not fortunate enough to receive university training now had ready access to their philosophical and moral positions, filtered, as they were, through the numerous treatises and works of fiction that influenced early modern Spanish society.

Early modern humanist writers, separated from the *Siete Partidas* by over two centuries, drew heavily on these classical thinkers in conceptualizing friendship. Roderigo de Encino's *Opusculum amicitiae* (Everyday Friendship, 1505), for example, displayed a trendy combination of Aristotelian and Ciceronian ideas. In this novel, the author held true to the Aristotelian tripartite division of friendship, providing his reading audience with practical advice on how to differentiate a good friend from a bad one. This distinction, he contended, was based primarily on the most valued attributes of friendship—namely, discretion, loyalty, and love.[72] Francisco de Castilla's *Tratado de la amiricia* (A Treaty on Friendship, 1508) similarly adopted Aristotle's tripartite division of friendship, focusing mainly on class as the defining factor in friendship. Interestingly enough, Castilla took inspiration from the *Siete Partidas* in arguing that friendship also functioned on a larger societal scale as between rulers and those they ruled.

Two of the better-known Spanish writers, Garcilasco de la Vega (1501–36) and Cervantes (1547–1616), equally borrowed from classical interpretations of friendship.[73] Because Garcilaso received a rudimentary humanistic education,

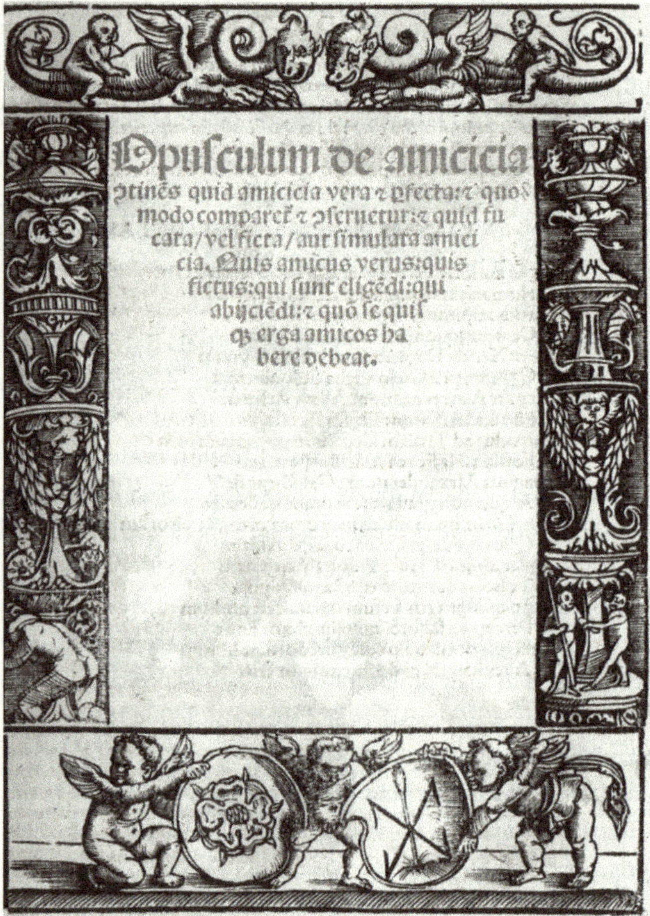

FIGURE 1 Front cover of Roderigo de Encino's *Opusculum amicitiae* (1505)

which would have exposed him to classical conceptions of amity, one scholar has argued that he would have had a unique familiarity with these ideas. For example, true to Aristotle's second tier of friendship, Garcilaso maintained that a friendship based solely on pleasure was not "true" friendship. Yet, while he characterized several types of friendships as "*amistad perfecta*," he believed that it was only perfect if it was practiced among men, since Garcilaso rejected the idea that men and women could ever be friends of the most perfect kind.

Cervantes's literary works, also written from a humanist perspective, were similarly full of references to ideal friendship. In his first book, *La Galatea*

(1585), he portrayed "los dos amigos Silerio and Timbrio" as a depiction of perfect friendship because of Silerio's willingness to sacrifice his life for Timbrio, unsheathing his sword and charging the guards when he saw Timbrio being taken to the gallows.[74] In *Don Quixote*, written between 1605 and 1615, Cervantes again reintroduced a paradigmatic version of friendship to describe the relationship between Don Quixote and his squire, Sancho Panza, as one of intimate loyalty and devotion. This friendship, which was conceptualized by both men as being unequal, was leveled, much like that of Enkidu and Gilgamesh or Achilles and Patroclus, because of their mutual love for one another.

During their epic journey together, while at an inn, they are told the unusual story of *El curioso impertinente* (The Impertinently Curious Man) named Anselmo.[75] As the tale went, Anselmo, a Florentine nobleman, was obsessed with the idea of testing his wife's fidelity. Hoping to put her devotion to the test, he devised an ill-conceived plot in which he tempted his wife Camila with his friend Lotario. Playing the ever-devoted friend, Lotario yielded to Anselmo's whims but, much to Lotario's surprise, ended up falling in love with Camila. Camila reciprocated the sentiment, engaging Lotario in a drawn-out affair behind her husband's back. But this was only the half of it. In blatant disregard to the classical ideals of loyalty and honor, Lotario simultaneously sought to maintain both his affair with Camila and his friendship with Anselmo, hoping Anselmo would be none the wiser. By incorporating this short story into the larger narrative of *Don Quixote*, Cervantes intended to showcase an inferior friendship that was the inverse of ideal.[76]

Friendship in Mesoamerica and New Spain

Nahuatl dictionaries define *amigo* (friend) as *teicniuh* and *ycniuhtli*; *amistad* (friendship) as *ycniuhtlamatini*, *ytechnemachoni*, and *necniuhtiloni*; *amigo eternal* (lifelong friend) as *tonalecapo*, *noyolloicniuh*, *noyolicniuh*, and *notechicniuh*; *mi particular amigo* (my good friend) as *notonalecapo*; *amigos de novela* (iconic or ideal friends) as *tlatomocuicuitlauiani* and *tlatolli quietetemotinemi*; *ganar amigos* (to win over friends) as *pret oninoteicniuhti*; and *el acto de descubrir el secreto al amigo* (the act of discovering a friend's secret) as *neteyollotiliztlie*.[77] These unique friendship categories were reflected in Nahuatl poetry, which was frequently sung at gatherings by wise men and *cuicapicque* (forgers of songs). As discussed in the introduction to this book, the following poem addressed the notion of self-discovery through friendship by knowing "our faces," reflecting the Aristotelian and Ciceronian adage of knowing or perfecting ourselves by means of a congenial friend.

> Let us have friends here!
> It is the time to know our faces.
> Only with flowers
> Can our song enrapture.
> We will have gone to His house,
> but our word
> shall live here on earth.
> We will go, leaving behind
> our grief, our song.
> For this will be known,
> the song shall remain real.
> We will have gone to His house,
> but our word
> shall live here on earth.[78]

The speaker in this poem prescribed friendship both as a venue through which we can better come to know ourselves and as a treatment to life's many struggles.

Nahua poets, much like Christian scholars of the Middle Ages, also addressed the idea of friendship as being between an individual and their community. As the following poem titled "Song of Brotherhood" makes clear, through the ritual act of gift giving and dance, humans would form the necessary bonds of amity required to come to terms with their own mortality. Here the speaker eagerly gave himself over in friendship to the community, so cherishing his ties with them that he promised to take their memory with him into to the "region of the dead."

> I am come, oh my friends,
> with necklaces I entwine you,
> with feathers of the macaw I adorn you,
> a precious bird, I dress with feathers,
> I paint with gold,
> I embrace mankind.
> With trembling quetzal feathers,

with circlets of song,
I give myself to the community.
I will carry you with me to the place
where we all,
someday,
all must betake ourselves,
to the region of the dead.
Our life has only been loaned to us![79]

"Temilotzin's Poem" (below), which was composed a few years before the Spanish Conquest by an Aztec warrior and companion of Cuahutémoc, expressed the notion of sacrifice in friendship.

I am come too,
here I am standing;
now I am going to forge songs,
make a stem flowering with songs,
oh my friends!
God has sent me as a messenger.
I am transformed into a poem,
I, Temilotzin.
I am come too,
to make friends here.[80]

The author of this poem seems to have adopted a dual identity as both human and poem. In this way, this particular poet was better able to spread the message of friendship—a task bequeathed to humanity by the divine. Indeed, Nahuatl poetry was itself considered to be a gift from the gods.

Finally, the importance of friendship for connecting with ourselves and with our communities left many poets concerned about its potential absence in the afterworld. Would there be friendship there? If not, how then would they come to know themselves? The following poem expressed this concern.

Will I have to go like the flowers that perish?
Will nothing remain of my name?
Nothing of my fame here on earth?
At least my flowers, at least my songs!

Earth is the region of the fleeting moment.
Is it also thus in the place
where in some way one lives?
Is there joy there, is there friendship?
Or is it only here on earth
we come to know our faces?[81]

The angst of friendship lost and the process of "mirroring" represented familiar themes within Nahuatl poetry. While friendship was highly prized among the Mexica, and in many ways echoed several of the same themes found throughout the Old World, there is no scholarship that I am aware of that speaks specifically and at length about the philosophy of friendship as it was practiced among pre-Columbian peoples.

In like manner, early modern European dictionaries sought to identify the nature, quality, and purpose of friendship, largely by emphasizing its wide usage and variability. Antonio de Nebrija's 1495 Spanish dictionary, for instance, recognized thirteen adaptations of friendship, including references to male–female friendships.[82] Henríquez's 1679 edition contained as many as twenty-two variations, underscoring friendship ideals such as *amigos de taza y vino* (drinking friends), *el amigo hasta el altar* (a close friend up to the point of marriage), *amigo de honra* (an honorable/virtuous friend), and *amigo de buenas letras* (an educated friend).[83] The Royal Spanish Academy, which published its own dictionary between 1726 and 1739, defined friendship simply as being comprised of love, benevolence, confidence, and reciprocity.[84] The definitional evolution of friendship reflected the cultural ethos of the time in which it was penned and, I would argue, was significantly influenced by the extant corpus of moral literature. Since most Europeans, both educated and uneducated alike, received many of their cultural perceptions about friendship from this type of literature, definitions of friendship can confidently be interpreted as reflections of the larger intellectual and literary trends of the time.

During the sixteenth century, Spanish colonists migrating to the New World recognized friendship largely through its literary adaptations. Thanks to the scholarship of Irving Leonard, we have fairly reliable information on what these early settlers were reading at the time of their arrival. A ship manifesto from 1585 shows that the books onboard seagoing vessels bound for the Americas ranged in themes from adventures of chivalry, such as Garci Rodríguez de Montalvo's *Amadís de Gaula*, Jerónimo Fernández's *Don Belianis*, and Alfonso de Villegas's

Flos santorum (the latter of which was used by Jesuit missionaries well into the eighteenth century), to more highbrowed authors, such as Lope de Vega, Boscan, Juan de Mena, Quevedo, Cervantes, Ovid, Homer, Terence, Cicero, and Aristotle.[85] For Leonard, literature of this sort represented an indispensable agent in the diffusion of Renaissance Europe to the New World, implanting a specific version of Hispanic civilization that sought to highlight its most noble and admirable qualities.[86] During the various cross-Atlantic voyages, which lasted anywhere from one to two months, confined passengers entertained themselves by playing musical instruments, organizing cockfights, and by performing mock bullfights. They also spent long hours reading the most celebrated literary oeuvres, either in silence or aloud to attentive listeners.

Finding themselves amid a new social context, European colonists and intellectuals were compelled to reconceptualize the meaning and purpose of friendship. The conquest of the Americas, coupled with the rise of Renaissance humanism, the Protestant Reformation, and the growth of skepticism, created an intellectual web that was uniquely tailored to the Hispanic world.[87] This ideological netting, which was "original, idiosyncratic, and complex," obliged Spanish intellectuals to turn away from larger European developments in philosophy, ensuring that their frame of reference would be thoroughly American and Iberian in orientation.[88] In particular, it was Spain's encounter with the New World and its indigenous populations that most profoundly influenced the trajectory of their early philosophical inquiries. Of greatest import were questions such as the following: What rights did these people have? Should Christianity be imposed on them? Should they be treated as slaves? Who was the rightful owner of the riches that hitherto had belonged to them? What should the conquerors make of the Natives' laws and traditions? These ethical concerns required a hard-nosed scholarly approach to which humanism and scholasticism provided two contrasting yet interconnected methodologies.[89]

Despite their unique New World orientation, Spanish settlers, intellectuals, and administrators continued to rely on classical thinkers in coming to terms with where the Indian fit on the social ladder. According to Anthony Pagden, by using Greek legal discourse—in particular the Platonic ideal of an organic society composed of various parts that together strengthen the whole—Spaniards had a ready-set prescription for conveniently positioning Indians into a formulaic social pyramid.[90] The following social pyramid, taken from Aristotle, Plato, Cicero, Augustine, and Aquinas's understanding of society as organic and corporatist and filtered through the *Fuero Real* (1255), highlights the logic behind this restructuring of society.

God

Archangels

Angels

Cherubim

Seraphim

Principalities

Princes

Nobility

Artisans

Craftsmen

Merchants

Soldiers

Bureaucrats

Peasants

Slaves

Lions, foxes, dolphins

Lesser animals

Trees, vegetables

Inanimate objects[91]

Following this classical and medieval blueprint, which was ordained by God and therefore inviolable, European settlers used such characteristics as urbanity, language, scholarship, religion, and friendship to distinguish the "civilized" from the "barbaric."[92] In Plato's *Republic* this natural tendency toward forming social hierarchies had been represented by means of the *thymos*, a word that can be translated as "spirit," and which represented a fundamental part of the human soul. According to political theorist Francis Fukuyama, this Greek term, which he calls "megalothymia," functioned under the premise that some people— mostly nobles and aristocrats—were inherently superior to those of lower social rank and must therefore be respected as such in order to attain an ordered and harmonious society.[93]

The process of reconstructing the colonial world along such rigid lines began in the immediate years following the military conquest of America as Spanish intellectuals and legal jurists set in motion a series of vigorous intellectual debates.[94] These scholars zealously sought "to mould the developing colonial society in accordance with its own aspirations, and its own high sense."[95] At the core of these debates was an attempt to understand the nature of the American Indian in terms of both his potential labor and his behavioral expressions.[96] The Crown took careful note of these incredibly important disputations, for it was by means of their philosophical resolutions that legal prescriptions were formalized and implemented.

The most (in)famous of these early neo-Aristotelian thinkers was Juan Ginés de Sepúlveda (1494–1573). Sepúlveda, a highly accomplished humanist scholar trained at Bologna, utilized Aristotelian logic to aggressively argue that the Natives of the New World belonged to the category of natural barbarians or slaves.[97] Due to this extreme social designation, Natives were best served under the protection of Spaniards for whom, in exchange for their support and tutelage, they would have to work as slaves. In making this argument, Sepúlveda was following in the theological footsteps of men like Scottish philosopher and theologian John Mair (1467–1550) and Juan de Quevedo (1450–1519), a Franciscan priest and the first bishop of Santa María de La Antigua del Darién in Panama—both of whom had previously used Aristotelian thought to exemplify the "barbarity" of the Native. Using incredibly blunt and exacting language, Sepúlveda outlined his impression of America's Indians: "These barbarians of the New World . . . in prudence, intelligence, virtue and humanity are as inferior to the Spanish as are children to adults and women to men. The difference between them is as great as between a wild, cruel people and the most merciful, between the grossly intemperate and the most continent and temperate, and, I am tempted to say, between men and monkeys."[98] By means of these irreverent words Sepúlveda had effectively reduced the Indians of the New World to mere animals—an overtly callused strategy for promoting their continued social and political subordination.

Sepúlveda's arguments about the inherent inferiority of Indians were not without refutation. Bartolomé de Las Casas (1484–1566), while also relying on the philosophical urgings of Aristotle, Cicero, and other classical scholars, argued in favor of their humanity.[99] From the time he enrolled in the Dominican Order in 1523, Las Casas had devoted much of his time to studying the works of Aristotle, integrating his ideas and philosophy into several of his own scholarly works.[100] For Las Casas, the designation of "barbarian" was fully without merit, for did not the Natives have cities, politics, and religion—the very accoutrements of civilization? The level of civilization possessed by the Aztecs and the

Incas was, Las Casas believed, equivalent to that of the Greeks and the Romans. Furthermore, had not Spaniards behaved in such a violent and detestable manner that they too, if properly reasoned out, could also be considered barbarians?[101] Michel de Montaigne's famous 1580 essay *Des cannibales* (On Cannibals) had ardently reiterated this claim, asserting that the Natives of the New World were superior to Europeans in their goodness, liberality, and loyalty. A few years later, Dominican friar Luis de Granada (1504–88) in his *Breve tratado* (1588) took as evident that all the indigenous peoples of the New World possessed reason, "which is a natural light which God instilled in our understanding, and which no man lacks."[102] While Las Casas agreed with Sepúlveda that the Spanish monarch had a legitimate right to rule over the New World, he warned the Crown that if it continued to sanction the enslavement of its American subjects, it would legally invalidate its right to govern. As a humanist influenced by classical and religious sources, Las Casas belonged to a group of illustrious thinkers that included the likes of Fray Julián Garcés, Friar Juan de Zumárraga, Vasco de Quiroga, and Francisco Hernández. These men were all independently influenced by the works of scholars such as Erasmus of Rotterdam, Constantino Ponce, Thomas More, and, going further back, Plato and Aristotle.[103]

According to Ivy Schweitzer, the idea of "natural slavery," which had been advanced by neo-Aristotelians like Sepúlveda, "operated like the inverse of perfect friendship and governed how European explorers preconceived and later saw the indigenous people they encountered in the Americas."[104] Because most Europeans regarded sameness and equality as central to their overall conceptualization of friendship, Schweitzer maintains that it became difficult if not impossible for eighteenth-century Anglo thinkers to envisage themselves forming friendships with Natives. For them, the vast racial and behavioral differences between themselves and Native Americans pointed to a cultural imbalance that was simply too much to overcome.[105] But in New Spain things were considerably different. Largely because of the rapid progression of *mestisaje* (race mixture), which made racial difference less striking, Spaniards and criollos were able to respond to their cultural disparity with Natives in a much more nuanced, sophisticated, and often ambiguous way. Here is where the "ironies of Empire" most plainly manifested themselves, for at the same time as Spaniards and criollos promoted the notion of friendship with Natives, they also advocated for the Platonic ideal of an organic social hierarchy. Because Natives were integral to the economic and political life of the empire, the colonial discourse on civilization necessitated the idealization (though not necessarily the implementation) of relations of amity, particularly between Indians and Spaniards and, as time wore on, between colonials and the Crown.[106] In New Spain, then, the rhetoric of friendship took on a political, cultural, and economic importance not found among the English of North America.

Throughout Spanish America, the archetype of high civilization, such as it was described by classical scholars, became etched into the very pane of colonial thought and administration. The prejudices that emerged from this elevated point of reference were as evident along the southern edges of South America as they were on the northern borders of New Spain.[107] In northern Sonora, for instance, while O'odham and Sobaipuri communities tilled the mission fields and attended Mass—qualities, many believed, demonstrative of a civilized existence—they regularly "returned to the wilds" when it suited them, usually around harvest time.[108] For colonial administrators, this patent inconsistency pointed to their inherently "barbarous nature," which only further reinforced the perception that, despite bouts of civilized undertakings, their true intentions were always unknowable and disingenuous. Thus, while Jesuit missionary Andrés Pérez de Ribas (1575–1655), citing religious and classical scholars such as St. Paul, Augustine, Cicero, and Horace, believed that the "barbarous" nations of Sinaloa had the potential of exhibiting "Christian friendship" toward Europeans if only instructed in the proper methods of "civilization," others believed that this was simply not enough.[109] Pérez de Ribas's assessment of Native barbarism echoed the thoughts of earlier intellectuals such as José de Acosta, who in his *De Procuranda Indorum Salute* (1588) cast the Natives of the New World as "barbarous" largely because of their ignorance of Christian civilization.[110] Throughout the colonial period, critics of men like Acosta and Pérez de Ribas embraced the view that while civilizing Natives was indeed the proper first step toward achieving a lasting peace, it needed to be accompanied by the complete annihilation of their old customs. On the Bolivian frontier, Spanish functionary Francisco de Paula Sanz (1745–1810) noted that while tribute-paying Indians seemed to have adopted the rough trappings of civilization, the fact that they continued to speak their native languages and don their traditional garb only reinforced their "barbarity."[111] In order to unfetter them from their own "backwardness," it was imperative that such conventional practices be eradicated. Archbishop of Mexico Manuel José Rubio y Salinas (1703–65) anticipated Paula Sanz's call to civilize Natives when during his tenure as archbishop (1749–65) he oversaw the creation of some 237 Spanish-language schools throughout central New Spain. The goal of these schools was straightforward enough: the complete eradication of *lenguas bárbaras* (savage tongues). Only in this way, he held, would Indians be properly introduced into "civil life," thus facilitating their eventual commercial and cultural integration into the empire.[112]

As Pagden writes, "The close association in the Christian mind between belief and certain types of social behavior meant . . . that there were those who were prepared to argue that the forced introduction into 'civility' was legitimate as the preliminary and necessary condition of voluntary conversion."[113] Whether this meant that their old customs should be respected, so as to avoid any resentment and derision toward the missionary enterprise, or completely eradicated became a major source of debate. The borrowing of the term *barbarian* from Aristotle thus provided Spaniards and criollos with a useful framework for negating those more tradition-bound societies any meaningful social status or full-fledged political sovereignty.

With Aristotelian logic in mind, the Laws of the Indies (1513), amended first in 1523 and then again in 1573 and 1680, were established. The final version, the *Recopilación de las Leyes de los Reynos de Indias* (Compilation of the Laws of the Kingdoms of the Indies), was a set of 6,377 laws subdivided into nine books. Book IV of the Laws set forth 148 ordinances that dealt largely with city planning. Generally speaking, it represented the most comprehensive set of instructions ever created for the founding and building of towns in the Americas and "in terms of their widespread application and persistence probably the most effective planning documents in the history of mankind."[114] This section of the Laws made numerous civilizational demands of Natives, of which living in a city was at the forefront—recall that cities were, according to Aristotle, places where friendship and civil society merged. It also sought to civilize Spaniards and Natives by governing the nature of their interactions. Efforts at regulating Spanish–Native interactions had been previously attempted through the Laws of Burgos (1512) and the New Laws (1542). Book IV of the Laws of the Indies built on these legal documents by promoting civilized behavior and friendship as central components in the development of cities. While ordinances 15–31 instructed Spaniards on the formal issues of encountering, greeting, teaching, and punishing the indigenous populations of the New World, ordinances 136–39 addressed friendship specifically. Ordinance 136, for instance, stated that "if natives should resolve to take a defensive position toward the [new] settlement, they should be made aware of how we intend to settle, not to do damage to them nor take away their lands, but instead gain their friendship and teach them how to live civilly."[115] This ordinance made it clear that the onus of "gaining" friendship belonged to Spaniards. But how would they "gain" the friendship of the very people whose land they had just usurped? The following ordinance (137) suggested an answer, linking fear with respect and friendship. It stipulated that "they [the Spaniards] should be so feared that they [the Indians] will not dare offend them, but instead they will respect them and desire their friendship."[116] By means of this Machiavellian approach that mixed fear with love, Spaniards would eventually acquire the much-desired friendship of Natives.[117]

Following from this, ordinances 138 and 139 proposed that prior to the completion of a settlement, Spaniards should ensure that any form of antagonism between them and the relocated Natives be eliminated. Spaniards should then obtain information on

> the diversity of nations, languages, sects, and prejudices of the natives within the province, and about the lords they may pledge allegiance to, and by means of commerce and exchange, [the Spaniards] should try to establish friendship with them [the Indians], showing great love and caressing them and also giving them things in barter that will attract their interest, and not showing greediness for their things. [The Spaniards] should establish friendship and alliances with the principal lords and other influential persons who would be most useful in the pacification of the land.

In an almost complete reversal of ordinance 137, ordinance 138 clearly stated that friendship should be established through "love and caressing." The logic here was apparent if rather self-serving and shortsighted. Whereas ordinance 137 underscored fear as a tool for establishing an initial presence in heavily populated indigenous areas, ordinance 138 proposed that once the settlement had been fully established, the relationship should evolve into one of love and compassion—as if the memory of their subjugation and relocation would simply be forgotten and forgiven. Furthermore, this ordinance assumed both a strategic connection (an alliance) and an emotional closeness (friendship); both were interconnected, but they represented separate strategies in the process of settlement.

In Book Four of his *Milicia y descipción de las Indias* (1599), Bernardo de Vargas Machuca (1557–1622), a former soldier who had lived in the New World for more than twenty years, offered a similar instructional manual for the foundation of towns.[118] Like the Laws of the Indies, Machuca had argued that settlers seeking to establish a town should, as an initial first step, assure the Indians of their peaceful intentions. Settlers should be practical, negotiating when necessary favorable peace terms with Native communities. But they should also be savvy to the complexities of indigenous politics, always strategizing on how best to exploit existing tribal rivalries. As with Book Four of the Laws of the Indies, there is simply no escaping the transparently calculated and manipulative method undergirding Spanish policy. The extent to which indigenous peoples understood such duplicitous tactics, developing in response their own counterstrategies, is an intriguing proposition worthy of further study.

To facilitate the "civilizing mission," Machuca continued, Indians should build their houses near religious institutions such as churches or missions. With the tacit endorsement of the local Indian chieftain, the Spanish caudillo should then erect a tree trunk whereby he would sink his knife into it and proclaim his right to rule and punish. He would then declare, "I hereby found this community in the name of his Majesty, and in his royal name I shall protect it and keep peace and justice among all its inhabitants, Spaniards, conquerors, settlers, residents, and outsiders, and all its native population as well. I shall administer even-handed justice to the poor and the rich, to the humble and the exalted, and I shall protect their widows and orphans."[119] To formally establish possession of the community, the caudillo would then proceed to slash bushes in sight of everyone, thereby placing the community under royal jurisdiction.

This kind of symbolic ownership of the land had its antecedents in the Old World, being first implemented outside of Europe in 1464 when Diego de Herrera (1417–85) took possession of the Canary Islands by raising the royal standard, stamping the ground with his feet, and cutting the branches off of several trees.[120] In other parts of the New World, Spanish caudillos threw stones to delimit the extent of their rule. Once these symbolic gestures were concluded and the land was officially under the authority of the Spanish caudillo, he would, according to the *Milicia*, brandish his sword and challenge any opponents to a duel. Following this, "a cross would then be erected at the site of the future church, Mass said to impress the Indians, and the caudillo's cabildo appointments announced."[121] Overall, Book Four of the *Milicia* adumbrated the highly structured, ritualistic, and hierarchical nature of Spanish-American city-building policies, the reach of royal and ecclesiastical power, and "the role of urban centres in appropriating territory and recruiting native peoples for the economic needs of settlers and for the political and 'civilizing' purposes of empire."[122]

Book One through Book Four of the *Milicia*, much like Book Four of the Laws of the Indies and the *Siete Partidas*, represented one part of a larger

FIGURE 2 Front cover to Bernardo de Vargas Machuca's
Milicia y descipción de las Indias (1599)

"civilizing process" occurring throughout the whole of Spanish America. In all three of these foundational texts, which were responsible in many ways for outlining the contours of Spanish settlement and colonialism in the New World, the association between the civilizing mission and friendship occupied an important role. In fact, two centuries after the first printing of the Laws of the Indies and the *Milicia*, Spaniards colonizing Sonora continued to see their mission as a civilizing one. For them, civilizing the desert required the transportation, establishment, and, if necessary, imposition of Spanish institutions, culture, and customs onto the "barbarian" Natives. In the process, settlers were expected to utilize the land to their advantage, extracting as much mineral wealth as possible.[123] Anthropologist Edward Spicer has argued that this single concept (civilizing the Native) remained relatively consistent from the sixteenth through the nineteenth century.[124] However, while the practical outlines of civilizing Natives didn't change much over the early colonial period, its ideological impetus did, being reconfigured during the so-called Age of Reason. This transitional period, which embraced much of the eighteenth century, introduced a renewed ethos into the conventional civilizing formula. In an effort to make reason the cornerstone of human interaction, enlightened scholars and administrators openly rejected fear as a means of winning over Natives, preferring relationships founded on love and friendship.[125] Here again, however, we see the conflictual relationship between ideology and practice because while the most enlightened of these scholars favored reason, a majority of seasoned soldiers and administrators continued to prefer the mixed strategy of friendship and violence that had worked well for them over the previous two centuries.

Through representations of friendship taken from classical philosophers, early modern religious thinkers, legal codes and city-planning documents, and humanist writers, a new sociopolitical layout was being established. But it was fraught with confounding hurdles, particularly because at its core rested a deep, irreconcilable contradiction. On one hand, colonial philosophies of friendship, which occupied a prominent place within the social tapestry of New Spain, sought to disempower those deemed racially inferior precisely by defining their inadequacy as friends. Throughout the colonial period, Spanish scholars and administrators used Old World interpretations of friendship as ideological instruments from which to systematically exclude, dehumanize, and set in place restrictive behavioral standards on Indians and other non-Europeans. Spanish-American colonial thinkers carefully utilized amity and its attendant emotional and behavioral characteristics as a tool of effective government, recasting it as an essential feature of civilized life. Through a process of fashioned self-promotion Spaniards conveniently placed themselves atop the civilizational pyramid, using their elevated social position to exploit non-Europeans, who, by virtue of their "barbaric" status, were incapable of understanding notions of true friendship and thus of contributing to the formation of civil society. Without recourse to the intellectual construction of friendship, Indians, blacks, and *castas* (mixed-race people) could not connect with their fellows, thus remaining outside the realm of official political discourse. On the other hand, Spaniards continued to demand that individual Native leaders, and indeed entire communities, adopt and adhere to idealized European conceptions of friendship as a primary step toward embracing a new standard of civilization. By extension, adopting this new civilizational standard would facilitate the formation of civil society. This uniquely colonial paradox, which remained unresolved for much of the colonial period, set the stage for the development of a society that perforce necessitated nuance, contradiction, and irony in order to function.

While the behavioral and ideological expectations of friendship remained important means of moral and political authority for Spanish settlers, missionaries, and magistrates, these leaders were soon forced to realize a workable arrangement between archetype and practice, especially at the edges of empire where ideology often played second fiddle to the demands of survival. Along New Spain's northern frontier, Spaniards utilized two forms of friendship to their advantage: the first centered on its practicality, giving credence to the necessity for Indian knowledge of the local landscape, assistance in military matters, and labor; the second focused on the strategic implementation of Western ideals of friendship as a tool for establishing specific standards of behavior and by implication of promoting European civilization. By incorporating "violent" and "nonviolent" Indians into their emotional economy of friendship, Spaniards skillfully colonized the very notion, turning it into a subtle form of subjugation, while creating specific behavioral expectations founded on Old World rules of fellowship. "For the subjects of the Spanish empire," writes Alejandro Cañeque, "love and friendship were not, as we nowadays tend to assume, personal feelings devoid of political meaning but rather very strict forms of codifying power exchanges and of conditioning social behavior."[126]

In addition to demarcating idealized relations between Indians and Spaniards, friendship was also conceived as being between the king and his New World subjects. Because Aristotle's works, the *Siete Partidas*, and the literary oeuvres of men like Francisco de Castilla and Cervantes had argued that friendship was possible among socially unequal persons, seventeenth-century Spanish administrators utilized this validation to highlight a metaphorical relationship between a sovereign and his subjects as one of friendship. A seventeenth-century manual on how a ruler should rule his people titled *Quien deua a quien más amor, el Príncipe a los vassallos, o los vassallos al Príncipe?* (Who owes who the most love, the ruler to his vassals, or the vassals to the ruler?) argued that while a sovereign was entrusted with the protection of his vassals' lives and honor, the vassals were in turn compelled to provide unadulterated love and complete loyalty to their king.[127]

Such benevolence between the king and his subjects was addressed in the *Siete Partidas* through three fundamental proclamations: "First, by conferring benefits upon them [vassals], and doing them favors . . . it is eminently proper that he [the king] bestow favors upon them. . . . Second, by showing compassion upon them . . . he will be to them as a father who brings up his children in love, and punishes them with mercy. . . . Third, by having pity upon them, and remitting at times the penalty which they deserve."[128] Sixteenth-century humanist Desiderius Erasmus (1464–1536) later suggested that an ideal monarch should not gauge the state of the kingdom in material terms; rather, he noted, "a king must assure that the people conduct themselves in an honorable and disciplined fashion, disdaining greed and living together in harmony. True happiness could only be spiritual, while the prince's esteem rested on his 'kindness and beneficence.'"[129] The proper role of the Christian state was therefore that of "'admiration, kindness, and protection.'"[130]

According to Cañeque, by the seventeenth century this type of emotional relationship between the king and his subjects began to be conceived of as one of friendship. Juan Pablo Gil-Osle adds that within the seventeenth-century Spanish literary ideal of friendship, "the rhetoric of patronage and the rhetoric of friendship were two sides of the same coin."[131] Therefore, the relationship between the king and his vassals was in actuality one of political and spiritual reciprocity. For Gil-Osle, it is only through an understanding of early modern notions of political patronage that we can fully comprehend the ways in which friendship doubled as a system of clientism and as a rhetorical tool for influencing moral behavior.

Miguel Lastaria's 1804 *Documentos para la historia Argentina* clearly conveys this sentiment, noting that the Spanish as much as the Portuguese sought to establish solid ties of friendship with their respective monarchies.[132] According to Lastaria, this feeling extended to the South American Indians of the Chaco, who he believed desperately wanted nothing more than friendship and familiarity with the Spanish.[133] For Lastaria nothing ingratiated "God as much as the conversion of these infidels, and nothing is more desired from this Catholic monarchy than their reduction . . . to these infidels are given the name of friends and they are to be treated as one's own children."[134] But as Lastaria argued, friendship with the Natives was something that operated along an evolving scale, which was dependent on a number of specific behavioral attributes. To best determine the quality of any given friendship, then, Lastaria divided Indians into fourteen different "degrees of progress," with the final stage being conceived of as the "adult stage of civilization." According to this calculation, Spaniards occupied the top position, unconquered Indians the lowest. The remaining Indians "were ranked according to the degree to which they had absorbed Christianity and other Spanish ways, beginning with Indians who had accepted baptism but fled the missions and thus became 'wild Indians.'"[135]

Along the northern and southern edges of Spain's colonial empire, friendship had by the eighteenth century elevated one behavioral aspect above all others. If the empire was to be successful, it needed all its residents to be loyal. Spaniards required Natives to be loyal to them as individuals as well as devoted subjects of the Crown. Loyalty to Crown and Church, therefore, represented the most basic commitment Spanish administrators and missionaries required of their Indian charges, and it could be demonstrated in myriad ways. The most explicit of these was in maintaining outwardly peaceful relations with Spaniards while conversely articulating an animosity toward indios enemigos.[136] Loyalty, as J. H. Elliott has argued, took on cultlike status in the New World as Spanish administrators sought to control the actions and political devotion of its vassals. This ideal was so strong, Elliott maintains, that it took "deep root in the political culture of the emerging colonial world."[137] Along the northern frontier, it was the enlightened administrator José de Gálvez (1720–87) who carried forward this proposition, implementing policies that aimed to keep Indians in a sustained state of loyalty.

Because Indian settlements in colonial Sonora consisted of small *rancherías* (hamlets) scattered about a vast terrain and made up of diverse linguistic groups, loyalty was seen as the most elementary and therefore essential requirement for every Indian to profess if the colonial project was to have any measure of success. For Sonora's settler population, absolute loyalty to Crown and Church represented the basis of Indian friendship writ large. As a number of scholars have argued, during the colonial period "Spain evolved a complex set of laws, royal orders, and heavily bureaucratized religious, military, and civil institutions to cope with a single problem: how to make loyal Spanish subjects out of native peoples."[138] The concept of loyalty was not, however, a straightforward one. As the following chapters highlight, it was conceived of in slightly different terms by missionaries who relied on its religious and intellectual idiosyncrasies and by administrators and settlers who embraced its more pragmatic applications. Due to the isolated, violent, and ecologically unforgiving nature of the frontier, uncertain loyalties represented an enormous liability that could prove deadly. As the eighteenth century progressed, and as rival European empires jockeyed for control over North America, loyalty as a philosophical concept and as a practical expectation attained even greater importance. Of greatest concern for Spanish officials during this time was the possibility that Indians, particularly those from New Mexico and Texas, might, because of poor treatment, form new and perhaps more advantageous friendships with their imperial rivals.[139]

At their foundation, then, friendships between Indians and Spaniards approximated something akin to a client–patron relationship; seldom did they resemble the tender bonds of comradeship, though they certainly did in a number of cases, as we shall see later in this book.[140] More important for the development of civil society was the way in which the rhetoric of friendship was systematically employed to encourage metaphorical relationships, as those between individuals (usually a leader of some sort) and entire communities, particularly Spanish ones. The main goal behind the intellectual construction of friendship was as much to structure individual and communal behavior as to limit the extent of Native power and influence. This large-scale ideational construction of friendship derived from the Hapsburg model of administration, where a slow, inefficient, and incompetent colonial bureaucracy was tolerated so long as its colonial subjects remained loyal.[141] Loyalty in Sonora originated from this generalized archetype. Interethnic friendships could thus prove to be fruitful nonzero-sum games in which both parties benefited or, in terms of game theory, won from their mutual association.[142] However, given the unpredictable nature of the Sonoran environment, nonzero-sum relationships could rapidly turn into zero-sum games, for it paid to be loyal so long as it paid to be loyal.

Conclusion

Though classical and religious friendship ideals dominated much of the colonial period, they met their first major intellectual challenge at the turn of the nineteenth century with the publication of Latin America's first picaresque novel, *El periquillo sarniento* (The Mangy Parrot). To be sure, scholars such as Don Carlos Sigüenza y Góngora (1645–1700) and Sor Juana Inéz de la Cruz

(1648–95) had been avid critics of classical and religious ideas (see chapter 3), but the popular and vernacular nature of this particular novel made its message widely accessible to most colonial readers. This novel, which broke from the established European literary canon, traced the adventures and misadventures of a young boy named Pedro Sarmiento. Through this young boy, José Joaquín Fernández de Lizardi (1776–1827) challenged classical ideals of friendship by presenting an autochthonous version of amity that utilized everyday experiences from the perspective of the lower classes. The friendships expressed in this novel were inspired by personal necessity; they were often short-lived and, in many cases, exploitative. But they possessed an important element of sincerity and authenticity that was lacking in their more idealized counterparts.

Throughout the novel, readers engaged with a version of friendship that was at times genuine and humorous and at others vulgar and crude. At one point in the novel Pedro states, "These devilish friends who led me astray and who lead so many astray in this world are expert in the cursed art of cloaking vices with the names of virtues. They call dissipation liberality; gambling honest entertainment, no matter how many savings are lost; lewdness, courtliness; drunkenness, pleasure; arrogance, authority; shallowness, dignity."[143] In effect, Lizardi was directly challenging idealized interpretations of friendship, celebrating in their stead the more authentic, albeit often immoral and corrupt, forms of amity that he believed accurately portrayed the reality of nineteenth-century Mexico. Here then was a popular novel that privileged everyday friendships over the more illustrious and heroic forms with which this chapter began.

The ideological roots of friendship in Northern New Spain can thus be traced back to its earliest European and Native societies and to their philosophical and literary traditions. From the *Epic of Gilgamesh* to *El periqullo sarniento*, Old World ideological influences shaped the way in which Europeans and later criollos conceptualized friendship in the New World. For Native Americans, friendship ideals were found both in their literature and poetry and in their traditional rituals that involved dance and gifting. Taken together, both Continental influences coalesced along the frontiers of America, creating in the process a specific brand of friendship that privileged loyalty and behavior as its primary components. In this way, loyalty to individual Spaniards, Jesuit missionaries, and the king became conceptualized as a form of "Christian friendship," forming the centerpiece of the missionizing project. In order for Indians to fully embrace Catholic Christianity, many believed that Natives first needed to have accepted the accoutrements of civilization, of which friendship was an essential ingredient.

Aristotle had argued that friendship was integral to the development of the Greek polis, and so it was that "Christian friendship" represented a specific style of engagement and behavior on the frontier. The creation of the Spanish Empire in the New World was, therefore, as much about conquest, colonization, *mestiaje* (race mixture), and exploitation as it was about ideas and emotion. The following chapter highlights the manner in which ideas about civilization, Christianity, and friendship coalesced as settlers, administrators, and missionaries attempted to promote a version of civil society that emphasized order, obedience, and loyalty among its multiethnic populations.

CHAPTER TWO

Civilizing the Frontier

Soldiers, Missionaries, and Indios Amigos

No one has greater love than this, to lay down one's life for one's friends. You are my friends if you do what I command you. I do not call you servants any longer, because the servant does not know what the master is doing; but I have called you friends, because I have made known to you everything that I have heard from my Father.

—John 15:12–15, NRSV

AS EUROPEAN INTELLECTUALS DEBATED THE NATURE OF THE Indian and the meaning of the Spanish Conquest, conquistadores and settlers reassessed the legacy of *La Reconquista* (the reconquest: 711–1492) and its civilizing mission. For close to eight hundred years, defenders of Christendom had been engaged in intermittent warfare against the Islamic armies of southern Spain and North Africa, striking the final victorious blow to Al-Andalus on January 2, 1492. That year proved historic for the Spanish monarchs, Ferdinand (1452–1516) and Isabella (1451–1504). In an effort to streamline Iberian Catholicism and modernize the Spanish state, they signed the Alhambra Decree that March, expelling all practicing Jews from the peninsula. Seven months later, Christopher Columbus (1451–1506) landed on an island in the Caribbean, initiating the conquest of the Americas. Castilians and Aragoneses were more than eager to conceptualize this new discovery as a divine offering to the recently unified Spanish Crown, gifted to the Catholic monarchs for their victory over the Moors and so that they may continue converting infidels over to the one "true" religion. The election of Charles V in 1519 further intensified the feeling of divine favor.[1]

Early Hispanic writers such as Jesuit theologian José de Acosta (1539–1600) added to this state of generalized euphoria when he declared that "God so loved Castile" that he had given her an entire new world, so that with all its newfound wealth and vast natural resources, Castile could continue to defend European Catholicism against the heresies of the Turks and the Protestants. Other intellectuals such as Franciscan missionary and historian Gerónimo de Mendieta (1525–1604) took a slightly more pious approach, writing in his *Historia eclesiástica indiana* (1596) that "God gave the Indies to Spain in order that she might cultivate a profit from the mines of so many Indian souls."[2] The papal bull *Inter caetera*, issued on May 4, 1493, by Pope Alexander VI (1431–1503), gave Castile full political sovereignty over the New World and its indigenous populations. The following year the Spanish and Portuguese monarchs signed the Treaty of Tordesillas, officially moving the line of demarcation fifty leagues west of its original position and by implication eliminating all other European rivals from staking claim to this new land. Incensed by the pope's audacity in sanctioning such an exclusionary treaty, King Francis I (1494–1547) famously demanded to be shown the pertinent clause in Adam's will that excluded France from its equal share of wealth from the Americas. Despite imperial scheming over access to the New World, the full significance of this momentous discovery registered at a methodically slow pace as learned men from throughout Europe struggled to come to grips with its immeasurable implications.[3]

Throughout the Americas the spirit of *La Reconquista* was renewed in the militant ethos of conquistadores and *adelantados* (a military title held by those conquistadores who were the first to reconnoiter an area) who hoped to obtain wealth and titles of nobility from the land and its indigenous peoples. "I have not come to till the land like a peasant," wrote Hernán Cortés, echoing the sentiment of other like-minded adventurers.[4] In *La araucana*, published in three parts from 1569 to 1589, Alonso de Ercilla (1533–94) celebrated the heroism of *La Reconquista* by equating its intrepid character with the battles that were then raging between Spaniards and Indians along the Chilean frontier. The violent legacy of this eight-hundred-year battle with Islam in effect militarized Hispanic society while simultaneously fortifying its aristocratic character, particularly the idea that "wealth should be gained by plunder or the forced labor" of its subjugated populations.[5] This militaristic mindset, which went hand in hand with Spain's religious mission to Christianize and civilize those within its path, dated back to the Old Testament "when Yahweh sanctioned the Hebrew's conquest of Canaan."[6] Constantine (306–37) continued the practice of conversion through conquest when he used the incredible might of the Roman army to defend and expand the reaches of the Church. Charlemagne (768–814) did the same when from 772 to 804 he overthrew the Saxons and converted them to Catholic Christianity. Similarly, during the thirteenth century, Teutonic knight-monks who had been transferred from Jerusalem to the Baltic proceeded to conquer and convert its native populations. Thus "when emperor Charles V (1516–1556) campaigned against the Ottoman Turks in the Mediterranean or sanctioned the deeds of the conquistadores in the New World, he was fulfilling the ancient ideology of *cruzada* or holy war."[7] Later, Phillip II's (1527–98) Mediterranean policy of maintaining defensive forts along the Spanish frontier while fostering peace agreements with Muslim rulers from North Africa would be replicated in all those lands residing under the imposing shadow of the holy cross.[8]

Sustained efforts at bringing New Spain under the fold of Catholic Christianity through conquest began in central Mexico. Throughout the sixteenth and seventeenth centuries, military forays ventured north and south of the capital as ambitious men with extravagant dreams sought to make names for themselves. In 1523, two years after the fall of Tenochtitlán, Pedro de Alvarado (1485–1541), an Extremeño from Badajoz and the architect of the Toxcatl massacre, set off for Guatemala and El Salvador.[9] Through the brutal exploitation of indigenous communities and the skillful manipulation of their internal rivalries, Alvarado achieved measured successes, eventually attaining the governorship of Guatemala in 1527. Thirteen years later, Francisco Vázquez de Coronado y Luján (1510–1554), a thirty-year-old Spanish adventurer and governor of Nueva Galicia, led a group of about 260 settlers, 60 soldiers, and as many as 2,000 indios amigos into New Mexico in search of the fabled seven cities of Cíbola.[10] Many died along the way, and even though his expedition took him deep into the heart of North America, there was ultimately no city of gold—there was no Cíbola, no Gran Quivirá. In fact, there was little mineral wealth at all. This unfortunate reality, coupled with fierce opposition from a number of Native groups, convinced him to abandon the venture after only two years. Native hostility to the Coronado expedition was not entirely unjustified, for while many spurned the harsh treatment of Coronado's men, others retained vivid memories of the entrada (expedition into an unknown or unsettled area) of Nuño Beltrán de Guzmán (1490–1558), an Indian slaver of the worst sort who, accompanied by a sturdy contingent of Spanish soldiers and fifteen thousand Native allies, blazed a trail of destruction through Michoacán, Jalisco, Zacatecas, Nayarit, and Sinaloa.[11]

It took more than forty years for the Crown to commission another expedition to the north. In 1581 Francisco Sánchez Chamuscado and Fray Agustín Rodríguez made their way into New Mexico looking for "lost souls" and mineral wealth—the dual engines of northward advancement. Aside from documenting the landscape and identifying a number of new indigenous groups, their expedition was largely uneventful.[12] The following year, Antonio de Espejo journeyed north in search of the already martyred Fray Rodríguez, who had decided to stay with the Natives when Chamuscado and his nine Spanish soldiers retreated back to the mining town of Santa Bárbara, Chihuahua. Both expeditions lasted only a few months and from the Spanish perspective proved inconsequential. Unsanctioned expeditions in the early 1590s, such as the one by Gaspar Castaño de Sosa and a later one by Captains Leyva de Bonilla and Antonio Gutiérrez, yielded similar outcomes. Despite the inability to effectively colonize the north during these early years, two small Spanish settlements (San Miguel de Culiacán and San Sebastián) were eventually established in Sinaloa.

It was not until 1598 when Juan de Oñate y Salazar (1550–1626), a forty-eight-year-old miner and entrepreneur from Zacatecas, finally realized the colonization of the far north. His initial expedition into New Mexico possibly numbered seven thousand head of livestock and more than five hundred colonists comprised of soldiers, women, children, servants, and slaves.[13] Ten Franciscan missionaries also accompanied the group. Unlike the various *adelantados* who had preceded him, Oñate was somewhat successful in establishing a number of Spanish colonies during his tenure as governor (1598–1607). But, as was the case with so many of these early settlements, in order to convince settlers to remain among the impoverished Pueblo communities of the region, Oñate felt himself compelled to promise them ample opportunities for wealth. When his promises fell hollow, all but the most ardent abandoned the struggling province. By 1630 only 250 Spaniards remained in Santa Fe. The lack of mineral wealth, the distance from material and cultural centers, the difficult and harsh climate, and the presence of hostile indigenous groups represented irreconcilable challenges for many of New Mexico's earliest Spanish pioneers.[14]

The eagerness with which so many colonists abandoned New Mexico came as somewhat of a surprise to Oñate given that initially things seemed so promising. As was common among many of the indigenous communities throughout the northern frontier, Natives graciously welcomed Oñate's expedition with food and lodging. The Zuni, wrote Oñate, "received us very well with maize, tortillas, beans and quantities of rabbits and hares, of which there were a great many. They were very amiable people and all rendered obedience to his Majesty." They were not the only ones to behave in such an outwardly friendly manner. Other tribes further inland also "came out to receive us with tortillas, scattering fine flour upon us and upon our horses as a token of peace and friendship."[15] It was, argues one scholar, through the "limits of hospitality" and "goodwill" that the far northern frontier was "defined in the minds of Spaniards."[16] These mental and affective "limits" acted as useful guideposts and maps in the Spanish imagination, allowing them to delimit the territorial extent of their authority. But such perceptual maps were difficult to decipher because they were constantly fluctuating amid the ambiguities of indigenous pleasantries and the vicissitudes of colonial rule.

Integral to the dual process of civilization and Christianization was the economic exploitation of the land. In 1546, Spanish commander Juan de Tolosa set up camp at the foot of a mountain near Zacatecas called La Bufa. Making every effort to befriend local Natives, Tolosa was soon repaid for his kindness when he was escorted to a site with "live rocks" that turned out to be deposits of silver ore.[17] The discovery of silver at La Bufa made Tolosa an extremely wealthy man, but more importantly it transformed Zacatecas into one of the richest mining centers in all of New Spain. Thirty-nine years later, due to its impressive growth, it was given the designation of a *ciudad* (city).[18] Subsequently known as the "mother of the frontier," the discovery of silver at Zacatecas was instrumental in the continued northward advance of Spanish colonization. At Santa Bárbara, Chihuahua, rich silver deposits along the valley of Río Conchos began drawing in Spaniards from all over New Spain during the 1560s. A little less than a century later, in the early 1630s, silver was discovered in San José de Parral, converting that mining district into a boomtown and eventually the de facto center of government for Nueva Vizcaya. These mining communities were the first large-scale permanent settlements in northern New Spain, encompassing all the settlers and miners within a five- to fifteen-mile radius.[19]

The desire to find silver and other lucrative minerals, as had been discovered in Zacatecas, Chihuahua, and Durango, continued to loom large in the minds of Spanish settlers. It was this omnipresent dream that ultimately led to the conquest and colonization of Sonora. By 1678, the Spanish population of Sonora had approached three thousand.[20] In 1683, a silver strike at Los Frailes in southern Sonora led to the founding of the *real de minas* (mining town or district) of Nuestra Señora de la Concepción de los Álamos. A century later, Álamos had become "the wealthiest and most powerful Spanish community in the Southwest," with a Royal Treasury (established in 1769), a bishop (1779), and a population of more than five thousand inhabitants—three-fifths of which were Spanish. Like Zacatecas and Parral, Álamos soon "developed into an urban center, with cobblestone streets, high-ceilinged mansions and a magnificent church where wealthy miners and merchants formed one of the competing-yet-interlocking urban élites that dominated the late-18th and 19th century politics in Sinaloa and Sonora."[21] Productive mining centers such as Álamos created a cottage industry with haciendas and ranches springing up in the vicinity of functioning mines in order to provide workers with essential foodstuffs and clothing.[22]

Unfortunately, the growth of the mining industry in northern New Spain coincided with the rapid destruction of its few forested areas, drastically altering the natural environment. Mining, particularly vein mining, required large amounts of timber for scaffolding and for fuel in its processing plants.[23] It also necessitated large amounts of water. In Sonora, entire communities of Yaquis, Mayos, Opatas, Edeves, and Pimas were resettled so that mine owners could have enough workers. While the process of relocation created new communities, it weakened or destroyed long-standing ethnic boundaries.[24] In addition, the increased consumption of both surface and underground water sources, partly due to a combination of mining, large-scale farming, and animal husbandry, led to protracted conflict with and among those indigenous communities who had had access to reliable sources of water for generations. Settlers further altered the human and cultural terrain in several crucial ways. First, they unknowingly introduced European pathogens such as smallpox and typhus, leading to a precipitous decline in the indigenous population. Second, and in the wake of this biological catastrophe, Europeans incorporated into the local ecology foreign foodstuffs such as wheat and grapes and alien livestock such as horses, sheep, pigs, and cattle. These domesticated animals, which ate much of the protective natural grasses and shrubs, had a major impact on the ecology of the region, increasing runoff from summer rains and by implication intensifying soil erosion. These same animals were also notorious for trampling indigenous gardens and plots, becoming a constant source of irritation for many Indian communities. Further altering the demographic landscape of the frontier was the arrival of indigenous settlers from central Mexico, particularly Tlaxcallans. These groups mixed into frontier society in a number of ways. Eventually they set up their own colonies: San Estéban de Nueva Tlaxcala and Santa María de Parras, Coahuila, among others. Frontier settlers also found it necessary to incorporate local Indian captives into their fledgling societies. At local festivals and trade fairs held throughout the northern frontier, captured Indians, mostly women and children from enemy tribes, were sold to Spanish households to be

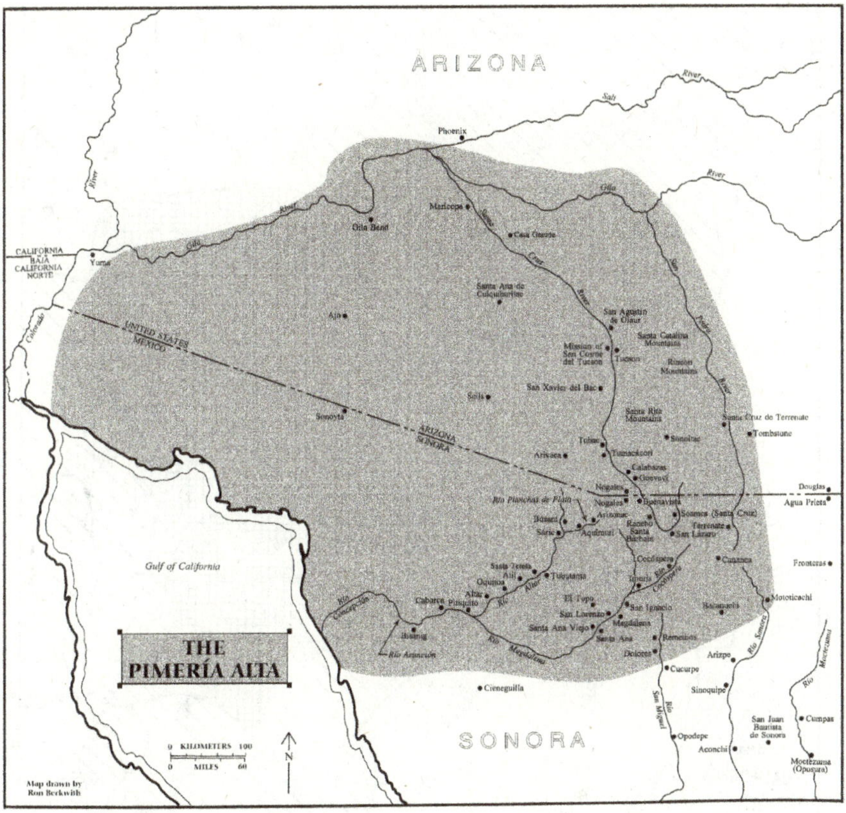

MAP 1 Map of the Pimería Alta, circa 1750. With permission from the Southwestern Mission Research Center.

used as domestic laborers. These *criados* (servants) were then incorporated into borderland society, adding to the already byzantine mixture of ethnic and racial groups inhabiting the area.[25]

Civilization and Christian Friendship

The conquest and colonization of Sinaloa and Sonora began roughly three years after Oñate settled New Mexico. In 1601 Captain Diego Martínez de Hurdaide (b. 1568)—a hardnosed military man whom one scholar has described as being short in stature with bowed legs and a deformed foot but nonetheless incredibly

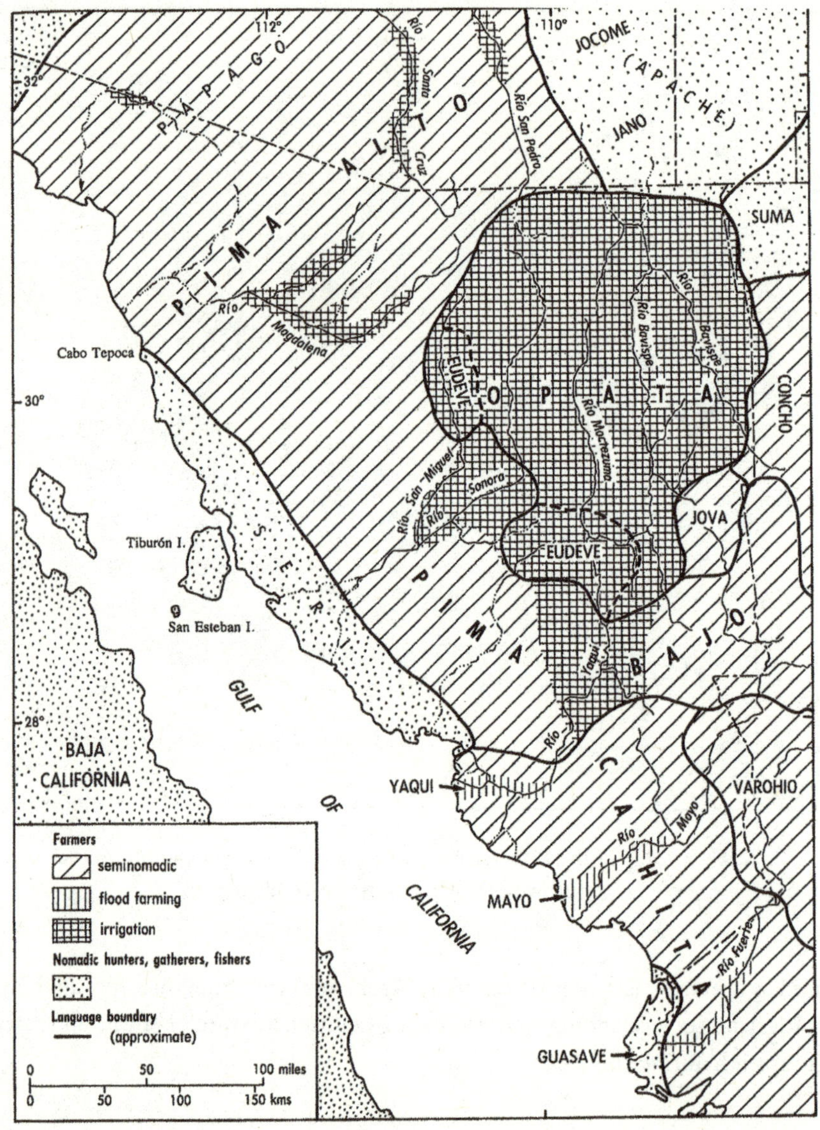

MAP 2 Map of indigenous tribes and modes of subsistence in Robert C. West, *Sonora: Its Geographical Personality* (Austin: University of Texas Press, 1993), 17. With permission from the University of Texas Press.

strong—made his official entrada into Sinaloa.[26] The legend of his incredible strength apparently arose from a number of instances in which he made a public show of picking up Indians by their hair as he galloped beside them on his horse.[27] In Sinaloa, Hurdaide and his men—a combination of Spanish soldiers and central Mexican indigenous allies—initially encountered openly hostile Native communities. One such group were the Zuaque Indians whom the Spanish seem to have feared, both because they were responsible for the murder of several Spanish settlers and their Native allies and because of their unpredictability: "they sometimes seemed to want friendship . . . and at other times they rejected offers of alliance with contempt."[28] This well-established Native strategy of calculated impulsivity remained at the center of Spanish–Native relations throughout much of the colonial period, keeping Spaniards guessing as to Native intentions. Unfortunately, for the Zuaque, such ambiguity greatly frustrated Hurdaide, who in an act of calculated brutality set an ambush, capturing forty-two men. Contemplating how best to send a forceful message to what he determined to be unreliable and therefore dangerous foes, Hurdaide hung all forty-two. He then ordered that they "remain there, swinging in the sun and wind, as a warning to all those who stood in his way."[29]

Such public displays of violence, while potentially beneficial in promoting a narrative of Spanish dominance, were not a good long-term strategy for the colonization of the province. Ordinances 136–39 of Book Four of the Laws of the Indies had made it clear that fear and friendship should represent two sides of the same coin. That a healthy fear of Spanish power would over time mature into a sincere respect and obedience on the part of Natives was nothing short of wishful thinking, however. Nonetheless, whether through familiarity of planning ordinances or by means of on-the-ground experiences, Hurdaide eventually modified his brutal "civilizing" methods in favor of a strategy that mixed terror with kindness. According to Andrés Pérez de Ribas, though Hurdaide was a tough and ferocious captain, he also sought to win over Native groups such as the Mayo with "affection and friendship" in the hopes of establishing "political government in their numerous pueblos."[30] His reputation for violence being well established, Hurdaide had also become a highly skilled negotiator, utilizing the rhetoric of amity as a way of pacifying local hostilities. Hurdaide's mission, wrote Pérez de Ribas, which would complement Pérez's own, was to militarily pacify the Natives of the province in order to introduce them to a Spanish style of "government and civility."[31]

For Pérez de Ribas, civilizing the Natives of the region was essential because only by embracing the accoutrements of civilization—that is, urbanity, language, religion, and friendship—would they be fully prepared to receive the Lord's gospel. According to the Comprehensive Order for New Discoveries (1573), the task of bringing "civilization" to the Natives belonged to the Jesuits; to Captain Hurdaide and others of his military ilk fell the responsibility of reinforcing the "civilizing mission," which would be accomplished by means of the pacification of Native hostilities and through the establishment of civil government.[32] Cementing "a good and loyal friendship" with the local indigenous people was, therefore, paramount if Pérez de Ribas and others of his Order were ever to produce a fruitful harvest of souls.[33] Despite his best intentions, however, the "friendship" Hurdaide established with the Mayo remained tenuous. But it set an important precedent for the way in which the rest of Sinaloa and Sonora would eventually be colonized.

Speaking strictly from a religious perspective, the notion of ideal friendship was best conceived of through the rose-colored lens of religious drama—a drama that pitted the devout against the subversive designs of the devil. Thus, for men like Pérez de Ribas, the idea of "Christian friendship," both between Indians and Spaniards and among the disparate Native groups of the region, represented a necessary precondition for the successful colonization of the frontier. When a Mayo Indian came to see him in order to complain about the fact that the Yaqui were using Mayo scalps during their ritual celebrations, Pérez de Ribas immediately recognized this as a failure of "Christian friendship." Because he found the accusation made by the Mayo Native sufficiently credible, he summoned two Yaqui leaders to appear before him. "I," Pérez de Ribas wrote, "said that they [the Mayo] were justified in their complaint, and because they dealt with one another in Christian friendship and brotherhood, which demands that they forget hatred and war, it was wrong to hang on to such things from the past."[34]

The concept of Christian friendship, which was a central component in Pérez de Ribas's conceptualization of civilization, was reminiscent of early Christian thinkers who saw the community of believers as a brotherhood. According to Pérez de Ribas, in response to his appeals to "Christian friendship," the Yaqui immediately collected all manner of relics, scalps, and any other offensive "articles of superstition" and burned them. This act of contrition apparently satisfied the Mayo, who "returned [to their lands] satisfied in their complaint and confirmed in the Christian friendship that they had established with the Yaqui, who demonstrated quite well how much they had welcomed Christianity."[35]

That Pérez de Ribas simply glossed over long-held antagonisms between the Mayo and the Yaqui in order to focus exclusively on the benefits of "Christian friendship" highlights the extent to which he believed that, through the imposition of a religiously inspired comradeship, ancient hostilities, no matter what their origin or history, could be quelled.

Unlike the Mayo, the Yaqui maintained a more paradoxical reputation within the political and religious landscape of northern New Spain. According to Evelyn Hu-DeHart, the Yaquis "were the most populous, most powerful, and most feared nation in the northwest, having thrice repelled presidial Captain Hurdaide and his frontier soldiers."[36] Indeed, Pérez de Ribas described them as a tribe "so populous, warlike and arrogant that never had [they had] commerce nor friendship with the Spaniards."[37] It is through such comments that we come to appreciate Pérez de Ribas's incisive vision of civilization, for according to him "commerce and friendship" represented two sides of the same coin that, if properly controlled for, would eventually lead to peace and to the establishment of civil society. This rendering of civil society only had value, however, because the popular perception of Yaqui ferocity and intransigence could be set against their "very good character, grateful[ness] and loyal[ty]."[38] Taking notice of the peaceful relationship that the Mayo had established with Hurdaide, the Yaqui decided that they too would sue for peace and perhaps like the Mayo achieve a lasting "friendship" with Hurdaide. Several Yaqui women were thus sent to negotiate peace terms with the captain. Aided in their endeavor by a number of Mayo leaders who acted as middlemen in the negotiations, these female emissaries successfully set the stage for full-blown diplomatic discussions. Several days later, various Yaqui caciques visited Hurdaide, who in a calculated display of friendship invited them into his home, allowing them to stay there for the duration of their visit. Such outward and public displays of friendship as allowing them into his home ensured that peace would eventually be established. But peace came at a significant cost to the Yaqui, for in addition to having to return to the Spanish all the horses they had previously stolen, they would also have to surrender two of their main leaders: Lautaro and Babilonio. According to Hurdaide, these two men had been responsible for much of the discord that had taken place between the Spanish and the Yaqui over the past several years. In the name of peace and friendship the Yaqui complied, knowing full well that once the transfer was completed both men would be summarily executed. These were the types of Faustian bargains Yaqui caciques made on a daily basis—some they could live with, whereas others would require violence to undo.

For military and religious leaders like Hurdaide and Pérez de Ribas, then, friendship was synonymous with civilization, the construction of civic life, and ultimately the formation of a Christian brotherhood among the various ethnic sectors of frontier society. But for precontact Indians, friendship had a different set of social meanings. As we saw in the previous chapter, indigenous groups from Texas to California used dance as a way of cementing their friendships and loyalties. Others, however, used sport. For example, Jesuit missionary Gonzalo de Tapia (1561–94), who took great interest in studying the social and material culture of Sinaloa's various indigenous groups, was particularly interested in the intertribal competitions and games they played. He was especially struck by a game they called *correr el palo* (run the stick), in which Indians from one tribe would challenge those from another in kicking a stick from village to village, often at distances of more than a league.[39] In this way, communal friendships were established and solidified.

In a report from 1701, Jesuit priest Juan María de Salvatierra (1648–1717) documented among the Indians from lower California the long-standing presence of a friendship ritual they called *el Mico*. While reconnoitering lower California, Salvatierra came upon this unique ceremony. Following the *Mico* as it traveled from town to town, Salvatierra interviewed a number of Natives as to its meaning and purpose. As he was told on a number of occasions, this highly symbolic performance was designed for the sole purpose of forging friendships throughout the region. In fact, as Salvatierra wrote, the very word *Mico* translated into Spanish as "friendship." Wrote Salvatierra:

It is known that this dance continues to the end of California or San Lucas, [but] it is not known [exactly] where in the northern lands it starts. [The dance] is performed with the little heads of birds and animals and various bird feathers found in different regions, and if there is any other curiosity it has to do with the ornaments of the Mico. In this way [some people from] the northern rancherías travel one or two days and deliver the ornaments of el Mico to other rancherías further [south]. They receive the guests presenting them with many large troughs as a dish for their seeds, [then] one and another dance solemnly with the ritual ornaments. After [that], the first [dancers] return to their land, and the second [group of] dancers, in this same way, travel with the Mico toward the [south]. They are received with the same solemnity. And in this way, they move [the ornaments of el Mico] from hand to hand until they reach the edge of the land, meeting and confirming their friendships, and quelling antagonisms between nations.[40]

For Salvatierra, the fact that the Natives of this region celebrated friendship indicated to him that they maintained the capacity for sustained relationships—a truly positive sign, for it facilitated their future instruction in the ideals of Christian friendship. Unfortunately, friendship rituals such as *el Mico* do not seem to have survived the Spanish colonization of lower California as the negative impacts of colonialism fundamentally rearranged their long-held friendship patterns.

In 1626 Pedro de Perea (d. 1644) succeeded Hurdaide as captain of the presidio of Sinaloa. Within a decade he was reconnoitering lands along the Río Bavispe, pushing the Sonoran frontier to its northernmost limits. His brutal military tactics were no less noteworthy than those of Hurdaide, though his unpleasant temperament put him at odds with the Jesuits. More importantly, what Perea lacked in diplomatic ability he made up for in boldfaced ambition. In 1637 Perea gained rights to the colonization of Sonora, becoming its *alcalde mayor* (principal municipal officer). In addition to his title as alcalde, which granted him a significant amount of power, Perea was given the title of chief officer, administrator, commander in chief of the militia, chief justice, budget director, and planning czar.[41] As part of his vast administrative duties, he was tasked with founding a town. He was also expected to "construct appropriate fortifications, introduce European agriculture, open mines and refineries, and provide for the propagation of Spanish culture."[42] To this end, Perea brought in twelve New Mexican families to help with the initial settlement of the province, enticing them with large tracts of land.

While the acquisition of land along fertile river valleys allowed early colonists to establish a firm foothold in Sonora, it severely affected Native subsistence practices. When water was later redirected from Native communities and free-range livestock introduced into the landscape, indigenous communities took it upon themselves to fight back through a combination of legal maneuverings and the outright threat of violence. These early settlers were committed to making their fortune off this barren land. In addition, with the full backing of the Crown, they also "considered their mission a license to civilize the region, i.e., establish an enclave of Spanish culture, institute European customs and norms to guide the 'barbarian' native peoples."[43] Their desire to make their fortune in mining meant that they would need access not only to the best and most valuable land but also to prized sources of water.

Unlike Durango, Sinaloa, New Mexico, or Chihuahua, where the encomienda system (a grant of Indian labor) had a visible presence, in Sonora it never took root. This was partially the result of Jesuit opposition. But whereas the Crown placed heavy restrictions on the theft of indigenous lands throughout much of Mexico, in Sonora it supported settlers in such endeavors. The logic behind this endorsement made a great deal of imperial sense: the Crown believed that once settlers became landowners they would naturally seek to protect their property from both rival European empires and hostile Indians, thus serving as an alternative to the expensive military units that resided in the province's various presidios. As David Yetman explains, granting land to the militia led these settlers "to establish roots and a permanence more reliable than could be expected from mere soldiers."[44] The use of colonists as soldiers and vice versa formed an important part of the imperial strategy for the colonization of the northern frontier. Thus the Crown placed a high value both on their ability to function as defenders of empire and as purveyors of civilization. Few of these early settlers, writes Anthony Pagden, "had any doubt that the Christian religion and the European way of living were far superior to anything known to any non-European. Few also doubted that it was the duty of the Europeans to export both religion and civility everywhere and by every means possible."[45] Just like missionaries and professional soldiers, the "civilizing mission" also belonged to Spanish and mestizo settlers who saw themselves as the "principal architects of frontier society," responsible for "setting its tone and determining and dominating its institutions."[46]

Though land was a major draw for Spanish colonists, it was not enough to drive widespread interest in the region. The prospect of getting rich off of gold and silver, however, led to the establishment of Spanish enclaves throughout the land. Spaniards began to pan for gold and silver along the San Miguel and Sonora River valleys during the 1640s; a decade later they had established themselves at San Juan Bautista, Nacozari, and Bacanuche.[47] Sonora's earliest settlers would have to wait, however, until 1736 before a rich outcropping of silver ore was discovered along the Santa Cruz River. The local indigenous people, today known as the O'odham, called this river 'Al onag, or "Place of the Small Spring." The discovery of silver deposits that year brought in diverse immigrants of from all over Mexico. Because most of these men were of limited financial means, they found themselves unable to return to central Mexico if their goals of acquiring financial success failed to materialize. To Jesuit missionary Ignaz Pfefferkorn (1726–98), these ethnically mixed immigrants, who desperately desired to be categorized as Spanish, were nothing more than common vagabonds of the lowest caliber whose presence only jeopardized their efforts at civilizing Sonora and at guiding Natives toward the light of the Holy Faith.[48] Still, mining remained the main reason why Spanish settlers came to northwestern Sonora, a place they eventually came to know as the Pimería Alta, named after the Pima (O'odham) people living there (see map 1). The term *Pima* was derived from the word *pimahaitu*, which ironically meant "nothing."[49]

But while settlers "civilized" the landscape by introducing commerce, the Spanish language, and European customs, they also, according to Pérez de Ribas and Pfefferkorn, also brought with them an extreme form of greed and perfidy. Jesuit missionaries much preferred their own particular brand of civility that fundamentally lacked the "malice and hypocrisy" represented by Spanish settlers.[50] Indeed, they made it a common practice to regularly remind their Indian charges that should they choose a life of sin with settlers over that of the mission community, they would unquestionably fall from God's grace.[51] The widely held belief that Spanish settlers corrupted Natives more than they actually civilized them meant that, as far as the Jesuits were concerned, they should be in charge of the "civilizing mission" or at the very least of constructing its moral scaffold. When Indians did manage to stray from mission communities to join settlers, Jesuits, perhaps rather conveniently, attributed this to their willful ignorance, laziness, and backwardness or, conversely, to the vile and sneaky character of settlers who lured them away with false promises and material goods.

In order to effectively colonize, civilize, and Christianize (in that order) the frontier, soldiers, missionaries, and settlers all depended heavily on indios amigos. The concept of an indio amigo(s) originated in the early years of the colonial period and was widely utilized by Spanish soldiers and administrators throughout much of colonial Spanish America. It became especially prominent along its northern and southern edges. María Laura Cutrera and Silvia Ratto have discussed the role of indios amigos along the frontiers of Argentina during the early years of independence.[52] Andrea Ruíz Esquide has similarly highlighted their role along the Araucanian frontier in northern Chile.[53] The institutionalization of friendship along South America's frontier regions also led to the development of formal friendship roles between Spaniards and Natives. Abelardo Levaggi, for instance, has analyzed the role that *el capitán de amigos* (captain of friends) played along the Chilean frontier. Officially created in 1647, *el capitán de amigos* was an administrative and military position created to address the problem of maintaining peace with unconquered indigenous groups. These *capitanes* were typically Spanish men chosen from within the military ranks. Their job responsibilities consisted of keeping the peace, acting as translators and informants, and defending the interests of Indians. However, the *capitán*'s central role, as Levaggi tells us, was to be a "friend to indigenous leaders in both name and action."[54]

The political and military adoption of indios amigos was also common along the northern peripheries of New Spain. In her work on the Mixton War (1540–42), Ida Altman describes them as military confederates of the Spanish. She had no reason to read any further into these associations, especially given the fact that these "amigos" were conscripted through "force and intimidation."[55] However, in Sonora not all indios amigos were conscripted in this manner, and many benefited from their role as amigos. As noted earlier, indios amigos accompanied Coronado on his expedition through New Mexico. Their motivations for joining Spaniards on such excursions ranged from the potential for personal profit (the Crown allowed indios amigos to keep Indian captives) to exemptions from tribute payment for entire communities.[56] In general, indios amigos were essential to the colonization process of the northern frontier. Without them the frontier would not have advanced and may have even been pushed back.

Soldiers relied heavily on indios amigos to act as guides in reconnoitering the landscape—after all, they knew the landscape better than anyone else; they knew the location of valuable sources of food and water; they understood the social and ethnic composition of the frontier; they operated as translators, helping to forge alliances with other indigenous groups; and they acted as allies in skirmishes against indios enemigos. Indians also performed the critically important task of harvesting crops, and in many cases they assisted in the day-to-day activities of governance. For their part, Natives embraced their associations with soldiers and settlers for the freedom it gave them from their daily mission chores (Indians were periodically taken on military campaigns), for the business opportunities (licit and illicit) it presented, and for the prestige that it brought.

Identifying their Native allies as indios amigos also maintained an important psychological logic of its own. Throughout the colonial period the rhetoric of friendship helped Spaniards order and structure their mental worlds by creating useful binaries such as friends and enemies (indios amigos and indios enemigos). The mental construction of the "friendly Indian" and the later dichotomy between "*indios de paz*" and "*indios de guerra*" (peaceful Indians and warlike Indians) sustained Spaniards in the high stakes game of survival, to say nothing of their need to justify and legitimize their presence in Sonora.[57] This process of ordering and simplification, which began with the Crown's efforts at creating racial hierarchies and highly structured cities during the early portion of the six-teenth century,[58] gained increasing importance along frontier zones like Sonora where having too many options at one's disposal could prove disastrous; it simply took too long to decipher between shades of gray. To the European mind, it was far easier to understand their social surroundings through a bifurcated lens—and so it became essential that there exist only two kinds of Indians: good Indians and bad ones. But, while such an artificial simplification was essential for the social and administrative construction of the frontier, more seasoned Spaniards and mestizos were far too tuned-in to simply look past the gray spaces in-between, for that too would have been needlessly irresponsible and dangerous. In order to survive in this impulsive environment, it was essential that one understand and master nuance, and that could only be done by learning how to navigate a world that constantly juggled artificial simplicity with actual complexity. Over time, Natives too developed the skill to navigate between these two extremes. While many indigenous groups maintained a conception of "us and them," they did not, as Mark Simmons has argued, maintain "a strict division of the universe into opposing forces of good and evil."[59] Therefore, in not seeing Spaniards as either good or evil but as something in-between, Indians were well equipped to better negotiate, traverse, and, ultimately, manipulate the social and intellectual expectations of friendship.

The fear of indios enemigos also necessitated the development of streamlined mental "maps" that would help in demarcating hostile versus friendly Indian territory. Such physical and mental maps were important for those soldiers and missionaries intent on reconnoitering territory previously visited by Europeans. Father Eusebio Kino's (1645–1711) letters and maps, for example, which identified the locations of friendly tribal groups, were later used by missionaries like Father Juan María de Salvatierra (1648–1717) to locate and rekindle previously established relationships.[60] In much the same way as Juliana Barr has argued that physical maps highlighted the extent to which Indians dominated the Texas landscape, mental maps served to effectively delineate the extent of Spanish influence in Sonora, thereby defining the limits of Spanish imperialism. Men like Kino and Salvatierra had taken great pains to reconnoiter and map the land. In the process, they interviewed Natives about a whole host of issues such as the location of watering holes, food supplies, the layout of the land, and Indian rivalries.[61] They also exerted a great deal of time and energy baptizing Natives, preaching the Christian gospel, giving them gifts and supplies, setting up alliances and friendships, and making promises for their eventual return. In return, Natives made substantial gifts of their own to the Jesuits, which often included their children. For Jesuits, there was no surer sign of friendship than the gift of a Native child to baptize and raise in the Holy Faith.

Thus, for colonial residents of the frontier, friendly Indians, or indios amigos, became vital to the overall success and colonization of the province. Interethnic friendships then developed along four tracks of interaction: (1) the understanding that there existed good and bad Indians, that those who were hostile to the Spanish were bad and those who were welcoming were good; (2) the notion that Indians who were friendly and sincere in their friendship with the Spanish were natural enemies of their enemies and would therefore help defend them against indios enemigos; (3) the idea that Indians, with their vast reservoir of knowledge, would help Spaniards exploit the landscape and develop the economy of the frontier; and (4) that Natives represented fertile land, ripe for a spiritual harvest, as well as a potential labor pool.

A Jesuit Empire: Ideology, Power, and the Logic of Friendship

In 1524 Hernán Cortés orchestrated a public meeting with Martin de Valencia—one of the original twelve Franciscans to arrive in Mexico—at the entrance to the city of Mexico-Tenochtitlán. Within the purview of everyone present, including Native dignitaries and such luminaries as Bernardo de Sahagun, Torbido de Benavente (Motolinía—"the poor one"), Andres de Olmos, and Pedro de Gante, Cortés proceeded to humble himself before the impoverished missionary.[62] Cortes's showmanship was both characteristic of his grandiose style and suggestive of his genius. By means of this public spectacle, Cortés had sought to convey a very important message to all those Indians in attendance: the power and majesty of the Christian faith would transform them into civilized beings. To those in attendance it was made clear that what these first-generation missionaries embodied in simplicity, they made up for in spiritual and moral authority.[63] Self-identified as millenarians and devotees of the eschatological ideas of Cistercian abbot Joachim of Fiore (1135–1202), these early mendicants fully adopted the idea that the end times—or more precisely, the Age of the Holy Ghost—was drawing near. Their zealotry and missionizing fervor mirrored their ideology, for it was left to them to "compel" Natives to receive the Holy Faith, thereby preparing them for the imminent arrival of

Christ.[64] In order to accomplish this task, these early Franciscans labored vigorously to "establish in the New World a New Jerusalem, free from corrupting secular influences."[65]

As an Order the Franciscans were the first to arrive to New Spain, establishing over the course of three centuries an impressive string of mission communities from California to Florida, baptizing, as they claimed, tens of thousands of Natives.[66] But in the end, they would not be New Spain's most influential or celebrated Order. That title would be won by the Society of Jesus (officially founded in 1540, established in New Spain in 1571). Their success came at the annoyance of many, particularly of their Franciscan, Dominican, and Augustinian counterparts who unabashedly reproached them for dealing exclusively with the elite of Spanish society.[67] This accusation was only partially true. While the Jesuits did find a ready niche in the education of some of the most renowned criollos of the colonial period, they also created their own "utopias" in the most remote corners of the American continent. Over time, the Jesuit Order developed into an incredibly wealthy and powerful society. By the mid-seventeenth century, they maintained a steady income of 119,500 pesos from the various rental properties they owned, properties that totaled twenty-five times the value of its yearly income.[68] Additionally, because the Order required its members to vow absolute obedience to the pope, the Crown never fully trusted them, eventually expelling them from the whole of the Americas in 1767. According to David Brading and Jacques Lafaye, the Jesuits' major accomplishment in New Spain came in their ability to develop a unique creole consciousness, itself firmly rooted in the image of Our Holy Lady of Guadalupe whose motto "*Non fecit taliter omni nationi*" (Other nations are not thus blessed) convinced criollos of their rightful place as the true heirs of colonial society.[69]

Unlike other religious Orders, Jesuits missionized in some of the most remote places on earth. They could be found in China, Japan, India, Brazil, Paraguay, and New Spain, and at their height in 1749, they counted on 22,600 members.[70] They were also ethnically diverse. In New Spain, many of the Jesuits, especially starting in the late seventeenth century, came from Italy and Central Europe—Father Eusebio Kino was, for example, Austrian. Not to be denied opportunities for evangelization and martyrdom, they sought out the mission fields in far northwest Mexico. By 1613 they had begun to make deep inroads into Sinaloa and Sonora.[71] The following year, the Sons of Loyola, led by Pérez de Ribas, entered Yaqui territory, being some of the very first Europeans to arrive in the Sonoran Desert.[72] Their basic goal, as Robert Jackson tells us, was "to radically alter the religious beliefs and the cultural, social, and economic organization of the Indian converts who settled or were settled in the mission." As far as the Crown was concerned, Jesuits were there to pacify, convert, and introduce Natives to European culture all in an effort to prepare the frontier for the eventual arrival of Spanish settlers.[73] Of course this was easier said than done as Jesuits were met with resistance on a number of fronts, particularly from groups such as the Yaqui, Seris, Janos, Sumas, and Jocomes, who were particularly resistant to their missionizing agenda.

Herbert E. Bolton, writing during the early portion of the twentieth century, unreservedly asserted that "river by river, valley by valley, canyon by canyon, tribe by tribe, these harbingers of Christian civilization advanced into the realm of heathendom."[74] Bolton's hagiographic account of the Jesuits—described by him as warriors of Christ who by holy mandate were sent to guide the Natives from out of their darkness—was a welcome historiographical contribution to a profession that had hitherto sidestepped North America's Spanish origins. But it was deeply flawed. While it lauded missionaries for their efforts at bringing European civilization to the borderlands, it undervalued the intellectual and cultural contributions of Natives. His scholarship, important as it remains to us today, was the product of an earlier time when the histories of nonelites, women, children, and their cultural practices remained but mere curiosities.[75]

The extent to which their ambitious objectives were accomplished was reflected in their own unique missionizing ideology. By means of a heroized rhetoric that relished agricultural metaphors, Jesuits sought out a fruitful harvest of Indian souls from the "Lord's vineyard." According to religious scholar Brandon Bayne, these religious men "watered these seedlings [Indian converts] with the sweat, tears, and blood of many daily and more dramatic sacrifices. Indian loyalty and cases of edification, especially in the midst of suffering, testified to their ripeness as fruit. Taken together, Jesuits imagined their missions as fields and vineyards that would one day teem with the bounty of indigenous Christians."[76] This perspective was heavily influenced by Old World martyrdom ideologies, most of which stretched back to the earliest accounts of Peter, Paul, and Ignatius, all of whom believed that through the drama of sacrificial death "new life would spring."[77] Jesuits then used this tradition of Christian martyrdom as a way of understanding and making sense of the death and violence that seemed ubiquitous along the frontier. Martyrdom was simply the necessary price of ensuring eternal salvation for the Natives; it represented the necessary sacrifice to ensure the propagation of the faith.[78]

But a bountiful harvest would take time. Jesuits thus saw in the barren desert landscape a reflection of the impoverished state of Christianity in Sonora. It was up to them to nourish Sonora's Native seedlings with their own martyred blood. Indeed, by means of a forthright devotion, they believed that they needed "to give life to get life."[79] It was through this kind of dramatized rhetoric that missionaries infused their faith-laden message with raw emotion. Luis de Granada (1504–88), a sixteenth-century Spanish scholar who used Cicero as his intellectual model, wrote in Book Three of his *Ecclesiasticae rhetoricae* (1576) that emotions were central to missionary success, particularly since emotion was the only true way to motivate men to action.[80] However, for Granada the measured use of emotion remained the sole provenance of Europeans since only they were sophisticated enough to understand and digest its deepest meanings—Indian neophytes were simply too ignorant to truly comprehend the inner life. In his *Breve tratado* (1583), Granada addressed this issue by writing a treatise for the propagation of the faith to Native newcomers. Here Granada proposed that the message that would foster conversion had to be simple and straightforward, devoid of either complex rhetoric or calls to emotion. "The variations between the *Ecclesiasticae* and the *Breve tratado*," notes Don Paul Abbott, "strongly suggest that rhetoric would be reserved for Europeans, while only a simpler catechistic approach would be appropriate for the Amerindians."[81]

As Jesuits spread the Lord's gospel along the Río San Miguel, they took great pains to reconnoiter the land, baptize so-called lost souls, and build wooden and adobe structures for the worship of a vague and mysterious god. To facilitate this process, they built alliances and friendships with indigenous leaders and entire communities, encouraging military leaders to do the same. Such strategic connections allowed for the processes of pacification, civilization, and Christianization to advance at a steady pace. It was, therefore, as spiritual wardens to their "lost" Indian charges that the Sons of Loyola understood their divine mandate. Their religious conceptualization of amity was thus refracted through the lens of spiritual paternalism and martyrdom. It was also filtered through a long lineage of Christian theologians and scholars. Still, the relationship between Jesuits and Natives was one of inescapable contradictions, as Raphael Brewster Folsom has laid out for us:

> The Jesuits wanted to protect Indians from the Spanish conquerors, but they refused to take up arms in times of war. The Jesuits expressed admiration for many aspects of indigenous culture and went to extraordinary lengths to learn

native languages. Yet they also went out of their way to offend native elders and tried to commandeer the sacred rites of native towns. The Jesuits risked death to care for the sick, the elderly, and the dying, yet they lashed out at Indians whose sex lives they disapproved of. It took many years for native peoples to make sense of these strange men.[82]

The best way to "water these seedlings" was by means of *reducción*—the congregation of Indians into towns and villages so as to educate them in the political, cultural, and social ideals of the Old World. For Jesuits, congregating Natives into towns was important because it was impossible, they believed, to properly educate and Christianize nomadic Indians. Unsettled Natives simply did not have the capacity to engage with the truths of the Holy Faith. Reducing Indians into towns and mission communities helped establish the social parameters for appropriate comportment, namely, that they live a peaceful and stable family-oriented life under the moral constraints of Christian friendship. Because there remained a rather close association in the European mind between belief and social behavior, many Europeans were perfectly willing to acknowledge that forcing Natives to accept "civility" was a legitimate goal in order to stimulate a voluntary conversion.[83] Towns were to be the basis upon which Spanish imperialism was to be enacted, since, as many saw it, it was contrary to nature "for human beings to live far away from society."[84]

Aristotle had highlighted the intimate connection between civilization and friendship when he proposed in his *Politics* that "man is a political animal" (*zo͞on politikon*), being that it was man's relationship to man that alone guaranteed his humanity, "for all true men must connect with their fellows because men are, by their very nature, connecting animals, just as they are city-building, social animals."[85] This civilizational model was particularly applicable along the extreme edges of empire. Settlers and Jesuit missionaries thus attempted to gather dispersed Indians into towns and mission communities, the better to instruct them in the "civilized arts." Roman poet Virgil (70–19 BCE) had undergirded these intellectual efforts when he officiously wrote: "To rule nations with imperium these shall be thy arts, oh Romans; to humble the proud with war and to crown peace and justice to the weak."[86] Spain's American empire, which was colonized by means of this Roman ideal, was an attempt to create new Spains throughout the land. However, the philosophical posture that allowed the Spanish monarchy to see itself as the new Roman Empire in the Americas—heroically imposing order and civilizing Natives—changed over the course of the colonial period as Spaniards came to realize the necessity for Indian cooperation and friendship in advancing the Spanish frontier. "Throughout the Spanish-American mainland by the 1790s," writes David Weber, "numerous indigenous peoples had been incorporated rather than eliminated, and most of the Natives who still lived independently along the borders of Spain's American empire had come to some form of accommodation with the Hispanic world, and it with them."[87]

The Laws of the Indies had mandated the reduction of Indians into the mission system, which was designed as a social institution from which to begin the organization of Indians into towns, along the lines of the corporate structure of the Spanish pueblo. They were also ideal places from which to inculcate proper work habits, ideas about sedentary life, urban habits, and civic responsibilities.[88] Already existing indigenous towns and *rancherías* were to be renamed to emphasize European possession and new establishments were to be given Catholic saints names for the day on which they were founded. Once Natives resettled in mission communities, they were then to be given a plot of land for their subsistence. In exchange, they were expected to work three days a week tilling mission fields, looking after mission livestock, and facilitating day-to-day mission activities.[89] In this respect, missionaries became, according to Richard Morse, "the most successful agents of Hispanicization and Christianization."[90] Only through the rigid enforcement of civilizing policies, believed many Jesuits, would the Natives exit their "cultural backwardness" and embrace the European civic ideals of friendship. Since, according to the Greeks and Romans, virtue and friendship could only be practiced in cities, many early European settlers saw the establishment of towns as the first step toward colonizing the frontier. As Anthony Pagden notes, these establishments were "communities governed by the rule of law which demanded adherence to a particular kind of life, that of the 'civil society' (*societas civilis*), and which were closely identified with the physical location the citizens happened to inhabit."[91] For Augustine it was the "City of God" that constituted the spiritual foundation for civil society; for Aquinas the city represented the "perfect community."[92] This urban ideal held a powerful sway over Latin American intellectuals even as late as the nineteenth century, when scholars such as Domingo Faustino Sarmiento (1811–88) declared that cities represented the only viable receptacles of European culture.[93]

Through this urbanization/civilization process, Jesuits and settlers believed they would turn Indians into Hispanicized mestizos capable of fully embracing the word of Christ and the precepts of "civilized life." Jesuits understood that providing Indians with material goods would facilitate their conversion. As

Yetman writes, by controlling the regional economy Jesuits controlled the economic development of Sonora, ensuring that the region would become a "Jesuit empire."[94] Unfortunately, Jesuits also understood that it was the economy—the selling and trading of goods—that would form the basis of Indian–settler contact. Such relationships, as Pérez de Ribas had warned, had the potential to derail their moral and religious empire by diverting Natives away from missions and toward mining towns and ranches. From the perspective of several missionaries, those Natives who refused to be incorporated into the mission community, and instead chose to remain outside its purview, were to be severely punished. The battle over indigenous labor would be at the center of Jesuit–settler conflict for much of the colonial period, exacerbating over the course of the eighteenth century as the population of settlers began to vastly outnumber that of missionaries. Overall, the process of reduction required a tremendous effort, but one that at least initially inspired Jesuits as they envisioned a civilized outpost at the edges of Christendom.[95] "The intention behind forming reducciónes," writes Charles Polzer, "was to 'lead the Indian back' from the mountains and woods into a community where he could better learn the rudiments of Christian belief and the elementary forms of Spanish social and political organization."[96]

One of the most renowned missionaries to work along the Sonoran frontier was Father Eusebio Francisco Kino (1645–1711). Fond of winning over Natives with gifts in order to attract them to mission life, Kino understood the connection between material acculturation and the conversion of Indians. As Henry Kamen observes, the gifting of items such as iron tools, bells, clothing, musical instruments, and food "established a bond of hospitality that created an obligation to friendship."[97] Kino's extensive body of writings tell of the kindness and friendship with which he was frequently received as he reconnoitered the desert. For Kino, the hospitality that the Natives extended toward him was a clear manifestation of their friendship.[98] Unlike early Jesuits whose missionary ideology was dominated by an agricultural worldview, Kino was more practical in outlook and—as one of his biggest critics, Francisco Xavier de Mora, argued—politically motivated (see chapter 3).

Indian groups throughout the Pimería welcomed Jesuit missionaries in a very similar manner for much of the colonial period. First, it was common for the Natives to send out scouters to see how far away the missionaries were, in some cases providing them with escorts as they neared their communities. Prior to their arrival, the Indians would clean the roads, awaiting them in two straight lines with crosses and arches. As the visitors entered the indigenous *rancherías* they were typically greeted with food and lodging. Three ramadas (arbors) awaited them: one with food, one for lodging, and one as the kitchen. Following a period of rest, the missionaries would be given *párvulos* (children) to baptize.[99] Here is how Kino describes such meetings:

> We passed through San Cosme del Tucson, through another large ranchería, through many cornfields, abundant fields of corn and beans, and watermelon and squash that grow in these environs. After five leagues of travel we arrived at a very good house that they had prepared for us, [made] of wood and palm-mat, [and] well swept. And with much generosity they gave us abundantly of their foods and were very prompt to what we desired. [They] gave their obedience to El Rey Nuesto Señor, and having given them a good speech we gave them some trinkets in recompense for our previous journey, which they greatly appreciated; [thereafter] we proceeded with our trip. On the twenty-eighth, after mass, we passed through the ranchería of San Clemente located to the northwest; we [stopped there] to drink some water. And the Indians, having given their obedience to El Rey Nuestro Señor, received us with the same affection as their antecedents. At about four in the afternoon, having traveled fifteen leagues, we arrived at the ranchería of Santa Catalina Cuituabagu. More than two leagues of Indians come out to receive us, and having the road well aligned, they placed arches and crosses for us. [They] had a very good house made of wood and palm-mat, which had an abundance of their foods; having a corral we gathered some animals. And in everything they gave examples of their longing to see us, and of their great loyalty.[100]

In an early letter to the king, Kino wrote of the Indians that "by means of these many and repeated journeys and missions which I have made to all parts, without special expense to the royal estate, they remain reduced to our friendship and obedience to the royal Crown, and with a desire to receive our holy faith."[101] As with Pérez de Ribas, for Kino friendship meant accepting the word of God by means of baptism. Kino noted in his *Favores Celestiales* that he sent messengers to different parts of the Pimería with "friendly invitations, requesting that they should endeavor likewise to become Christians . . . for I had come to aid them in order that they might be eternally saved."[102] In 1693, when Kino visited the western Sobaipuris, he befriended their leader, El Soba. Kino later wrote of them as being "so friendly that, having come thirty, forty, and fifty leagues' journey from the north to see us, they gave us their infants to baptize."[103]

Like Kino, Juan María de Salvatierra befriended Indians through the practice of gifting. Once befriended they would then be sent back to their lands "far inland, and all of them received gifts from the two Fathers [Salvatierra and Kino] so that they [the Natives] would give good advice to, and befriend, those [other indigenous] people who [live] through where we were [later] going to pass."[104] Indigenous leaders, in this case, were used as vessels for facilitating peace and fostering friendships throughout the region. For missionaries like Kino and Salvatierra, the most basic understanding of Indian friendship was clearly within the framework of proper Christian behavior. Warmly and eagerly welcoming Spaniards into their *rancherías*, providing them with food and a ramada to rest in, and giving them their children to baptize—Jesuits came to understand all these acts as signs of friendship. For the various indigenous communities keenly attuned to the nuances of colonialism, it simply made logical sense to maintain amicable relationships with missionaries, until the point that it was no longer beneficial to do so.

In 1748, several years after Kino's death, the Bavarian Jesuit Jacobo Sedelmayr (1703–79) traveled through the Pimería and into Yuma territory, where he encountered what he could only describe as idealized signs of friendship. Sedelmayr was just as rigorous in his missionizing efforts as Kino was. From 1737 to 1754 Sedelmayr carried out eight missionizing entradas into unknown Indian territory. Once there he sought to reduce them from their scattered villages to mission communities along the rivers of Sonora. Accompanied by fifteen Spanish soldiers, he entered Yuma territory in the vicinity of the Gila River valley, fully expecting to be received, as so many missionaries before him had been, with open arms. As was customary among missionaries reconnoitering the land, he sent an Indian guide ahead of his party to inform the Cocomaricopas of his arrival. Per his instructions, the Indian guide was to inform the Natives of their peaceful intentions. To this end, Sedelmayr sent a sign with the indigenous guide that read "ICSSU, Amigo."[105] To his delight, the Cocomaricopas welcomed them, returning Sedelmayr's friendly gesture by clearing the roads and coming out in mass to greet them. Three hundred men and two women met the party at the outskirts of their village. Sedelmayr soon discovered that they had strong commercial ties with the Pimas (Tohono O'odham), to whom they sold mesquite and other food stuffs; the Pimas then sold it at a profit to Spaniards. This was to Sedelmayr a sign of their industriousness and of their ability to engage in civilized behavior.

During his conversations with the Natives, Sedelmayr was informed that, while they desired to receive more missionaries in the lands, the one thing they needed more than anything else was horses. Sedelmayr, who was taken by their sincerity and eager to convert them, informed them that if they engaged in friendship with Christians, they would in time gain access to the horses they so desired. No sooner had Sedelmayr conveyed his practical advice on how to get access to horses than Father Phelipe de Uparah took it upon himself to chastise them about their immoral marriage practices, reciting to them the sanctity of the sixth commandment. In doing this, Uparah was simply following in the long line of missionaries who saw themselves as civilizing agents. The pattern had long been established: befriend Natives, civilize them by reducing them into towns, introduce ideas of Christian friendship and political government, promote Christian moral practices, and finally, fully Christianize them in the doctrine.[106]

The civilizing goals of Jesuit missionaries like Pérez de Ribas, Kino, Salvatierra, and Sedelmayr, among many others, remained fairly consistent throughout the colonial period and were to some extent taken up by the Franciscans, who took over after they were expelled in 1767. Writing during the late eighteenth century, Franciscan friar Diego Bringas noted that there was a dire need to promote good behavior among the Indians of Sonora in order to help the vast dominions of His Royal Majesty flourish. This was because the mission continued to be inhabited by "heathens" outside the reach of Spanish authority.[107] It was essential to educate Natives in proper farming techniques so as to curtail their idleness, encourage vigorous workers, and ensure that Indians follow the laws of the Crown, thereby fostering "civil society." They should therefore embrace peace and become agile workers in ranches and mines of the province as well as traders; they should be "weaned away from insubordination, lack of foresight, distrust, and 'instability' and encouraged to live in settlements with uniform and straight streets 'in order to avoid disorderly appearance.' . . . Indians should also be made to work for private as well as community good." Such industriousness, Bringas argued, would bring them "true happiness." They should also be punished for any excesses they should commit; they should be expected to be fully clothed and to avoid drinking and gambling; and they should be expected to become fully acculturated and Hispanicized Indians, embracing learning, the Catholic faith, and the Spanish language.[108]

Aristotle's notion of the polis was as influential in sixteenth-century New Spain as it was in the eighteenth century. Throughout the colonial period, then, the connection between friendship and civilization was made quite clear and reinforced through various secular and religious efforts. Soldiers like Hurdaide and Perea were tasked with pacifying the land, keeping indios enemigos at bay, and maintaining friendships with Native leaders in order to institute political government; settlers were asked to be emissaries of European culture and ideals, using friendship as a way of keeping Natives close and economically useful; and missionaries used friendship (Christian friendship) as a way of spreading the faith.

Conclusion

During the early years of colonial rule the Spanish borderlands came to depend on a sophisticated, nuanced, and highly precarious economy of emotion. By looking at the "emotional economy" of various indigenous and European communities, we are presented with a useful framework for more fully understanding people's actions and behaviors through shared feelings of friendship and disdain. While emotions can be difficult to decipher, particularly in a colonial context where various cultural and intellectual conceptualizations of affect existed side by side, and frequently in contradistinction to one another, they nonetheless provide a vital framework for coming to terms with how people used the emotional properties of friendship to their advantage. By undervaluing emotion as a necessary category of inquiry, recent scholarship on the economic and political forces that helped shape the borderlands does not fully appreciate the internal machinations of negotiation, manipulation, and fabrication that occurred all along the frontier. By addressing the nexus between friendship, the colonial economy, and the ideological development of civil society, this chapter has laid some important groundwork for understanding how emotion became integral in the formation of the frontier. Actions such as risking one's life for another, gifting, or performing outward signs of respect and deference all manifested a general goodwill and loyalty that could be easily understood in a colonial setting where the vagaries of language were often be difficult to decipher.

Examining the idiosyncrasies of friendship along the frontier offers us a unique opportunity for better understanding how Spanish, Indian, and mixed-race people molded and restructured their social, ideological, and emotional worlds. This consideration is made concrete by way of five issues of central importance, which taken together conditioned the fluid applicability of friendship. First, of all the indigenous groups in Sonora the Pimas were perhaps the most open to religious conversion and willing to join Spaniards as allies. This amenability allowed them to better negotiate power and authority. Second, European residents of Sonora, being distant and disconnected from national centers of population and viceregal authority, were forced to negotiate the limits of power at the local level and with local actors.[109] Third, an isolated and often lonely existence far from "civilized life," which for the Hapsburgs represented an important cornerstone in monarchical legitimacy, made life difficult for those who had a deep-rooted penchant for urban living, making friendship a logical aspiration through which to amend the loneliness of the frontier.[110] Fourth, a high level of social interaction among ethnically, linguistically, and culturally diverse people made associations based on amity a necessary precondition for economic and political functioning. Without the development of interethnic alliances and friendships, the frontier would have become a wasteland of violence and hardship. And fifth, the frontier's harsh ecological features, which fostered major struggles over resources such as water and food, made cooperation and fidelity a necessary condition of life there. As a nonhuman actor, the environment played a pivotal role in how people compromised, fought, and befriended one another. As the following chapters show, not only did emotion set the stage for the ways in which friendship was understood and performed, but it could also be used as a tool for reinforcing ethical and moral behavior.

CHAPTER THREE

The Many Faces of Betrayal

Kino and the Coded World of Friendship

Amicus Plato, amicus Aristoteles, magis amica veritas. (Plato is my friend, Aristotle is my friend, but my greatest friend is truth.)

—Isaac Newton, Cambridge Student Notebook

THE ABOVE ADAGE, WRITTEN ON THE FRONT PAGE OF ISAAC Newton's (1642–1727) notebook while studying at Cambridge (1661–68), reflects an adherence to the "new science" sweeping throughout much of Europe. Meant to echo Aristotle's previous critique of Plato's theory of the Forms, Newton's candid words were central to his vision of the professional scholar. While academics of Newton's caliber belonged to a rather exclusive society, it was their scholarly responsibility, so he believed, that they publicly assess the leading ideas of their day in the most honest and forthright manner possible, even if their critiques risked offending colleagues and friends. In this way, one's scholarly reputation rested largely on the expert evaluation of like-minded competitors. This laborious process was essential in the noble pursuit of truth, for truth, not love or devotion, represented the penultimate endpoint of friendship among academics. It was important, however, that these academic friendships adhere to a very specific code of ethical behavior whereby reason and not emotion or malice structured one's scholarly critiques. This early modern variation on friendship differed in many ways from previous types (discussed in chapter 1) that placed great emphasis on equality or on the notion of a second self. To comprehend Newton's vision for friendship, then, is to understand his goal for knowledge, for both were intimately intertwined.

In this chapter, I scrutinize idealized forms of friendship among intellectuals to reveal the ways in which knowledge and scholarship interfaced with notions of authority, status, and the lived experience. Through the personage of Jesuit missionary Eusebio Francisco Kino (1645–1711), this chapter displays the inner dynamics of power in relations of amity by peering into the civic spaces where ideology and behavior came into conflict. This task is accomplished by looking at the associations between Kino and two men: Don Carlos de Sigüenza y Góngora (1645–1700) and Francisco Xavier de Mora. Through the purview of betrayal, which operationally functioned as an inverted diagram of ideal friendship, I expose a different set of codes, ethics, and expectations that endured among New Spain's intellectual elite. As the following pages highlight, in colonial New Spain friendships among men of letters and of faith were as essential in the development of civil society as they were potential obstacles to the advancement of one's reputation.

Science, Authority, and the Politics of Friendship

Imbued with a missionary fervor from a young age, Eusebio Francisco Kino arrived in Mexico City on May 1, 1681. His prodigious abilities as a mathematician had landed him a professorship at the University of Ingolstadt five years earlier, but he had declined this prestigious post in order to bring "the light of the Gospel to the heathen in a remote and inhospitable region of the globe."[1] Initially, it was China that occupied the Austrian's attention. Kino had expressed his desire for the Far East in his many letters to the Duchess of Aviro, his patroness at the time.[2] But, alas, China would not be in the cards. In a game of chance with Reverend Father Anthony Kerschpamer, Kino sealed his own destiny: "I told Father Anthony to choose the mission which he preferred; he insisted that I make the first choice. After contending for some time in this pious effort to give the other the preference, we thought of drawing lots to decide our destiny. Accordingly, 'Mexico' was written on one slip and 'Philippines' on the other. On drawing lots, Father Anthony got the 'Philippines,' and I 'Mexico.'"[3]

Already a well-respected scholar, Kino was met with great fanfare upon his arrival to New Spain's colonial capital. One man in particular, Don Carlos Sigüenza y Góngora, distinguished scholar of mathematics and astrology at the University of Mexico, led the welcoming party. His sincere longing to meet Kino was, according to Irving Leonard, guided by "a certain loneliness . . . for it cannot be said that men of comparable learning abounded in the viceroyalty of

New Spain."[4] At the time of Kino's arrival Sigüenza had just been awarded the title of Chief Cosmographer of the Realm, a title that represented a significant level of prestige and respect. Here, then—as Sigüenza saw it on the day he welcomed his European colleague to New Spain—were two men of equal intellectual footing who, as it were, happened to share many things in common: both were the same age (thirty-six), both were mathematicians, both were amateur geographers, and both had received their formal education from the Society of Jesus.[5] And so it was that the Creole scholar, eager for intellectual engagement, welcomed Kino into his home—where they apparently had long conversations on a variety of scholarly topics—introduced him to his friends, loaned him his personal collection of maps (most of which were of the northern frontier, to where Kino was soon to embark), and defended his colleague's reputation, all "in an act of intellectual hospitality."[6]

For Sigüenza, acts of generosity among scholars, and in particular the loaning of academic material to a respected colleague, embodied the requisite ethical behavior for members of the intellectual elite who inhabited an imagined "scientific republic." Within this conceptual space, citizenship was determined by a particular style of friendship that rested, as Anna More writes, on acts of generosity, scholarship, and reasoned dissent and on the development of one another's intellectual reputations.[7] Properly regulated friendships among scholars that emphasized decorum, reason, and civilized conduct were particularly important given that there was a "propensity for debates among members of early modern scientific communities to devolve into resentment or violent, ad hominem attacks, but equally, when conflict was avoided, to serve as models for civil society."[8] Alternatively, forging a close friendship with a distinguished scholar could prove academically advantageous. To have someone of Kino's stature and reputation attest to or write a positive endorsement of one's own work could, as Erika Rummel argues, mean the difference between a successful or unsuccessful publication.[9]

In the highly competitive world of ideas, friendships had a number of added purposes as well, some honorable, others less so. Using fifteenth-century professor of poetry Marineo Siculo as a case study, Rummel notes how it became common practice for scholars like Siculo to steal a friend's unpublished work in order to present it to a willing publisher. In this way, the scholar of the stolen academic piece would be able to sit back and wait to see how his work would be received.[10] If received well, the author would forgive the friend for the brazen theft. But if rejected by the academic community, the author could claim that his treatise had been stolen and was yet unfinished, or that it was not ready for publication. Conversely, he could simply say that it had never been intended to be published in the first place, and that it merely represented a series of personal musings. Here is what Helius Eobanus Hesus (1488–1540), a leading German humanist of the sixteenth century, wrote about one such incident:

> A few days ago, gentle reader, when I paid a casual visit to a friend and, as one does, looked at the newest material on his desk, it so happened that there fell into my hands a letter from the excellent theologian Johann Lang (you know how great a man he is). It was addressed to the great jurist Martin of Margareten, rector of the gymnasium, but had apparently not yet been sent off. When I had read it through diligently and avidly, as I usually read everything the man writes, I thought it was worthy of being immediately printed in as many copies as possible and put into the hands of scholars . . . So here is the letter, dear reader, full of piety and learning, made available to you, so that you might read it before it reaches the man for whom it was intended. You may blame me (if it is a culpable deed and not rather an act of charity) . . . indeed I'll gladly and willingly shoulder the responsibility for any fault or crime this involves, if I may thereby provide a service to you and your studies.[11]

As Rummel notes, Lang's letter was by no means meant to be a private correspondence. The intent was for it to be published, only not by the author—who "in defending liberal studies would have come off as a prude"—but rather by some "well-intentioned thief."[12] Were Sigüenza's efforts at befriending Kino, then, the sincere acts of an attentive friend or the strategic maneuverings of a self-promoting scholar who hoped to expand the scope of his academic fame?

The peculiar world that both Kino and Sigüenza took their scholarly inspiration from constituted the keystone in their rickety relationship. This was a world in which the fate of man was no longer subject to the unknowable designs of the divine; it was a world in which rote memorization, a devoted faith in the authority of classical scholars, and excessive ornamentation in forms of rhetoric went hand in hand with the latest discoveries in heliocentric science, experimental mathematics, and Cartesian doubt. This was, in other words, an age in the midst of transition, or as many scholars have postulated, the beginnings of a second Axial Age.[13] Yet, it was precisely the ambiguity and eccentricity of this era that fostered a "prodigious creativity" in both Spain and America.[14] As Leonard notes, Sigüenza represented the archetypical Baroque scholar, whereas

Kino remained firmly committed to the authority of the ancients. Both men represented the best of their age, yet, true to form, they embraced vastly different perspectives on the world.[15] While Sigüenza's worldview continued to be influenced by the "religious dogma and pious faith" of the seventeenth century, in matters of science he embodied the ethos of the Age of Reason.[16] In fact, Sigüenza frequently criticized his academic colleagues for maintaining such blind devotion to classical scholarship simply "because some ancient scholar held this or that to be true."[17]

In 1680, the year the Pueblo Revolt shook the very foundations of Spanish authority in the kingdom of New Mexico, the "Great Comet" appeared in the sky.[18] Visible for months, its ethereal glare stirred both men, separated by the vastness of an ocean, to independently embark on the process of mapping and cataloguing the comet's route, length, and duration.[19] Sigüenza published his findings first. In 1681, shortly after the comet disappeared from the heavens, Sigüenza wrote his *Manifesto filosófico contra los cometas despojados del imperio que tenían sobre los tímidos* (Philosophical manifest against comets stripped of their dominion over the timid), dedicated to the Marchioness of La Laguna. He dedicated this work to the marchioness in order to eliminate any fears she might have that comets foreshadowed misfortune and calamity. In his treatise, Sigüenza argued that these celestial events were wholly natural phenomena—an ideological position that was still fairly unique for the time. As Leonard tells us, "This kind of skepticism was rare in the Baroque world of seventeenth century Mexico, and it was a little subversive in a culture in which Theology, as the 'Queen of Sciences,' still reigned supreme."[20] By using such a reasoned, scientific, and logic-driven approach in coming to terms with the nature of the comet, Sigüenza had openly and implicitly challenged all those scholars who relied on the authority of classical scholarship in deducing their arguments. In this way, he was inadvertently walking a fine line between the rejection of ancient authority and the modern directives of reason.[21]

Soon after the publication of Sigüenza's treatise, Don Martín de la Torre, a Flemish scholar living in Yucatan, produced a response titled *Manifesto Cristiano en favor de los cometas mantenidos en su natural significación* (Christian manifest in favor of comets maintained in their natural significance), in which he argued that comets were nothing less than warnings from God. Sigüenza countered these arguments in his *Belerofonte matemático contra la Quimera Astrológica de Don Martín de la Torre* (Mathematical Bellerophon against the Astrological Quimera of Don Martín de la Torre) where he juxtaposed the sophistication of his scientific and logic-driven approach against what he saw as the inferior and irredeemably conformist scholarship of his colleague. According to historian José Rojas Garcidueñas, Sigüenza's essay, which had a limited circulation and was never published, devastated Martín de la Torre so completely that the Flemish scholar never attempted a reply.[22] Similarly, when Don José Escobar Salmerón—another one of his colleagues, this time at the University of Mexico—wrote a competing treatise declaring that comets were wholly composed of dead bodies and human perspiration, Sigüenza, as if to elevate himself above such sterile debates, sardonically advised Mexicans to "avoid sweating!"[23] Such theories, bizarre as they may seem to us today, were a part of the academic parlance of the day. Even the highly revered European intellectual Athanasius Kircher (1602–80), whom both men greatly admired, held that comets were "exhalations of clouds, rivers, and seas of the terrestrial globe and that they come from evaporations of the planets."[24]

But it was Kino's competing essay on the comet titled *Exposición astronómica* (Astronomical Exposition) that unwittingly set the stage for a confrontation over the intellectual and cultural parameters of scientific authority and of the ethics and expectations of academic friendship.[25] While Sigüenza had argued that comets were wholly natural phenomena disassociated from the supernatural in every meaningful way, Kino held the contrary view; namely, that comets were divinely inspired and thus signs of imminent disaster and evil.[26] Taking impetus from celebrated thinkers like Seneca and Aristotle, Kino used the authority of the ancients to support and justify his scholarly position. In a letter to Father Luis Espinosa, he commented that the comet "signifies many calamities for Europe and means, in particular for three or four countries, unproductiveness, famine, storms and several earthquakes, disturbances on a vast scale, fevers, epidemics and numerous death, especially of eminent persons. . . . The fact that the comet is so colossal means that its evil effects will be all the more universal and affect more people and countries."[27] Furthermore, due to the comet's length and duration, it was virtually assured that its negative effects would "plague mankind for many years to come."[28] Kino, unlike Sigüenza, adhered to the Hapsburg model of scholarship "with its reliance on the symbolic logic of the political and religious authority of the court."[29]

According to Sigüenza, prior to Kino's departure to the northern frontier, the Austrian scientist visited his home in order to personally deliver to him a copy of his *Exposición*. Book gifting of this sort, especially if it was done in a sacred space like a home, had since ancient times been widely recognized as a sign of friendship. And perhaps Kino meant it as such.[30] But that is not how Sigüenza would come to understand it. For him, Kino's scholarly offering, which outlined an opposing perspective on the comet, was nothing less than a challenge to a *duelo literario* (literary duel), which Sigüenza openly embraced as being essential to advancing the cause of science. Wrote Sigüenza:

> With all certainty I was convinced that the most revered and learned fathers of the Company of Jesus, who are such patrons of the truth, would not take this controversy badly, since it takes place between two individuals and two mathematicians without going any farther that that; and all the more so because the duels that occasionally occur between those who pore over books are not only common but indeed licit and even necessary since one is assisted in them.[31]

But this was no standard scholarly duel. During the time that Kino was writing his *Exposición*, he apparently never mentioned it to Sigüenza, a rather strange omission given that the Creole scholar had just recently finished his own work on the same topic. Instead, Sigüenza came to hear about Kino's work from several of his academic colleagues who warned him of Kino's intention to challenge his *Manifesto*. At some level, this clandestine approach must have struck Sigüenza as a bit underhanded. But no matter, as a member of the larger scientific community, Sigüenza dutifully read Kino's *Exposición*, and his critiques of Kino's academic theories, which relied on the authority of classical scholarship, were entirely warranted. But the fact that Kino apparently scorned Sigüenza's own theoretical positions by not fully addressing them in his *Exposición* was to him an unpardonable affront. To Sigüenza, this blatant omission was the equivalent of Kino having cast him aside as a second-rate scholar and therefore undeserving of his intellectual energies. To be fair, it's quite possible that Kino never actually read Sigüenza's treatise. Kino attested to that very fact in his *Inocente, apostolica y gloriosa muerte del V. Pe. Francisco Xavier Saeta* (Innocent, apostolic, and glorious death of the Venerable Father Francisco Xavier Saeta) written fourteen years later, when he wrote that he never intended to offend the Mexican thinker, whose book he did not remember having read. But Sigüenza was convinced that he had, and his argument for Kino's betrayal of their academic friendship rested firmly on that premise.

Not only did Sigüenza believe that Kino had flagrantly dismissed his scholarship, but he also believed that the Austrian had purposely mocked him. According to Sigüenza, even though Kino never mentioned his name throughout his treatise, it was obvious to him that he was the source of Kino's derisive commentary. Sigüenza, for example, pointed to the fact that Kino had asserted that no scholar worth his salt could possibly hold an opposing view to his—the implication being, as Leonard tells us, that Sigüenza was worthless as a scholar.[32] But what followed was even more infuriating for Sigüenza. Kino wrote that the comet's nefarious message was evident to all "unless there be some *trabajosos Jucios* (dull wits) who cannot perceive it."[33] This statement, which Sigüenza believed was directed at him, was the equivalent of having been publicly called a *persona sin razón* (person without reason)—irrational, crazy, or worse, incompetent. In effect, such a contemptuous position was akin to Kino having revoked Sigüenza's membership in the transatlantic community of scholars. It also jeopardized his professional standing as a university professor and royal cosmographer. "I don't know," wrote Sigüenza, "whether to call it mockery or derision with which [Kino] speaks of me referring to my opinions."[34]

While Sigüenza saw Kino's *Exposición* as a patronizing rejection of his own scholarship, he also, and perhaps more importantly, saw it as a personal attack on his reputation as a scientist. In New Spain, as in much of Europe, one's academic reputation was of paramount importance; insults or rumors of incompetence could prove professionally disastrous. Because Kino's *Exposición* was read widely within scientific circles, Sigüenza felt compelled to respond publicly in order to defend his reputation, which Sigüenza apparently "valued as [if it were] my life."[35] Francis L. Ramos has written, "In the early modern Iberian world, public humiliation had political implications, and contemporaries at times declared war by embarrassing rivals publicly."[36] While Kino's treatise may not have been intended as an insult, Sigüenza saw Kino's contempt for his scholarship as a public humiliation. Among scholars of any historical period, the very impression of incompetence has often been enough to wreck a hard-earned reputation. Not responding to Kino's intellectual dual, then, would have been tantamount to admitting defeat and accepting dishonor and a devalued reputation. All this acrimony could have easily been avoided had a straightforward and logical critique of Sigüenza's *Manifesto* been set forth. A reasoned and civil counterargument would fit perfectly within the parameters of an imagined scientific republic, but not Kino's dismissive and disrespectful attack. To add insult to injury, Kino dedicated his work to the Marquis of La Laguna, husband to the marchioness, "thus setting the husband to liberate his wife from false counsel."[37] Wrote Sigüenza, "It appears that the Jesuit had come from Germany to this Septentronial

America to free her accidents from the deceit and air in which I had placed her [when I said that] comets should not be feared, as it was false that they foretell calamities and destruction."[38] Sigüenza, the highly revered Mexican savant, couldn't help but feel relegated to an inferior and somewhat shrunken position.

In response to Kino's *Exposición*, Sigüenza wrote his *Libra astronómica* (Astronomical balance), in which he defended himself against Kino's surreptitious accusation of scholarly ineptitude. Because Sigüenza felt that Kino's contempt toward him was personal, the full title of his book read: *Libra astronomica y philosóphica en que D. Carlos de Sigüenza y Góngora, Cosmógrapho, y Mathemático Regio en la Academia Mexicana, examina no solo lo que a su Manifiesto Philosóphico contra los Cometas opuso el R. P. Eusebio Francisco Kino de la Compañía de Jesus, sino lo que el mismo R. P. opinó y pretendió haver demonstrado en su Exposición Astronómica del Cometa del año de 1681* (Astronomical and philosophical balance in which Don Carlos de Sigüenza y Góngora, Cosmographer and Royal Mathematician of the Mexican Academy, examines not only in what to his Philosophical Manifesto Against Comets opposed by the Reverend Father Eusebio Francisco Kino of the Company of Jesus, but what the Reverend Father opined and pretended to have demonstrated in his Astronomical Exposition of the 1681 Comet). As the title highlights, Sigüenza's *Libra* was meant as a forceful rebuttal of Kino's *Exposición*. Unfortunately, due to its technical nature—the book opened with a series of complex mathematical and geometrical computations—Sigüenza was unable to find a publisher. His response remained unread for a decade. It was not until 1690 that an "admiring friend," Sebastián Guzmán y Cordova, a Spanish mathematician in the viceregal court, offered to foot the bill for publication.[39] Like Rummel's thieves, friends also served important financial roles in the competitive process of publication.

In this academic piece, Sigüenza forcefully argued against using the authority of the ancients in coming to terms with scientific phenomena, writing that they simply had no place in such endeavors. He also sought to defend his reputation. In order to respond to the apparent claim that he was irrational or uneducated, Sigüenza went through a litany of scholars that he drew from: men such as Kircher, Tycho, Descartes, Quevedo, Kepler, Caramuel (whom he described as "my great friend and most courteous correspondent"), Conrad, Confalonier, Pico della Mirondola, Gassendi, and Schott, among others.[40] His goal was not only to consult the most well-known and respected secular authorities of his day, but also to show Kino that he was no "dull-witt."

Sigüenza's passionate response, despite being out of character for someone who adhered so closely to the virtues of scholarly composure and reason, was unavoidable given the potential academic and social implications Kino's trivializing critique carried. The *Libra* was therefore clear in its outrage, beginning with these rather somber words: "*Nunca con más repugnancia, que en la ocacion presente tome la pluma en la mano*" (Never have I taken this pen in hand with more repugnance than on the present occasion).[41] According to Sigüenza, Kino, being European, openly disparaged Creole scholars like himself, considering them inherently inferior. His *Libra* was thus written in part to defend "'not only myself but also my patria and nation,' since the Jesuit clearly despised Mexico and Mexican scientists 'through being Spaniards . . . and because of this ignorance of the mathematical sciences.'"[42] Perhaps, Sigüenza believed, Kino had denigrated his scholarship because he had not attained his education in Europe, or because Kino could not possibly imagine that intellectuals of Sigüenza's prodigious abilities might "grow amidst the reeds and cat-tails on the margins of the Mexican pond!"[43]

Since Sigüenza was in 1681 already fairly well known among European scholars, it is not hard to understand why he felt betrayed by the condescension that Kino seemed to reserve for the Creoles of New Spain, treating them, as Sigüenza saw it, "as mere Indians," incapable of producing scholarship at the highest level.[44] And as if that were not enough to incite the Creole patriot's ire, Kino returned Sigüenza's maps of the northern frontier "incomplete and in shreds" and only through the great efforts of the rector of the Colegio de San Pedro and San Pablo, Francisco de Florencia, who sought them out for Sigüenza.[45] All these issues, both emotional and intellectual, were tediously laid out in his *Libra*.[46]

Sigüenza explained that his harsh tone in response to Kino derived from a sense of betrayal "when," believes More, "his expectations for intellectual friendship with the missionary, who was reputed to be a very eminent mathematician, did not come to fruition."[47] It became obvious to Sigüenza that he and Kino had a fundamentally different understanding of what such an imagined scientific republic of scholars entailed as well as of the rules regulating their ethical comportment. Anthony Grafton has outlined a similar code of ethics among those scholars who belonged to the European Republic of Letters. For Grafton, the Republic of Letters saw itself as Europe's first egalitarian society, where membership rested on the principles of openness, transparency, and the full citation of evidence.[48] Kino's bitter dismissal of Sigüenza's scholarship and his mocking tone was in no way acceptable in either in New Spain or in Europe. It simply had no place among men of letters, especially if made public.

As More maintains, Sigüenza had hoped to create a community of intellectual peers who were cosmopolitan and in vogue with the latest scientific ideas. This "imagined scientific republic" was to be structured in such a way as to create equivalence between core and periphery, principally through a unified adherence to ethical rules of behavior among men of learning where reason reigned paramount. The use of reason, as opposed to an adherence to the wisdom of the ancients, was the means through which Sigüenza could, as More attests, level the playing field, elevating New Spain to the position of Europe. In order for such equality to have merit, however, both sides had to agree to the same rules of behavior in relation to friendship and scholarship. Kino's flippant attack on Sigüenza's scholarship thus violated the most important tenant of academic friendship, that of reasoned and constructive dissent.

Despite Kino's supposed betrayal, Sigüenza wished to hold on to his dream of an self-contained intellectual community of equals. He ended his *Libra* with the following words: "*Y quedan los cometas libres de las infamas, que sin razón les imputan: y quedamos todos amigos, supuesto que*" (And all the comets remain free of calumny, which they have been assigned without the use of reason: and of course we all remain friends).[49] True to his words, when Father Pedro Van Hamme, a very learned man with a "fondness for mathematics," arrived the following year, Sigüenza made every effort to befriend him, sharing with him his ideas regarding the comet.[50] If this was a misunderstanding, as many contemporary scholars claim it was, it was an unfortunate one. As Ellen Schaffer writes, "One wishes it [the misunderstanding] could have been erased and that theirs could have been a warm, lifelong friendship."[51]

Kino on the Frontier: Friends and Foes

When Kino left Mexico City for the northern frontier, he became embroiled in yet another confrontation, this time with fellow Jesuit Father Francisco Xavier de Mora.[52] Prior to his departure to the frontier, Kino had been commissioned as royal cosmographer and tasked with surveying, delineating, and mapping the boundaries of California and Sonora and as missionary to the Natives of the region. After a rather uneventful reconnoitering attempt in California, Kino departed for Sonora in February 1687, six years after his initial confrontation with Sigüenza—he would spend the next twenty-four years of his life laboring among the Natives of that region. Soon after his arrival to Sonora, Kino directed the construction of his mission at Dolores. Known as *Nuestra Señora de los Dolores* (Our Lady of Sorrows), the mission was located along the San Miguel River because of its access to fertile land and because, as was the common practice among missionaries, it was near an Indian village.[53] Defense was also a major consideration for its location. Dolores was aptly constructed with the Sierra de Santa Teresa to the east, the Sierra del Torreón on the west, the Cerro Prieto to the south, and the rugged Sierra Azul on the north. Having established his mission, Kino energetically set himself on a project of exploration and conversion.

According to Herbert Eugene Bolton, Kino adopted a tireless work ethic, reconnoitering vast swaths of territory while enthusiastically extending the edges of Christendom to their furthest limits. During his time on the frontier, Kino made more than fifty journeys throughout the Pimería, all on horseback.[54] His individual trips were merciless, ranging from one hundred miles to more than one thousand.[55] And of the fifty expeditions Kino made throughout the Pimería, fourteen were into what is now Arizona. In 1700 Kino founded the mission of San Xavier del Bac, just south of modern-day Tucson. Due to his laudable accomplishments in Sonora and Arizona, Kino continues to be revered in both Mexico and the United States. In 1965 he was honored with a statue at the National Statuary Hall in Washington, D.C.

While Kino is widely credited with having traveled, reconnoitered, and mapped much of the Pimería Alta, he is also widely recognized as a historian, biographer, rancher, astronomer, theologian, geographer, and linguist. As a historian, Kino wrote a good deal about the Indians he ministered to, especially about their history and beliefs. He also wrote at length about his association with a number of men such as Admiral Atondo, Governor Jironza, Captains Manje and Bernal, and Fathers Juan Ugarte, Salvatierra, Francisco Maria Piccolo, and Saeta.[56] His *Inocente, apostolica y gloriosa muerte del V. Pe. Francisco Xavier Saeta*, which covered the history of the Pimería from 1687 to 1695, was composed of six parts and recounted the difficulties that missionaries like himself went through in reconnoitering and settling the Pimería. More importantly, it presented a narrative account of the events in Caborca that led to the Indian uprising of 1695 and to the eventual martyrdom of his good friend Father Francisco Xavier Saeta.[57] This work also provided important details on how he won over the Indians of the region. Later, in his *Favores Celestiales* (1703–4), Kino repeatedly claimed that the Indians were peaceful, and that they exhibited all evidence of friendship toward the missionaries.[58] Again, as we saw in the previous chapter, this was a very particular style of "Christian friendship" that celebrated civilized behavior and loyalty as the most important virtues. Kino's excessive praise of the indigenous peoples of Sonora earned him a great deal of criticism from secular and religious officials who claimed that he greatly exaggerated the positive qualities of both the land and its indigenous inhabitants. Much like the scholars of Newton's day envisioned a nascent form of civil society founded on relationships of amity among those members of a "scientific republic," so too did Jesuit missionaries, toiling along the edges of the Spanish Empire, imagine a "spiritual republic" where friendship was determined less by the rules of scholarship or those of loyalty and more by genuine acts of valor, martyrdom, and love for one another.

In 1610 Father Rodrigo de Cabredo had set forth a set of rules for proper missionary comportment. He stipulated, for instance, that Jesuits were to enter the missionizing field "two by two" in order to keep each other company and foster friendships with one other so as to avoid the ills of loneliness.[59] "This rule," writes Charles Polzer, "was tinged with Ignatian asceticism because one of the companions was to be subject to the other. The obedience-minded Jesuits were feeling the burden of isolated missionary existence."[60] Cabredo's rules emphasized constant communication among missionaries, which was primarily intended to ensure that their missionary asceticism, zeal, and behavior would not be corrupted. Close interaction among members of the Order was also "intended for the spiritual and human well-being of the men who had to live apart from the more familiar settings of Spanish daily life."[61] A later amendment to the 1610 Code, written in 1662, sought to regulate contact between missionaries and settlers, to govern commerce among them, and even to forbid the Fathers "from soliciting material goods for their welfare."[62] The sixteen paragraphs of Cabredo's 1662 Code were therefore designed to aid missionaries in their daily relations with Indians, settlers, and other men of the cloth in order to foster a more civil and peaceful society.[63]

Given Cabredo's emphasis on fostering friendships among the spiritually adept, Kino seems to have been successful in establishing fruitful associations with many of his contemporaries. Of Kino, Luis de Velarde (1677–1737) admiringly wrote:

He always took his food without salt, and with mixtures of herbs which made it more distasteful. No one ever saw in him any vice whatsoever, for the discovery of lands and the conversion of souls had purified him. These, then, are the virtues of Father Kino: he prayed much and was considered as without vice. He neither smoked nor took snuff, nor wine, nor slept in a bed. He was so austere that he never took wine except to celebrate mass, nor had any other bed than the sweet blankets of his horse for a mattress, and two Indian blankets [for a cover]. He never had more than two coarse shirts, because he gave everything as alms to the Indians. He was merciful to others, but cruel to himself.[64]

These words of praise emerged effortlessly from Velarde, even though he had apparently never met the man. Father Francisco Xavier Saeta (1664–95), who was the source of Kino's first book during his time in the Pimería, was also extremely fond of him. In one of his letters to Kino he wrote: "I am leaving for Matape, and I go in great haste, because of my eagerness to give your Reverence a thousand most cordial embraces. . . . Your reverence will pardon this very miserable note, which I am writing with a scrawl. Goodbye, my most loving father, *Humilimus ex corde*."[65] It seems clear from this short expert that theirs was a close and loving friendship. As friends they spent a good deal of time talking about their plans for the development of the Pimería, plans cut short by Saeta's abrupt martyrdom during the 1695 Pima uprising. After Saeta's death, Kino apparently went into a deep depression, but he retained enough wherewithal to unleash a massive manhunt for his companion's killers. Unfortunately, because Kino took on the role of a secular official in investigating the murder of his friend, he unwittingly created a number of enemies. In the months after the death of Saeta, Manuel Gonzáles, one of Kino's oldest friends, contemptuously wrote: "Who has said that a missionary can also play the part of an official?"[66] Similarly, for Francisco Xavier de Mora, Kino's behavior during and after the 1695 Pima uprising was anathema to the missionizing project.

Like Sigüenza, Mora believed that missionaries laboring at the edges of the Spanish Empire needed to adhere to a particular, idealized form of friendship where friends supported one other by adhering to a particular code of practical and spiritual ethics. Along the northern frontier, Mora labored intently to stamp out the "evils of paganism," public drunkenness, and the "violent" behavior of the Indians.[67] In order to prevent such "evils" from rearing their ugly head, Mora held that there needed to exist among all missionaries a unified and equal commitment to the missionizing enterprise.

According to Mora, he and Kino had initially maintained a good and amiable association, but their friendship soured in the years following the 1695 Pima uprising. Mora's concern over Kino's behavior initially began when Horacio Polici, then father visitor of the missions of Sonora, asked him to maintain a watchful eye over the "troublesome" missionary who was taking actions that were outside his religious mandate as a missionary.[68] But Polici was nothing if not practical, and he quickly understood that he needed Kino's established influence over the Natives of the region to restore peace. Thus, to Mora's utter surprise, Polici reactivated Kino's role as missionary, soldier, and explorer, giving him the authority he needed to quell the violence engulfing the Pimería in 1695. With the help of Native chiefs and indigenous allies, Kino successfully reestablished peace. To Mora's eyes, not only had Polici—who had originally ordered him to keep close tabs on Kino—betrayed him, but so had Kino, who was now in his estimation more of a soldier than a missionary and thus, according to him, not in accord with proper missionizing protocol. It was at this point that Mora broke from the celebrated missionary in order to write what can only be summed up as a fulminating diatribe against his former associate and friend.

In a 1696 letter to the provincial Juan de Palacios, Mora went to great lengths to describe Kino as a bad and detestable missionary, whose only interest was self-aggrandizement and promotion.[69] This highly contemptuous letter accused Kino of being an individualist who cared little for the proper ethical comportment expected of him as a member of the Society of Jesus. If for Mora victory over the devil resided in the ability to remain united as a religious Order committed to the goal of saving souls, Kino's individualistic actions hampered their overall strength. Kino, Mora continued, was ireful, domineering, stubborn, and not of an easygoing demeanor with his religious colleagues. Mora even accused Kino of mistreating the Indians under his charge, not by beating them, but rather by leaving his mission at Dolores for months at a time in order to reconnoiter the frontier, as if he were an explorer or a soldier. These long trips away from his mission were harmful because they left his Indian charges alone and without adequate supervision: "Well what free time would he have to rest in his home and pursue the administration of the Indians. It is very common the times that [Indians] die without confession, because the father is in another pueblo . . . how many children will remain without baptism, how many holy days without mass, how many without *doctrina*."[70]

Mora's critiques of his former friend did not stop there, however. He argued that Kino was mistaken regarding several issues of moral theology, that he abused his liturgical privileges far too often, that he spoke poor Pima, that he baptized much too freely without any follow-up, and that he was a manipulator because he had erroneously achieved the title of an exemplar missionary without having earned it. It is quite possible that Mora was envious of the missionary's success and fame. Or, perhaps Mora simply didn't understand the intricacies of the frontier in the same way Kino did. What is certain, however, is that Mora felt that Kino had betrayed the entire missionizing enterprise by disavowing the rules of ethical comportment and friendship among missionaries. Kino's goals, he believed, were for personal advancement and not for the overall good of the "spiritual republic." In particular, Mora was aggravated by the fact that Kino had made a poor habit of promising aid to his fellow missionaries without ever following through on his promises. Such a lack of commitment to his Jesuit brothers was inconceivable to Mora and represented for him a complete failure of friendship. Kino's various shortcomings, argued Mora, were a major reason for the high turnover of missionaries in the Pimería. Kino, he argued, was simply too concerned with his own reputation to care about the overall well-being of the Pimería and of the individual members of his Order.

Overall, Mora held that the Pimería would never advance with Kino as one of its main missionaries, for all he did, Mora wrote in a dismissive manner, was to go around handing gifts to the Indians and baptizing them so freely as to lose all meaning. This behavior, Mora continued, made Kino popular among the Indians but made his job in maintaining and advancing a "spiritual republic" virtually impossible. Reading through Kino's prodigious corpus of writings, it's undeniable that Kino was militaristic. After all, one of his closest companions and friends, Juan Mateo Manje (1670–1727), was a soldier; he did abandon his home base of Dolores for long periods at a time to reconnoiter the frontier; and he did baptize hundreds of Indians on his trips. Mora's sense of betrayal at Kino's behavior reveals his idea for what behaviors and actions he envisioned as being ideal. Once a friend, Mora eventually came to regard Kino as an enemy, not only of himself but of the entire Pimería.

In a rebuttal to Mora's accusations, Kino defended himself by claiming that the missionary was simply mistaken in his critiques of him.[71] In his *Favores Celestiales* Kino wrote that for Mora "human means have been so lacking that many times those whose duty it was to aid us have hindered us, and those who were our friends have become our enemies, placing obstacles in the way of everything and trying to make light of the whole affair."[72] As Polzer points out, the excess of rules and regulations along the frontier had by the early eighteenth century become so inconvenient and complex that they represented more of an obstacle than anything else.[73] Kino, it seems, never paid much heed to any particular set of rules. The frontier was simply too hostile and unpredictable a place for rules of such limiting quality. Because Kino did not abide by the coded, often-difficult-to-decipher rules of friendship on the frontier, he gained the envy, distrust, and revulsion of a number of his Jesuit brothers.

Conclusion

In both of the relationships addressed above, the dynamics of friendship come to life when analyzed in reverse through the purview of betrayal. Both Mora and Sigüenza felt betrayed by Kino, though in very different ways. Sigüenza had hoped to create a community of scholars who were in vogue with the latest philosophical and scientific trends of the time—a scientific republic. Mora hoped to maintain the integrity of a community of missionaries united in the struggle against the evil influences prevalent throughout the frontier—a spiritual republic. In both instances, the dynamics of power and authority intersected with the intellectual construction of ideal friendship. In Sigüenza's case, Kino's public attack on his scholarship left him with no other choice but to disavow their relationship in favor of a public scholarly duel so as to defend his hard-earned reputation. This public refutation was necessary because Kino had challenged not only his credibility as a scholar but his Creole patriotism as well. Mora's deep disdain toward Kino was prompted by Kino's particular style of missionizing that paid little heed to proper missionizing protocol. Kino's "selfish" behavior was to Mora an affront to their own personal friendship and to his commitment to the Natives he seemingly abandoned in order to play the part of an intrepid explorer. Because of his actions, Mora felt that Kino had betrayed his entire Order. These highly charged feelings of betrayal on the part of both Sigüenza and Mora show the extent to which socially constructed rules of amity with the aim of regulating behavior were everywhere in colonial society. They also show the extent to which Kino saw himself as existing outside the bounds of these socially and intellectually constructed bonds of fellowship. Interestingly, Kino seems to have paid only scant attention to the accusations leveled against him. It was Mora and Sigüenza who were the ones at pains to highlight Kino's supposed irresponsible and untrustworthy behavior.

While Kino was undoubtedly a part of these two "imagined" societies—namely, those of science and religion—both of which he was firmly dedicated to, his greatest passion was in pushing the Jesuit frontier northward, which, as we saw from Mora, elicited great criticism. Though Kino acted outside the bounds of these two ideological communities, he did find friendships in various places, especially among Indians and a few soldiers. By juxtaposing Kino's relationships of enmity with those of amity, we gain a clearer picture of just how complicated and emotionally charged was its ideological construction of colonial society. Friendships were important for a variety of reasons, but oftentimes the unspoken ethical codes of amity could be burdensome, confusing, and difficult to decipher. These codes only became visible when they were breached, provoking in the process strong emotional responses and feelings of betrayal.

Historians have talked at length about Kino. He is probably one of the most recognized figures of the northern frontier, but few have fully analyzed the wide spectrum of relationships he had with other missionaries, soldiers, and Indians, not all of whom admired him. By enlarging the scope of Kino's relationships in New Spain, we can better deduce the various types of social codes that existed in colonial society and the way in which they were perceived.

Overall, the scientific and religious communities outlined in this chapter offer a unique version of civil society that functioned conterminously with other idealized communities. In the following chapter we will see how morality fit into this already byzantine confluence of ideals and expectations.

CHAPTER FOUR

Internal Enemies

False Friendship and the Collapse of Moral Order

---

*Friendship is unnecessary, like philosophy, like art. . . . It has no survival value;
rather it is one of those things that give value to survival*

—C. S. Lewis, *The Four Loves*

ON JULY 19, 1686, DON FRANCISCO DEL CASTILLO BETANUER, *vecino* (Spanish resident) of Sonora, sent an urgent message to Juan de Theran, *capitán á guerra* (captain of war) in the valley of Bacanuchi, informing him that an Indian in his charge had reported to him that the Jocomes, Janos, and several Sumas—avowed enemies of the Spanish—had joined "in friendship" with their longtime rivals from the Pima nation of Quíbiri.[1] A so-called friendship between former adversaries presented a significant threat to an already unnerved European population whose numbers barely stretched beyond a few thousand. In Betanuer's mind the only possible rationale for a coalition of this magnitude was the complete annihilation of Spanish society, which at the time seemed like a very real possibility given recent events in New Mexico and elsewhere. No doubt he was troubled by the fact that the Pima Indians, long considered indios amigos of the Spanish, had betrayed their solemn vows of *obedienzia* (obedience) and loyalty in order to join forces with indios enemigos whose reputation for deception and violence had long been established in those parts. Though backsliding of this sort was not uncommon, for Spaniards living among frontier Indians it represented a serious threat to the development of civil society. The inherent difficulty in knowing when and why indios amigos might reverse course to become indios enemigos made life on the Spanish frontier particularly unpredictable and precarious.

Throughout the seventeenth and eighteenth centuries, European settlers, and in particular Jesuit missionaries, worked toward preventing such dangerous lapses in allegiance by befriending indigenous leaders or, at the very least, by winning their confidence and allegiance.[2] By learning their native languages, reinforcing a familiar supernatural and cosmological worldview, and adopting some of their long-held ritual practices, Jesuit missionaries throughout much of Spanish America made important inroads toward winning them over. By attempting to understand their ritual customs, "the better to preach the gospel on native terms," Jesuits also believed that in time they would wrench Natives from the rigid grip of the devil.[3] By this reckoning, early missionaries such as Andrés Peréz de Ribas and Gonzalo de Tapia (martyred in 1594 at the age of thirty-three) and later missionaries such as Juan de Salvatierra and Eusebio Kino were able to use their ties of amity with local indigenous leaders and groups in expanding their range of conversions, to say nothing of enhancing their chances of survival. This same logic held true on the southern edges of Spanish America. Working among the Guaraní of Brazil and Paraguay, Antonio Ruiz de Montoya noted that upon entering virgin territory "all their first efforts were directed to winning the friendship of the caciques, whose protection was often purchased by gifts of iron axes and other useful or attractive objects."[4] It was a commonly held article of belief by several of the missionizing Orders that Natives would naturally gravitate toward the embrace of the Holy Church if they were only treated humanely, safeguarded against settler abuse, and provided with tools, foodstuffs, and other supplies. The brutal Inquisitional trial of Carlos de Chichimecateotl of Texcoco (1535) set a far-reaching precedent for also excluding Natives from the powerful and potentially brutal hand of the Holy Inquisition.[5]

According to the Comprehensive Order for New Discoveries (1573), Franciscans and Jesuits would be responsible for setting the ethical standard for the exploration and pacification of the northern frontier. Though both Orders vigorously embraced their religious and ethical mandate, they maintained significant organizational differences. The Jesuits, for instance, who believed themselves as a cut above all others, saw themselves as "a religion of apostles," willingly sacrificing everything to the "task of winning souls" and "harvesting the Lord's vineyard."[6] In their mind, they were to act ethically, and through a policy of gentle persuasion they would win over the Natives. Later Bourbon reformers reified these established beliefs through enlightened policies, urgently professing the dangers of treating Indians like brutes, lest they become internal enemies.[7] Of course, all this represented an ideal, which was necessarily set against the sanguine backdrop of all-out war (*guerra a fuego y sangre*) should Indians prove recalcitrant. Naturally, then, for avowed indios amigos to be "in friendship" with indios enemigos represented a considerable obstacle to the ongoing process of missionization and settlement. But this is not what troubled Betanuer the most. Betanuer was most distraught by the disloyalty and "false friendship" of one Joseph Romo (better known as El Canito), governor and *capitán general* of the Pimas and leader of the 1686 alliance.

Indios amigos—indigenous leaders who openly professed loyalty and friendship toward Spanish officials—who became indios enemigos, such as Canito, were far more of a threat than unconquered Indian nations such as the Jocomes, Janos, or Sumas. An Indian amigo turned internal enemy, Canito was privy to a host of sensitive information such as knowledge of Spanish trade patterns, political and social hierarchies, internal rivalries, military strategy and technique, and social mores. Though the initial stages of the criminal investigation that followed the revelation of this "alarming" pact narrowed in on several coconspirators, Canito eventually emerged as the official face of the planned rebellion.

Identifying rebel leaders by name, describing their positions of authority, and isolating their stated reasons for rebelling was common practice in criminal investigations along the frontier.[8] It was also an essential component in the proper and efficient administration of empire. Spain's vast territorial possessions could only become a tangible reality through the production of such official criminal records and the various other administrative, cartographical, and legal documents produced for use in day-to-day operations.[9] Just as the *castellano* (Spanish) of Hernando de Talavera and Antonio de Nebrija became the official language of the Spanish empire (and not Latin), so too did colonial documents function as its universal currency.[10] Documenting the goings-on of the empire, especially along its furthest peripheries, was therefore vital in making these frontier areas visible to the Spanish king, whose continued commitment and support was indispensable to their overall success.[11] These valuable pieces of paper were then "consumed (and re-digested) by colonial bureaucrats, scribes, archivists, and historians—all of whom produce[d] their own carefully crafted narratives of truth, fact, fiction, and everything in between."[12] The fact that various often contradictory storylines emerged from criminal investigations like the Canito case, all of which were digested at differing levels of interest depending on who was dictating, writing, and reading them, suggests that these trials were wide open to interpretation and manipulation. With this kind of administrative irregularity in mind, scholars have tended to follow the lead of Natalie Zemon Davis, who has promoted the practice of reading in between the lines in order to find a more faithful interpretive understanding of historical events that cut through the formulaic rhetoric that comprised large sections of colonial documents. In this way, historians are better able to ascertain the coded meanings behind why people wrote and said what they did.[13]

In highlighting the fact that Canito had gained the confidence of the Spanish by skillfully performing his role as an indio amigo, Betanuer was using this criminal document as an opportunity to make visible, and therefore digestible, proper and improper applications of friendship. The fact that colonial magistrates also zeroed in on the "false friendship" of Canito as a major factor in the planning and preparation of this rebellion shows just how important the idea of friendship was to Sonora's Spanish ruling elite who, like Betanuer, benefited from a morally resolute society. While granting cultural brokers and "amigos" like Canito access to the inner workings of the colonial blueprint was necessary for the efficient functioning of civil administration, it remained a dangerous liability whose peril was magnified when potentially privileged information was shared with indios enemigos.[14] This vexing dilemma rested at the very core of Indian–Spanish relations throughout much of the colonial period.

In this chapter, I argue that the frequent literary usage of friendship during the seventeenth and eighteenth centuries, particularly in criminal investigations such as the Canito case, formed an important part of the colonial language of the northern frontier. Aside from serving a basic communicative function, the language of friendship also represented a moralizing mechanism for influencing, molding, and in many instances controlling indigenous behavior and their attitudes toward frontier settlers.[15] Concern over the significance of indigenous behaviors can be traced back to the earliest chroniclers of America, to men such as Gonzalo Fernández de Oviedo (1478–1557) and Francisco de Vitoria (1483–1546), who asked penetrating questions about why Indians behaved so differently from Europeans. As discussed in the previous chapters, the Spanish criteria for judging indigenous behavior was in large part derived from Greek and Roman models, infused as they were with all the ideological baggage and prejudices of its greatest thinkers. But in New Spain coming to terms with the variability of indigenous behaviors (particularly negative ones) was a convoluted issue that ran the full gamut of explanations, from those who believed that it was simply innate to their "inferior nature" as "natural slaves" to those who believed that because of their biological constitution they were more easily susceptible to influence from the devil to those who sought behavioral explanations in the human and physical environment.[16] Many held all three views at once. At the core of all these arguments, however, was the idea that Indians, with proper care and instruction, could be perfected, civilized, and ultimately made rational economic and political subjects of the Crown.

The strategic dissemination of friendship ideals and of their attendant moral responsibilities was another aspect of the larger "civilizing process" that took effect throughout much of New Spain.[17] The idea of civilizing men pervaded all three overseas empires—Spain, England, and France. The charter of the Virginia Company in 1609, for instance, issued the following statement: "Propagating of Christian religion to such people, as yet live in darkness and miserable ignorance of the true knowledge and worship of God and may in time bring the infidels and savages living in these parts to humane civility and to a settled and quiet government."[18] The notion of bringing the "barbarous" Indians to "quiet government" was right out of Pérez de Ribas.

In many ways, psychological mechanisms of social control such as constructed normative moral ideals—of which friendship was a core product—typically outweighed more exacting systems of coercion and persuasion.[19] "Conviction," writes Alfredo Jiménez, "rather than fear [was] the most permanent feeling working in favor of proper social behavior," because it was internalized in such a way that it incorporated "cultural values, mores, and goals by the individual through a psychological process that [made] them an inseparable part of oneself."[20] Such psychological tools for controlling behavior and affect formed the basis of what Susan Deeds has described as a "behavioral map"—a constantly shifting mental diagram that men and women utilized in order to better navigate and consequently manipulate the social intricacies of colonial society.[21]

Generally speaking, systemic psychological systems of control functioned best along remote frontier areas like Sonora that were distant from centers of viceregal authority and lacked a strong military or police force. They also had their greatest success in areas that were largely free from the weighty hand of the Inquisition, whose goal it was to supervise the faith and morals of Spanish society. These ideologically repressive but also unifying systems of controlling the moral ethos of a community formed the conceptual foundation of what Barbara Rosenwein has called an emotional community—that is, a group of varying size and ethnic composition in which "people adhere to the same norms of emotional expression and value—or devalue—the same or related emotions."[22] These values could be organic, evolving naturally from a shared history or trauma, or they could be imposed from without through conquest. According to Rosenwein, multiple emotional communities could, and often did, exist contemporaneously. They also changed with time. "Some come to the fore to dominate our sources, then recede in importance. Others are almost entirely hidden from us, though we may imagine they exist and may even see some of their effects on more visible groups."[23] Putting aside economic, political, or environmental explanations, Rosenwein's framework of "emotional communities" provides another important variable in determining why some indigenous communities allied with the Spanish and others didn't. The Spanish Empire also represented its own type of moral community writ large, which began at the very top with the king, who sought to justify his right to rule over frontier Indians by referring to his (and by extension Spain's) moral obligation to educate, civilize, and evangelize them. This obligation, as Alejandro Cañeque explains (see chapter 1), was couched in the moralized sentiments of reciprocity, love, loyalty, and friendship.[24] Along the Spanish frontier, such moralized language thus sought to reinforce the behavioral and attitudinal norms that regulated affect and, on a more practical plane, those of sex, marriage, racial indifference, and modes of authority.[25]

In *Suicide* (1897), Émile Durkheim showed how morality and, by association, loyalty, respect for authority, and sacredness were central in tying a community together. Sharing a moral compass, he believed, could unite a people irrespective of ethnicity.[26] By simply acknowledging and sometimes adopting the moral imperatives of Spaniards, Indians unwittingly entered their moral universe and, while never fully becoming European themselves or receiving many of its attendant benefits, at least in part became open to the idea of self-sacrifice for the good of the group. This process of emotional and moral association with Spaniards is clearly seen in the postconquest plays in which Tlaxcallans in central Mexico and Pueblos in New Mexico reinterpreted the Spanish Conquest, reimagining themselves as heroic players in an epic drama of good and evil.[27] Undoubtedly, it can be argued that this process of social and emotional identification worked in reverse as well, as Spaniards frequently adopted indigenous cultural values.[28] Such ideological commitments to a moral community, which were encouraged and defended by the Crown, are most clearly evident when we take into account the participation of indigenous leaders in important roles of judicial and administrative authority and in their presence within the ranks of the Church and the military.[29] For Indians to manipulate this constructed moral order was therefore a betrayal of the deepest sort.

But promoting and celebrating Westernized moral values such as loyalty, generosity, honesty, reciprocity, and trustworthiness—all of which were at the very center of the notion of friendship—was not an easy task to accomplish through conviction alone, as Jiménez has us believe. It often required a highly nuanced process of indoctrination and normalization through various legal, violent, and religious means. Spanish administrators, for instance, sought to impose moral authority through the sanctioned weight of official jurisprudence, the public and performative nature of criminal investigations and punishments, and the careful distribution of canes of office and administrative titles. Soldiers and settlers responded to breaks in the colonial pact with outright state-sanctioned violence or through the threat of retaliation and the promotion of "human trophies," which could be seen as a form of psychological warfare. Missionaries imposed their own system of religious behaviorism with all the moral heft of biblical orthodoxy. In fact, the Church, in all its physical and intellectual pageantry, represented an indispensable prop of the Spanish monarchy, "preaching obedience to the government and acquiescence to its social order."[30] Therefore, just as penal codes sought to create defined boundaries between acceptable and unacceptable forms of sexuality and familial relations among frontier residents,[31] so too did the full extension of public criminal investigations, such as the Canito case and others like it, influence the consumption and digestion of acceptable and unacceptable modes of morality. As I suggest in this chapter, the moralized and moralizing language of friendship on the frontier was not simply a function of etiquette, politeness, or the high-minded ideals of *civitas* (city life), though at some level it was also that;[32] it was, more to the point, an effective tool of civil administration and control.

Betanuer's characterization of this alliance as a "friendship" was thus prompted by his desire to incite moral outrage among Sonora's settler population. In so doing, he and others of his social and administrative ilk were methodically contributing to the development of a social standard by which to assess indigenous behavior, create moral legitimacy, and evoke loyalty and reciprocity among indigenous leaders and the communities they governed. In this way, they effectively placed themselves as the purveyors (second only to the Jesuits) of moral authority. As a *vecino*, not privy to official channels of power, Betanuer was able to influence his social surroundings by promoting efficient ethical and moral standards that undergirded the established social hierarchy and that were reinforced by the threat of settler violence. Moralized language, since it was almost always staged in such a way as to relay important information about power and authority, also constituted a socially meaningful act or "a type of performative utterance," necessarily collapsing words and gestures into a single expression or series of expressive actions.[33] Referring to someone as a friend was therefore more than a simple gesture of goodwill, since accepting this designation, and its attendant benefits, carried with it a series of specific responsibilities, behaviors, and ideals that rested atop a superimposed ethical, moral, and intellectual foundation.

European settlers sought refuge within this systematic distribution of ethics, propagandizing in the process the normalization of moral and immoral behavior and, by extension, of the spaces where said immoral behavior took place. The physical spaces where indios enemigos and, conversely, indios amigos resided, for instance, were seen by Spaniards through the bifurcated prism of good and evil. Sonya Lipsett-Rivera has highlighted how these types of ideological processes functioned in colonial Mexico City by looking at how social space, the built environment, and even the orientation of the furniture in one's home were seen through the lenses of morality and gender.[34] For Lipsett-Rivera, space is always an important factor in understanding social reality because it "influenced men and women and molded their behavior."[35] In the Canito case, for example, which I discuss in the following pages, the invitation of indios enemigos (Janos) into his home—a sacred and moral space that was largely unpoliceable—turned his house into a dangerous space of sedition. It was in the home, as we saw in the first chapter, where many of the most sacred friendship rites took place. And as we also saw in the second chapter, Hurdaide's attempt to befriend the Yaqui was initiated by means of an invitation into his home. French philosopher Gaston Bachelard's concept of the "poetics of space" plays an important role here. The idea that Bachelard postulated in his 1964 book was essentially that the quality and value afforded by the idea of the home was very much dependent on the social context in which it was found.[36] Thus, a home could in one context represent intimacy, secrecy, or security but within another, such as in a colonial setting, represent danger, sedition, and emotional withdrawal. Similarly, the fact that Canito attended "heathen" rituals that were located in isolated places, again outside the gaze of Spanish authorities, represented a threat to the artificially ordered social landscape upon which Spanish colonialism rested. Spatial formulas of this sort acquired emotional value and were often coupled with behavioral expressions of immoral comportment such as when Canito was accused of shaking hands with an indio enemigo right outside his home or, more to the point, when he strategically used the language of friendship in a deceptive and duplicitous manner in order to gain access to channels of authority and power.

As the process of colonization grew in complexity and sophistication, moral spaces and actions came to represent a wide range of different things and encompassed a number of communities, both Native and European.[37] Though morality was used as a tool of European colonization in reinforcing proper behavior and attitudes, it remained open to exploitation. For indigenous communities, survival not only necessitated a willingness and ability to adapt and accommodate to Spanish social expectations, but it required the keen and highly sophisticated skills of imitation and manipulation. In Sonora and Sinaloa, as one historian writes, "colonial domination itself had to become a subtle art in order to persist."[38] This "subtle art," however, was not the exclusive property of Spaniards. By cultivating strategic friendships through the moralized language of amity and by then holding Spaniards to these same ethical expectations, indigenous leaders, and oftentimes entire indigenous communities, entered into a highly nuanced and cosmopolitan discourse with the empire and its agents. As Joanne Rappaport and Tom Cummings maintain, colonial hybridity of this sort was not the exclusive product of Spanish culture being superimposed onto indigenous lifeways; rather, it more clearly resembled the nuanced process by which Natives consciously and strategically adopted a "range of foreign cultural forms."[39] Both Indians and Spaniards were, therefore, forced to change, adapt, and practice the subtle arts of deceit in ways that are not always obvious to us, but which were a central part of the negotiated ideological terrain of the frontier. It's through this type of morally deceptive yet deeply human behavior that we are able to peer into the constructed intellectual and emotional world of the "Spanish" frontier.

A Legacy of Violence on the Frontier

Because proclamations of violence against Europeans and their colonial institutions were not uncommon along the far-flung edges of Spain's American empire, it was imperative for European settlers, administrators, and soldiers to establish amicable ties with local indigenous leaders. Such efforts, however, failed as often as they succeeded. In the few instances when they were successful, friendships were generally short-lived, tenuous, uncertain, and highly susceptible to shifts in the colonial pact.[40] At every point along the path, interethnic friendships, either among groups or between individuals, were subject to exploitation and manipulation. Yet, despite the potential for misuse, the benefits of friendship almost always outweighed its drawbacks. Still, the uncertainty of strategic alliances and friendships kept both settlers and Natives in a state of constant preparedness, which perforce required them to become attuned to the subtle and not-so-subtle shifts in colonial power relations, and thus open to readjusting their alliances and friendships accordingly.[41] When readjustment failed, or when the dynamics of power swung too far in one direction or the other, violence commonly helped correct the imbalance.

One such shift, one of the most significant along the northern frontier, occurred in 1680. That year, several generations after initial contact and only six years prior to the formation of the Sonoran coalition, the Pueblo Indians of New Mexico—an alliance of Jemez, Keresan, Piro, Tewa, Tiwa, Zuni, and Hopi peoples—unleashed a brutal and highly organized rebellion against their Spanish overseers, leaving twenty-one Franciscan missionaries (half the total number in New Mexico) and just about four hundred settlers dead. Despite New Mexican governor Antonio de Otermín's attempt to warn Spanish settlers of the impending attack, the rebellion was too well planned and sudden for any effective countermeasures.[42] From the Spanish capital at Santa Fe, the remaining 1,946 settlers and Christianized Indian allies escaped with their lives to the Franciscan mission of El Paso del Norte, three hundred miles to the south.[43]

The widespread fear invoked by the events of 1680 emerged not just from the loss of life and targeted destruction of Spanish property, but from its highly secretive and organized nature. As news of the revolt spread throughout northern New Spain, unease over the potential for another Pueblo-like event pressed Viceroy Conde de Paredes into action. Due to a host of financial and administrative challenges, however, the viceroy was unable to mount an effective response. In neighboring Sonora, news of the revolt arrived with predictable haste. Francisco Agramont y Arce, former governor of Nueva Vizcaya and close associate of Governor Otermín, was among the first to receive word. On September 15, thirty-five days after Po'pay's Rebellion, Agramont y Arce sent Otermín a letter in which he thanked God for his safety and praised his valor in successfully shepherding his people to El Paso. Now a resident of Sonora, Agramont y Arce expressed a deep concern at a similar event taking place in his new backyard. Sonora's settler population also became filled with worry when they learned of these events. Their anxiety derived directly from the fact that "Indians built the vecinos' houses, watched over their children, cooked their meals, herded their cattle, tended their crops, broke rock in their mines, and fired their smelters."[44] They understood all too well that without an adequately maintained modus vivendi, their lives would be in peril.

The events of 1680 placed everyone, including the Pueblos themselves, on high alert. With the elimination of Spaniards from New Mexico, Pueblo communities unwittingly opened the door to Apache, Navajo, and Ute raiders, reestablishing ancient raiding patterns.[45] In Nueva Viscaya several military presidios were constructed to guard silver shipments to Mexico City.[46] As news of this momentous event spread throughout New Spain, in Mexico City, the epicenter of the American intellectual world, Kino and Sigüenza came to understand the revolt's origins from different perspectives. For Kino, the appearance of the Great Comet on the eleventh month of that year represented clear evidence of its providential nature, since comets, as we read in the previous chapter, were known to be ill omens of death and destruction, composed, so some believed, from the exhalations of clouds, rivers, and seas and possibly also from the evaporations of the planets.[47] Thus for Kino the appearance of the comet and the revolt were utterly connected. For Sigüenza, Kino's friend and intellectual peer at the time, this sort of deductive reasoning represented all that was wrong with adhering slavishly to classical modes of knowledge. While colonial centers like Mexico City and Lima were capable of accommodating simultaneous epistemological interpretations of events by referencing both scientific reason and the established knowledge of the ancients, this was not the case among frontier settlers. For them, scientific knowledge of the type Sigüenza promoted was of little use, for it was the established intellectual authority of the ancients, coupled as it was with emotion and intuition, that most adequately undergirded the simplified moral order of the frontier.

At the time of the Pueblo Revolt, most Sonorans adhered to Kino's providential interpretation of events. So, when in the following year *alcalde mayor* Lázaro Verdugo gathered the Spanish population of San Juan Bautista to inform them that he had heard from a loyal Indian named Javier that an uprising was being planned, they naturally understood this event through the simplified and moralized lens of religious design—perhaps, they thought, brought on by the machinations of the devil. Implicated in the conspiracy were the Jocomes, Janos, Sumas, and Pimas—the same four groups that would be involved in the Canito affair five years later. "The conspiracy of 1681," as David Yetman has called it, had as its central goal the expulsion of all Europeans and their gods from Sonora. Though no actual violence ever took place, the simple rumor of such an opportunely timed revolt laid the groundwork for an investigation that took several weeks to complete.

The investigation revealed a revolt that was three years in the making. Designed to take place in Chinapa (specifically chosen because of its proximity to several prominent mines), it was to be composed of pagan and Christianized Indians from the surrounding regions. The men tasked with investigating these reports and allegations quickly unearthed an intricate network of more than a dozen Indian coconspirators. Everywhere they looked, writes Yetman, "they found the seeds of sedition—plots; furtive communications with Sumas, Janos, Jocomes, and Apaches; envoys bringing tlátoles to every part of the province; clandestine convocos; Indians chupando in council circles."[48] This was undoubtedly a beleaguered society, rife with paranoia and anxiety. Because of this uncertainty, Verdugo immediately banned the use of bows and arrows for a year; those who were found guilty were then publicly shamed and punished in order to serve as examples to other would-be rebels.[49] Several of the supposed agitators were sent to work camps; others received lashes and were stripped of their canes of office; and still others—men like Ignacio Jojói—were tortured in an effort to extract information. Those who received the worst of it were hung, drawn, and quartered. Javier Jaure was tied up, beaten, and dragged through the streets to the calls of a *pregonero*—his "punishment was to continue until he was dead, after which his body was to be raised on a gallow and left untouched for eight days as an example to other Indians who might pretend to rise up against the Spaniards. No one was to offer any sacraments or to pay for burial expenses."[50] In all, sixteen men were executed.

Criminal cases of the sort that were produced in 1681 and again in 1686 remain important documents that reveal much about the conflicting political ideas, fears, anxieties, and rhetoric related to the administration of empire—of a European society that was perpetually teetering on the edge of catastrophe.[51] But was it really? As Yetman plainly suggests, the conspiracy of 1681 may have been nothing more than smoke and mirrors, more theater than reality. Verdugo, who was nearing the end of his tenure as *alcalde mayor*, desperately needed to secure a favorable pension, which was dependent on a positive *probranza de méritos* (evaluation) by his successor. With great political shrewdness he seems to have enlarged the scope and magnitude of the conspiracy in order to cast himself as the hero who saved Sonora.[52] He, in other words, had constructed an elaborate myth that was believable mainly because it fit squarely within the established narrative of the dangerous and violent frontier. Put differently,

Verdugo was fully engaged in the longtime practice of storytelling that represented a major part of the overall aesthetics of colonial rule. But if Verdugo could weave together such a conspiratorial tale full of danger and intrigue, couldn't Indians do the same?

As investigators in the 1686 Canito case soon found out, indigenous leaders were quite capable of contriving their own fantastic tales filled with betrayal, intrigue, and self-interest. Natives being interviewed during the fall months of 1686 were often savvy enough to use the platform of interrogation as a medium from which to air their own personal grievances and agendas against their enemies, making it difficult to determine who was telling the truth, who was saying what they thought the interrogator wanted to hear, and who was utilizing the opportunity for personal gain or revenge. The ability to manipulate the established moral order by constructing elaborate tales about vengeful Indians, Spaniards who turned into turkeys, ancient cave monsters, or people invoking the devil for help are just the kinds of mental calisthenics that colonial Sonorans perfected and validated on a daily basis. The better one maneuvered this mystical, ideological, and emotional universe, the better one fared.

A Dangerous Alliance Redux

In his impassioned 1686 letter to Captain Theran, Betanuer issued a stern warning: if immediate action was not taken to prevent this alliance from forming, all four nations would unite to attack the frontiers of Sonora, kill as many Spaniards as possible, and steal their horses. Obviously, the prospect of dying at the hands of indios enemigos was chilling, but so was the potential theft of their horses. Practically speaking, horses formed a significant portion of the frontier's social and cultural life, serving "as important symbols of status, masculinity, and freedom."[53] They were widely used by soldiers in their exploration and military operations; they were utilized by missionaries in their evangelizing ventures; and they were highly prized by local stock ranchers who represented the frontier's second-most important economic venture after mining. By the eighteenth century some of these ranches had grown into enormous estates covering hundreds of thousands of acres. The theft of Spanish horses was therefore no small matter for it severely restricted the ability of Spaniards to effectively colonize and settle the frontier.

Moreover, the theft of Spanish horses represented an affront to Spanish ideals of masculinity and to the honor associated with being a *caballero*. Indians frequently exploited this Spanish cultural archetype by subjecting Spaniards whose horses had been stolen to a barrage of insults and ridicule; Spaniards were, noted Betanuer, the constant target of "taunts and jeers" from enemy Indians. Natives ridiculed them for being too slow and perhaps too afraid to confront those defiant indios enemigos who had stolen their horses. In this way, Natives were directly challenging Spanish authority by putting their masculinity on trial. The group most responsible for stealing Spanish horses in Sonora during this time were the Apaches. According to Betanuer, in the previous eight months alone they had stolen over two hundred horses and mules. Because of these thefts both they and the Comanches had become highly efficient raiders, putting Spanish settlements in peril. If these thefts were not addressed, he warned, and if the Jocomes, Janos, Sumas, and Pimas were allowed to unite forces within the context of friendship, as they had attempted to do five years earlier, it was very possible that they would follow in the footsteps of the Apaches and Comanches. This potentially unmitigated disaster would believed Betanuer, undoubtedly lead to the demise of the province.

The investigation prompted by Betanuer's letter to Theran identified three Indians from the Pima nation as the main *indios tlatoleros* (Indian rabble rousers) aiding the Jocomes, Janos, and Sumas in their malicious plans. They went by the nicknames of El Coyote, El Malaya, and El Canito. According to El Seri, an Indian from the *ranchería* of Mototíchachi, El Coyote and El Malaya both lived in "sinful union" with women from the Jocome and Jano nations, which was the reason, he believed, why they had been so willing to collude with them. This intriguing allegation suggests that at least in some cases Pimas were willing to betray their vows of loyalty to their Spanish overseers in order to honor ritual or sentimental attachments of marriage with other indigenous groups. Such intertribal marriages or unions, as Lance Blyth has argued, were common along New Spain's northern frontier and formed a significant segment of their complex social networks and alliances.[54]

Of the three indios tlatoleros, El Coyote and Oôcaqui, commonly known as El Canito, elicited the most attention from Spanish authorities. One of the chief reasons behind such a targeted emphasis on these two men rested on the accusation that they had maliciously "enter[ed] into the confidence of Spaniards as friends," thus using their deceitful and disingenuous friendship as a tool of manipulation.[55] As this accusation implies, both men had skillfully adopted and assimilated the proper ethical comportment associated with Spanish conceptualizations of friendship. It also suggests that they somehow "entered" a morally restricted space (read: friendship) that was reserved exclusively for loyal members. Simply put, El Coyote and El Canito had behaved as friends, embodying the basic qualities and expectations of friendship, and as a result they were afforded a relative degree of respect and "confidence."[56] According to the testimony that followed, by means of their feigned friendship with the Spanish, these men gained valuable intelligence, which they then passed on to the Jocomes, Janos, and Sumas so that they could better organize their attacks on Spanish settlements. A major part of their duplicity involved the disavowal of their sworn commitment to thwart the escape of indios enemigos after they had attacked Spanish settlements. In fact, they had purposely granted the Jocomes, Janos, and Sumas free passage through their lands. At this point in the official investigation, the emphasis shifts squarely onto El Canito, perhaps because his deception had been the most compelling, having successfully entered the sphere of Spanish influence by earning the position of governor and *capitán general* of the Pimas.

As a strategy for survival it was essential for Spaniards to nourish amicable ties with Indian leaders—attaining their total commitment and loyalty as indios amigos—so as to effectively administer the province. Canito had fallen into that all-important category, obtaining in the process the implicit trust of his Spanish overseers. That Canito had callously feigned and manipulated his friendship with them was particularly distressing because it reified a very real concern— sincere friendships were being used as a kind of emotional and moral weapon. For many Spaniards Canito's perfidy became another reminder of their alarming vulnerability at the furthest edges of empire.[57]

But why did Canito, who possessed such an esteemed title and who maintained a significant degree of authority and respect among the Spanish, break his ties of loyalty and friendship? Obviously, his association with them represented a central source of his power and prestige. According to testimony taken from several indigenous declarants, a Spaniard (unnamed throughout the document) had hung Canito's brother several months earlier in retaliation for having killed a Spaniard. The death of his brother apparently caused Canito tremendous grief, and it awakened in him a desire for revenge. As the investigation soon exposed, Canito used the confidence he had built up through his friendship with Spanish authorities to avenge the murder of his brother.

In response to Betanuer's letter, Captain Theran spearheaded an intense and rather lengthy investigation into the accusations against Canito. His first witness, interrogated three days after he received the initial letter from Betanuer, was Pio Pio, a "loyal" Indian and governor of Cananea whom Theran considered to be "an affectionate friend of the Spaniards as is public and well known."[58] Under the scrutiny of interrogation, Pio Pio eagerly and rather quickly convicted Canito of crimes against the Spanish. He confessed that Canito had visited the Sumas where "he embraced" and spoke to prominent members of that nation, later joining them in a "drunken party." The reason he had followed Canito to the party, Pio Pio conveniently admitted, was to deter him from allying with the Sumas and to convince him that he should honor his commitment of loyalty to the king. Being an "affectionate friend" of the Spanish had afforded men like Pio Pio considerable social and material benefits. It was not, therefore, in his best interest to provide a testimony that would absolve Canito and potentially place the colonial structure in jeopardy. Pio Pio went on to state that on a separate occasion the Sumas had actually traveled to the *rancheria* of Ajos to visit Canito at his home where they spoke Castilian, "shook hands," and "where he [Canito] treated them like friends and relatives" by inviting them into his home.[59]

By making direct reference to the shaking of hands with enemies of the Crown, Pio Pio was intensifying the level of cooperation and friendship between Canito and indios enemigos. Given that this was a centuries-old tradition in the Old World, this ritual act would have been interpreted by Theran as a clear-cut act of friendship. It also shows the extent to which Indian leaders like Canito had skillfully adopted certain European friendship practices. The highly ritualized action of shaking hands has historically conveyed mutual goodwill and friendship.[60] Scholars are not entirely sure where the idea of the handshake first emerged, but it is depicted in Assyrian reliefs from as early as the ninth century BCE. Greeks and Romans also used the handshake as an ideal of friendship and loyalty.[61] Later, during the eighteenth and nineteenth centuries, American diplomats reinforced the handshake as a symbol of friendship by imprinting it on their "peace medals." These medals, which were used as tools of peace and diplomacy with Natives, highlighted the "duplicitous" rhetoric of friendship. Highly valued by American Indians, these medals "even more than flags or 'chief coats,' which were also distributed as gifts to Indian leaders, embodied an enduring connection between donor and recipient."[62]

After this clandestine meeting in which, according to Pio Pio, Canito and the Sumas solidified their friendship, Canito apparently instructed his visitors to

FIGURE 3 Thomas Jefferson Peace Medal, 1801, bronze, diameter 10.2 cm, Porcupine Quillwork added, ca. 1870, Oklahoma (24/1965). Courtesy of the National Museum of the American Indian.

join forces with the Jocomes and Janos so that together they could travel to the valley of Teurícache,[63] where they would steal Spanish horses and kill as many Christianized Indians and Spaniards as they could find. For his part, Canito promised to grant them free passage through Pima lands, since his authority as governor and *capitán general* allowed him to do so. And because of his close association with Spanish leaders, he promised to inform his newfound friends of Spanish intentions and of their current state of preparedness. As Pio Pio further relayed, in order to ease their passage through Pima lands, Canito would do all he could to preoccupy the Spanish with unrelated trivial matters. What those trivial matters consisted of, he does not say.

The fact that Canito had permitted indios enemigos into his home outraged Captain Joseph Romo de Vivar, Spanish *vecino*, miner of the valley of Bacanuchi, and owner of the hacienda on which Canito worked. Having discovered this brazen act of defiance on the part of Canito, which he interpreted as a betrayal of the highest order, Romo de Vivar promptly placed him in shackles. Not until the *alcalde mayor* ordered Romo de Viviar to release Canito a full month later was Canito finally freed. Canito, feeling embarrassed and disrespected by his incarceration, particularly because he possessed a title deserving of respect, immediately took to the hills of San Joseph, where he gave more bad *tlatoles* (speeches or consultations) to indios enemigos, redoubling his message of murder and theft.

Following Pio Pio's interrogation, which was easily the most damaging, Theran moved on to Sarguelles, "a heathen Indian from the Pima nation." While not entirely exonerating Canito for his disloyal behavior, Sarguelles had a slightly different story to tell. He asserted that it had been Canito's own kinsmen who were responsible for having pressured him into seeking revenge against the Spanish for his brother's hanging. Sarguelles stated that he had heard the Pima Indians say, "What [good] was he [Canito] in this world if he did not avenge the death that Spanish justice had given his brother?" Sarguelles added that he also heard Canito tell his kinsmen that in order to avenge his brother's death, he would first have to "become friends with the Sumas, Jocomes, and Janos in order to, with their help, destroy and finish [off] the horses of the Spaniards, incapacitating them so that they would not have what [they would need] to make war against them and that, seeing them on foot, [Canito] would, with all his friends, those [who were] confederates and friends of his, attack the Spaniards and kill them."[64] Canito's primary goal was, according to Sarguelles, to aid these groups in debilitating the Spanish by stealing their chief source of mobility.

Other Indian leaders, such as Sosoba, Indian governor of Huachuca, and Cabeza de Fraile, *topile* (minor judicial official) of Cocóspora, corroborated the testimonies of Pio Pio and Sarguelles. In like fashion, Usibácame, governor of Cocóspora, while verifying the belief that Canito had conducted these "wicked" actions because of his desire for revenge, also stated that he had heard that Canito was in constant communication with these "renowned enemies" of the Spanish Crown, allowing them free passage through Pima land so that they could kill Spaniards and Christianized Indians. Canito, he believed, would not be happy until he had fully avenged the assassination of his brother. More disturbing for Theran, however, was Usibácame's declaration that Canito had purposefully feigned his long-standing friendship with the Spaniards in order to gain valuable intelligence from them. With this privileged information he would warn the Jocomes, Janos, and Sumas of Spanish intentions. This was a serious accusation because it meant that Canito was effectively a double agent, feigning friendship with the Spanish in order to extract military knowledge that he would then pass on to the Jocomes, Janos, and Sumas, his "true" friends. If *he* could do this, then how many others were doing the same? Usibácame further alleged that "the governor of the Janos and Jocomes came to the place that they call Del Oso and there he became friends with Canito, and the two decided that the said governor of the Janos would go to the other rancherías of the Pimas and would make friendships with all of the governors of [said rancherías]."[65] Following Usibácame's confession, Theran became convinced that the chief reason behind creating a coalition of friendship among all the indigenous governors of the region was to promote a unified rebellion against the Spanish. All these declarations coincided on essentially the same point—Canito had used his friendship with the Spaniards in order to manipulate them, all the while forming new friendships with indios enemigos.

Following the initial round of testimonies, Captain Francisco Pacheco Zevallos, interim lieutenant to the *alcalde mayor* and *capitán á guerra* in the valley of Bacanuchi, arrested Canito for fomenting an uprising against the Spanish. Foremost among the list of crimes against Canito was being a false friend to the Spanish while fostering friendships with enemies of the Crown. While in prison, Canito was asked about the accusations leveled against him, about how at "the place of Los Ajos he had tried to become friends with six Indians of said rebel nations and ordered, as capitán general, that those of his nation become friends with said Jano Indians."[66] This was a serious concern for Spaniards because it suggested that, despite their efforts to cement the loyalty of individual Indian leaders, their loyalty was always unreliable at best. During the interrogation, which lasted several days, Canito was repeatedly reprimanded for having formed illicit friendships with indios enemigos.

Finally afforded the opportunity to defend himself, Canito refuted all accusations directed against him, vehemently denying any involvement with the "enemies of the Crown." He stated that while there were some Pima Indians who "all live together in great friendship with the enemies," he was not among them.[67] Unfortunately, Canito's denial of any involvement with the "enemies of the Crown" did not sit well with Zevallos, who remained unconvinced of Canito's innocence. Following protocol for the extraction of information from Indian rebels, he ordered that his confession be retaken, only this time under the administrative authority of an *auto de tormenta* (torture order); Canito was to be tortured until he revealed the truth. According to Alonso de Villadiego's 1720s *Instrucción política y práctica judicial*, members of the social elite such as administrative employees, those possessing titles of nobility, and pregnant women and children were exempt from torture.[68] However, since Indians were considered socially inferior and hence disreputable (*testigos viles*), even if they had been granted important distinctions and titles of governance as had Canito, they remained central targets for this practice.[69] The favored torture technique along the frontier was deceptively simple, requiring only two poles or sticks and a rope. With the pole on either side used for leverage, the rope was tied to either the legs, the arms, or the fingers and then, with measured resolve, slowly twisted. With each turn the rope tightened, methodically cutting off circulation to that part of the body.

Thoroughly tortured "on his thumbs," Canito was repeatedly asked why he "forced everyone from his nation to become friends with the Jano Indians."[70] Moreover, why as a loyal friend of the Spanish had he not informed them of the plot concocted against them and of the desire of the Pimas, Jocomes, Janos, and Sumas to attack and kill them? His response was straightforward if a little unbelievable: he simply stated that he had not notified them of this conspiracy because he feared for his life. According to Canito, his Pima kinsmen, who were the ones colluding with the enemies, had threatened to kill him if he revealed their whereabouts. This was simply not a credible excuse for someone of Canito's stature. No male leader worth his salt could cave to fear, not on the Spanish frontier where masculinity and valor were the most important attributes of a successful leader. Throughout what followed of the investigation, Canito stayed firm in his declaration of innocence. Unfortunately for Canito, Zevallos remained unconvinced. He believed, and perhaps rightly so, that Canito was purposely obscuring the truth, muddying it with sentimental pleas of ignorance and fear in order to evade punishment. Because of this, the tortures continued.

But Canito held steadfast. Throughout the questioning, which lasted several weeks, Canito remained resolute in his commitment of friendship and loyalty to the Spanish Crown, stating that his only goal was to protect them from the evil intentions of the Jocomes, Janos, and Sumas. He only wished to aid the Spanish in warring against these "enemies of the Crown." In fact, he maintained that it was he who had been wronged by his Pima kinsmen who had violently turned on him for not permitting them to form friendships with the enemies. He declared that "they [his kinsmen] had agreed that upon killing him [Canito], they would become friends [with the Sumas, Janos and Jocomes] in order to kill the Spaniards."[71]

Fatigued by Canito's narrative of events, which he believed to be untruthful, Zevallos appointed General Antonio Barba Figueroa to retake his confession. At this point the emphasis of the questioning shifted to Canito's acceptance of the Sumas into his house. Canito was asked by Figueroa how he "[could] deny the truth of [how] two years ago he admitted the Indians [who had] rebelled against the Crown into his house as friends . . . and gave them seeds so that they could plant crops."[72] Canito refuted such an accusation, asserting that when the Suma Indians arrived at his doorstep, he immediately demanded that they leave, never allowing these enemies of the Crown to enter the sanctity of his home. Nor did he ever shake hands with them as Pio Pio had asserted. The fact that the various versions of this story were not lining up meant that there were opposing interests at play. One or, more likely, several of the declarants were obviously lying.

During his defense, Canito stated that he never instructed his people to become friends of the indios enemigos. He reiterated time and again the general comment that "the Pimas are friends of the Spaniards."[73] To this statement he smartly added that as a fearful Christian—he apparently became a Christian during the trial and changed his named to Joseph Romo after his patron Joseph Romo de Vivar—he was obliged to tell the truth of his intentions, which at no time were malicious.[74] General Figueroa, also irritated by Canito's continued claims of innocence and convinced of the fact that Canito was colluding with the enemies, ordered that the torture proceed to his legs "below the shins with two crossed sticks with cords on the end of each one through which a stick is placed and turned around to give [torture]."[75] Canito was again ordered by

Figueroa to tell the truth. When Canito refused to admit fault, "the order was given for the cords to be tightened." Unable to bear the pain any longer, Canito confessed.[76]

Savvy to the ideological crosscurrents of his day, Canito blamed the devil for his actions. Blaming the devil for one's behavior made for compelling drama and was a common tactic for accused criminals throughout the colonial period. While Canito confessed that he wished to do harm to the Spaniards for what they had done to his brother, he had colluded and become friends with the enemies only "because the devil had deceived him" into doing so.[77] Blaming his actions on the devil was an astute move, for to suggest that the devil was behind his malicious actions rang true to Spanish ears. Missionaries in particular believed themselves engaged in an epic battle with this "enemy," their most cunning and ubiquitous foe. The devil was widely recognized as a clever manipulator who was actively involved in every aspect of society. In Spanish America, notes Jorge Cañizares-Esguerra, the devil was a very real presence, found in everything from the people to the landscape to its fruits and vegetables.[78]

After several months, the case was forwarded to the official courts under the authority of the *fiscal* (attorney) Marcos de Henao Zavala, who asked that the royal courts find Canito guilty as a "traitor to the royal Crown." Finding an Indian—one who had been an indio amigo of the Spanish and who had been given the position of *capitán general*—guilty of being a traitor was important if, argued Zavala, the province was to prosper. A conviction would send a strong message to other Indian leaders that disloyalty to their Spanish overseers and collusion with enemies of the Crown would be severely punished. It also reinforced the moral obligations of friendship. Throughout the investigation, Canito's friendship to both indios enemigos and to Spaniards had been a focal point of inquiry. Canito, Zavala somberly continued, had given the rebel Indians instruction to kill all the Spaniards in an effort to follow in the example of the Pueblo Indians.[79] As noted above, the legacy of the 1680 Pueblo Revolt created such a frenzied state of anxiety that most Spaniards believed that the "flames of rebellion" would eventually "engulf the entire northern frontier."[80] This concern was certainly behind the intensity of the Canito investigation.

During the final stages of the trial, Gerónimo García de Therán, *defensor de los indios* (Indian defender, not to be confused with Juan de Theran), argued that because the accusations brought against Canito were made by the local governor's *topiles* from the *rancherías* of Los Ajos, Cananea, Mototíchachi, Huachucha,

Santa María, Quebab, Cocospora, and Quitacar, all of whom were seeking to depose Canito of his administrative post, their testimonies were invalid. They were, in other words, fabricating fantastic but believable stories as a power play against Canito. Their disdain for him had apparently arisen from the fact that Canito had ordered them to stop going "around like deer and to instead plant a lot of corn." According to his *defensor*, by restricting their mobility and freedom "to go about like deer" and forcing them to instead work their plots, he was only doing the Crown's bidding. But because of Canito's restrictive policies, "they began to make their false declarations against him."[81] Thus, Therán argued, those declarants who had condemned Canito did so from false and self-interested pretenses; their testimonies, he argued, should be deemed unreliable.

By concocting such an elaborate story full of intrigue and conspiracy, Canito's kinsmen had ostensibly conspired to accuse him of crimes he did not commit. Again, it is difficult to untangle the web of competing narratives here, but it highlights the manner in which criminal investigations became moments and spaces from which to air grievances and accusations and in the process redefine relationships of power. Even if this was the case—that Canito was so obedient and loyal to his Spanish "friends" that he adopted highly restrictive governing policies that inhibited traditional indigenous modes of mobility—it shows the extent to which the Indian governors of Sonora highlighted the concept of friendship as a way of enhancing Canito's breach of proper behavioral expectations. It also shows just how well informed they were of these same behavioral expectations in regard to proper forms of amity. This manipulation of facts is only one side of the story that the present case alludes to, but it is a rather intriguing and important one.

García de Therán further noted that Canito had not ordered the Jocomes, Janos, and Sumas to attack the Spaniards; rather, these "rebel apostate nations" had proposed an alliance with the Pima of Quibiri, and because he feared his own kinsmen he did not inform the royal court. Furthermore, the *defensor* noted that at the time Canito had committed these alleged crimes, he was not a Christian and should therefore be released from prison—not being a Christian, the devil had full sway over his actions. Additionally, the only reason Canito confessed his guilt was because he had been tortured and only wished to end the pain. Despite Canito's vehement pledge of innocence, he was found guilty of being a traitor to the Royal Crown. The sentence handed down was harsh and widely publicized. According to the details of the sentence, Canito was condemned to death by hanging—an ironic end to a story that began with the hanging of his brother. He was to be placed on a saddled horse with his hands and feet tied and a noose strung around his neck, and he was to be paraded through the streets to the voice of a *pregonero* (town crier) who would make his crimes public until he reached the gallows where he was to be hung. The crime charged against him was straightforward: Canito was charged with organizing an uprising against the Royal Crown, in "cooperating in friendship with said enemies, [and in] giving and consenting to various *tlatoles* (speeches or discussions) about rebelling against the Spaniards."[82]

Finding the sentence excessively harsh, however, General Joseph de Neyra y Quiroga, governor of Nueva Vizcaya, commuted the sentence.[83] Canito was declared a *persona miserable* (a person incapable of understanding the severity of the accusations leveled against him) and thus unfit to receive the death penalty. Instead, he was condemned to two years in one of the mines in his jurisdiction. He was also forbidden from ever returning to Sonora. Canito was eventually sent to pay his debt as a laborer in the presidio located in the *real* (Spanish district) of Cuencamé. Given the severity of his crimes, however, it is not entirely clear why Canito's sentence was reduced. Some scholars have argued that the sentence was commuted due to economic considerations or perhaps because of good behavior. Another potential reason could be that Neyra y Quiroga feared that excessive punishment might result in wide-scale resentment, possibly provoking another uprising. Perhaps he simply had no desire to fuel the flames of another rebellion the likes of which had transpired in New Mexico six years earlier.

Conclusion

The narrative account of the 1681 conspiracy echoes many of the same issues present in the later Canito case. Both the conspiracy of 1681 and the Canito investigation of 1686 took place within a generalized atmosphere of anxiety and heightened vigilance that was pervasive along the Spanish borderlands for decades after the Pueblo Revolt. In both cases, Spanish interrogators utilized torture as a means by which to extract important information about the sequence of events leading up to the revolt and about possible coconspirators; in both cases, indigenous leaders used formulaic references to the devil to escape punishment; in both cases, the main conspirators indicated revenge to be the main reason for planning the revolt; in both cases, Spanish administrators pointed to the prevalence of dangerous "friendships" with enemy Indians as a central reason for the backsliding of indios amigos; and in both cases, Natives being interrogated reiterated pledges of friendship to their Spanish interrogators.[84]

As terrifying as they were to the Spanish, rumors of revolts also represented important opportunities for Indians and Spaniards. In the case of the former, spreading rumors of a potential revolt, whether authentic or false, had the effect of embroiling Spaniards in a lengthy, costly, and distracting investigation. Much like the Inquisition worked in Spain and the Americas, false reports of possible uprisings functioned in the same manner along the Spanish borderlands. Indians astutely used the lengthy criminal investigation that followed such rumors as venues from where to play out their frustrations with other Natives and Spaniards, accusing them (legitimately or illegitimately) of a variety of crimes and misdeeds. These accusations were almost always filtered through the purview of interrogators and scribes, after which a story emerged that was as much about the process of narrative form as it was about the accusation itself. Conversely, Spanish leaders such as Verdugo and, as we will see in the following chapter, Ortiz Parrilla could use the rumors of violence to enhance their own reputations as military commanders, maintain their jobs, and possibly also secure continued funding from the Crown. Unfortunately, it is extremely difficult to fully comprehend the reasoning and rationale behind why Indians and Spaniards spread such vicious and alarming rumors of violence, but we must remain open to considering a number of possibilities. Perhaps Indians simply sought release from the menial tasks of mission life, much like the practice of blaspheming allowed African slaves in the sugar mills of Pernambuco, Brazil, a brief reprieve from the daily doldrums of forced labor; perhaps the criminal investigation became a way to seek revenge on other Indians (their enemies or people they sought to eliminate from powerful positions) by subjecting them to the horrors of torture, which they knew accompanied criminal investigations; or perhaps rumors of violence by specific groups were designed to reinforce shaky loyalties and/or enhance one's reputation, as was the case for Verdugo and perhaps also for Theran.

As the Canito case highlights, the effective administration of Sonora required the vigilant management of interethnic relations of amity. These types of strategic friendships were essential to the administration of Sonora and could pay fruitful dividends, but they could also produce hazardous results. Even though Betanuer's allegation that the Jocomes, Janos, and Sumas were "joining in friendship" with the Pimas (under the leadership of Canito) was particularly troubling and presented a profound conundrum for the administration of Sonora, it was Canito's "false friendship" that became the central source of angst for them. For avowed indios amigos to be "in friendship" with indios enemigos represented a serious threat to Spanish hegemony because it held the potential to derail the process of colonization. In many ways, Canito resembled earlier indigenous agents of empire like Juan Lautaro, "who pretended to be a Christian" and was described by Pérez de Ribas as "astute, cunning, and very crafty" in his bid to attain power.[85] To this end, Lautaro utilized a series of tools such as "harmful lies about the captain" to great effect in "perverting" reduced Indians to revolt against the Spanish.

The specific and conceptual use of friendship throughout the case against Canito reveals its central importance to the administration of colonial Sonora. It also exemplifies the ways in which it was conceived, practiced, manipulated, and performed by its many residents. It was not uncommon for indigenous people to practice relationships of amity with Spaniards. Friendship provided Indians with an ideological mechanism with which to counter the negative effects of colonialism by opening up social space through which indigenous peoples were able to attain a measured level of power and influence. Indians used the benefits granted them through their friendship with Spaniards as a way to gain status and material rewards such as Spanish clothing and weapons. Susan Deeds has argued that Indians used a host of mixed strategies for adapting to and influencing colonial rule, which she has dubbed "mediated opportunism."[86] Friendship represented but one of these strategies.

Spaniards in turn utilized their friendships with individual Indian leaders, such as Canito, and with other indigenous groups as a way to maintain social order and stability—Indians were given positions of power and in return were expected to keep their Indian charges peaceful and loyal, facilitating for Spaniards the exploration and colonization of the province. Through the matrix of friendship, Spaniards utilized indigenous knowledge of the landscape; they also exploited Indians as laborers, intelligence operatives, soldiers, and guides. But Spaniards, like Indians, also practiced feigned friendships. In 1740, for example, two Jesuits attempted to convince a Mocobí cacique from Chile named Ariancaiquin to accept missionaries to his lands. Ariancaiquin's reply was telling: "The Spaniards have deceived our ancestors excessively. Their kindness was a falsehood and their friendship feigned. Of course, they only tried to make us slaves and kill us with whips, as if we were not human beings like them and did not have understanding. They used us as beasts of burden."[87]

Despite the potential for exploitation, both groups benefited from a nonzero-sum interplay, making the line between sincere and feigned friendship especially vague. Friendship, whatever its true intent, was useful and productive for all parties involved. But friendship, like most human relationships, needed to be maintained in balance. Amity between Indians and Spaniards worked only as long as the pros outweighed the cons. Once this balance was tipped in one direction over the other, friendship became unpredictable and disadvantageous to the offended party. As the offender, Canito's friendship with the Spanish proved to be a valuable resource for him if his intent, as the bulk of the testimony attests, was to kill as many Spaniards as possible. It is unclear from the present document, however, if Canito was a true and loyal friend to the Spanish who only turned on them after they killed his brother or if Canito disliked the Spanish from the beginning, becoming an astute student of Spanish ideals and cleverly performing his friendship with them in order to gain access to information, mobility, and power, waiting for the opportune time to exact his revenge.

While friendship as performance was integral to the European idea of civilization, the rhetoric of friendship was equally important in the creation of a moralized standard of behavior. As discussed earlier, in colonial New Spain, friendship reflected the manner in which Spanish administrators saw or understood the relationship between the sovereign and his subjects. In early modern societies, as Alejandro Cañeque maintains, power was not located in the arena of the state as much as it was confined to the aurora of the royal court and the king. This political system, which derived its magic from the persona of the king and his court, was based on a household administrative model of organization. Further, "it was distinguished by informal systems of power deeply enmeshed in patron-client relationships, and its technologies of legitimation were characterized by recourse to concepts such as *love* and *friendship* that set this system apart from modern forms of political organization."[88] The Canito case reflects the ways in which friendship and loyalty were inscribed onto indigenous behavioral modes of conduct as a way of colonizing emotion on the frontier. Batanuer's moral outrage at Canito's false friendship was thus partially performative, a clever way of inscribing onto indigenous and Spanish mentalities proper forms of behavior using friendship as a tool. But while the ideals of friendship were used to create a moralized standard of behavior among indigenous peoples, Indians utilized these same rules of behavior to manipulate Spanish forms of authority. They cleverly imitated these rules only to use them against their colonial adversaries. This seems to have been the case with Canito and a major reason why Spaniards found his actions so egregious. Throughout the colonial frontier, moral order was subject to changing standards, behaviors, and expectations about the meaning of things. Friendship was but one construct that throughout the colonial period imposed moral weight onto preexisting visions of the world.

CHAPTER FIVE

The Paradox of Friendship

Violence and the Ambiguities of Social Inequality

I am not afraid, in taking on the name of a friend, as some perchance may object, that I will incur the guilt of presumption, since unequals are not less bound by the sacred bonds of friendship than are equals.

—Dante, Letter to Can Grand, Lord of Verona

ON THE MORNING OF NOVEMBER 20, 1751, LUIS OACPICAGIGUA, governor of Sáric and *capitán general* of the Pimas Altos, gathered his kinsmen in a canyon along the outskirts of the town in order to proclaim a general uprising against all Spaniards and non-Pima Indians.[1] Their goal was straightforward: to drive as many of them as possible from Pima territory, thereby reclaiming their ancestral lands.[2] For more than a century Sonora's indigenous residents had angrily protested the theft of their lands by Spanish settlers.[3] Oacpicagigua's call for violence thus provided an opportunity for retribution. Following the initial gathering outside Sáric, Indian messengers were dispatched to the surrounding communities with instructions to circulate the message of rebellion. From there they were to depart with their families to the mountains of Boboquivari from which the insurgency would be based. That evening Oacpicagigua escorted eighteen Spanish residents into his home under the pretext that the town was about to be attacked by Apaches—as we have already seen, this was widely understood as a symbolic sign of friendship. Once inside, he and his coconspirators set fire to the thatched-roof structure, killing everyone inside.[4] The rebellion spread rapidly, engulfing much of the Pimería Alta within hours. While numerous Pimas enthusiastically joined the rebellion, hoping to redefine their inferior social standing vis-à-vis Spaniards, others preferred to remain loyal to the Spanish Crown, informing the *gente de razón* and the Jesuit missionaries of the impending danger headed their way.[5] Their warnings arrived too late.

On the first night, an estimated twenty-five *vecinos* lost their lives at Sáric, including the wife and children of the *mayordomo* (overseer) named Laureano.[6] Three Spanish families encountered a similar fate at Arivaca. At Caborca, *capitán de guerra* Luis Batiutuc led his own Pima cohorts in a general sweep against Spaniards, killing the resident priest, Thomás Tello, and eleven *gente de razón*. The next day Batiutuc and his men proceeded to the *real* (mining camp) of Oquitoa where, absent a resident priest, they killed twenty more Spaniards (mostly miners), taking their property and leaving the town in flames. At Tubutama, 125 Indian rebels under the leadership of Sebastián lit the mission church ablaze; Fathers Jacobo Sedelmayr (1703–79) and Juan Nentvig (1713–68) narrowly escaped with their lives. Pimas ransacked the church in Guevavi, making quick work of the church's furnishings—"mangling the *santos* and smashing the tabernacle"—while still taking time to kill all of Father Joseph Garrucho's (b. 1712) chickens and pigeons.[7] The violence spilled over to San Marcelo de Sonoyta, where the Pima insurgents clubbed Father Enrique Ruhen (1718–51) and his two Indian assistants to death, taking care to strip the church of its sacred ornaments before unceremoniously setting it ablaze. Two days later, Father Ignacio Keller (1702–59), missionary of Soamca, fearing the rebels might attack his mission next, pleaded with the lieutenant from the presidio at Terrenate, Isidoro Sánchez, for a military contingent. He was sent five men.[8]

The military presidios of Terrenate and Fronteras, those closest to the epicenter of violence, were ill prepared to respond to the uprising, as its soldiers were scattered about the region attending to other concerns.[9] Not that having soldiers present at their posts would have mattered, since most of Sonora's thirty-five thousand *pobladores* (settlers) lived in isolated communities far from military protection.[10] Furthermore, the fourteen Spanish *rancherías*, four villas, six military garrisons, and forty-one mining towns that dotted the vast desert landscape were enveloped by Sonora's fifty-four thousand indigenous residents.[11] Despite the lack of military support, Spanish settlers, incensed at what they saw as a betrayal on the part of their Indian subjects, took to the pueblos under attack. Within hours of the assault on Arivaca, a band of armed settlers from the valley of San Luis set out in aid of their fellow *vecinos*. But their indignation was outmatched by the military skill of the Pima insurgents. Halfway to their destination, their war party was routed by Oacpicagigua and his rebel army. With dedicated focus, Oacpicagigua bluntly outlined his objectives: *"Ea* [My] relatives," he declared, "Father Ignacio [Keller] has sent us the devil, which is the cause of this [rebellion] . . . the Spaniards have withdrawn, and in this way we go in their pursuit so as to finish them or be killed by them."[12]

It fell to Diego Ortiz Parrilla (1715–75), governor of the province of Sinaloa y Sonora, to put an end to the violence and punish Oacpicagigua and the rebels.[13] But to the consternation of the affected missionaries and Spanish residents, Ortiz Parrilla chose instead to negotiate. This remarkable decision, seen as "a strikingly un-Spanish campaign," became a source of intense controversy in the ensuing months and years, for in the minds of most Spaniards, and especially of those few Jesuit missionaries from the region, it was evident that the governor's judgment had been prejudiced by his personal bond of friendship with the Pima leader.[14]

The rebellion signaled a transitory shift in the hierarchical template of the Pimería Alta, temporarily redefining conventional relationships of power between both ethnic groups. Sensing this delicate swing in social influence, the Pima insurgents struck with a sense of immediacy, carrying out most of their attacks within one week of the rebellion's origin. Small skirmishes and hostilities followed intermittently for more than a year but were of little significance because the bulk of damage had already been done. All told, one hundred Spaniards, two Jesuit priests, and an indefinite number of Pimas lost their lives.[15] To the Crown and the Spanish residents of the Pimería, the revolt served as a stark reminder of their tenuous relationship with the Natives of the area; of the flagrant acrimony between Spanish soldiers, settlers, Indians, and those few men of the cloth—an animosity that was a constant source of tension for much of the colonial period; of the need for an increased military presence; and of the fragility of civil society.[16]

Despite declarations made by several Spanish witnesses and their indigenous allies about the causes of the revolt, there is little direct evidence to suggest that the insurgents desired to permanently eliminate Spanish forms of authority. No separatist sentiment seems to have existed among the Pima.[17] By 1751 indigenous and Spanish communities throughout the Pimería were simply too intricately woven together, making the idea of a nativist movement largely untenable.[18] In Sonora, writes Cynthia Radding, "the colonial regime endured with remarkable stability because indigenous peoples became stakeholders in its judicial and cultural institutions." There was not, therefore, "a clear choice between falling in line with the Spaniards or returning to a preconquest political order."[19] Both communities were intimately joined and quite frequently benefited from ongoing political, cultural, religious, biological, economic, social, and moral ties, lending credibility to the various, often contradictory reasons why Pimas joined the revolt. Some Indians, for instance, entered the struggle with a sense of justice in mind, hoping to right years of oppression and to renegotiate their inferior social standing; others joined the conflict with the simple goal of plunder and revenge; and still others willingly chose to go against their brethren during the revolt, preferring instead to remain loyal to the Spanish for a whole host of practical and ideological reasons. While revolts in Sonora like the ones that occurred in 1695 and 1751 differed from the Pueblo Revolt of 1680 in their inability to produce a unified front against the Spanish, they nonetheless remained "a serious challenge to the Spanish in Sonora" and "threatened the stability of the colonial order being created on the frontier."[20]

The exact reason why the revolt began at this particular time remains unclear. Brute physical abuse on the part of soldiers, years of land theft by Spanish settlers, the loss of political autonomy and cultural identity, and—perhaps most damaging—decades of psychological and physical exploitation at the hands of a few missionaries and their *mayordomos* all seem to have played a significant role. But, as Roberto Solmón contends, there remains no direct causal relationship.[21] This is a surprising conclusion given that Oacpicagigua clearly blamed Father Ignacio Keller for the rebellion, saying that it was he who had sent the devil— most likely a reference to Jesuit maltreatment. It's quite likely, as we shall see, that Oacpicagigua's combative relationship with Father Keller was simply the final affront that collapsed the tenuous social compact.

Most scholars have continued to tell the story of the 1751 Pima Rebellion as a straightforward narrative in which the revolt represented the logical outcome of oppression perpetrated by one group onto another.[22] While it is true that European colonialism deeply upset and in many cases devastated indigenous modes of existence, such tidy accounts far too often sidestep critical categories of agency by overlooking the ways in which Native peoples received, negotiated, and in many cases benefited from established networks of oppression. Laura Matthew has argued, for instance, that indigenous peoples in Guatemala were often considered to be both indigenous and foreign, Indians and conquistadores. There simply wasn't a clear-cut division between victor and vanquished or between oppressor and victim.[23] There were elements of this in Sonora as local and central Mexican Natives, Spaniards from various regions throughout Spain, and mestizos "mingled, became bilingual or multilingual, and moved in and out of ethnic groups," making it difficult to determine where one's loyalty ultimately lay.[24] We must, therefore, as anthropologists John Douglas and William Graves maintain, "turn away from simplistic models of colonialism drawn from world systems theory or models of domination and resistance."[25] Though conventional interpretations of rebellion remain important in underscoring some of the more recognizable patterns and processes of colonialism, they also tend to underemphasize its inherent ironies.[26]

In this chapter, I draw from the testimonies that followed the 1751 Pima Rebellion, locating these colonial ironies within the individual aspirations and fellowship of Luis Oacpicagigua (also known as Luis of Sáric) and Diego Ortiz Parrilla. Put simply, the 1751 Pima Revolt was surely the outcome of years of subjugation and land theft, but its unique origin, orientation, and character was the immediate product of the personal whims, vulnerabilities, and power politics exercised by both men, who were themselves fully engaged in the navigation and manipulation of the colonial nettings of power.[27] In the Americas, as Ivy Schweitzer writes, "utility and necessity forged formerly unthinkable alliances that shifted the meaning of 'likeness' and 'liking' and helped to evolve new forms of friendship."[28] A concentrated focus on this unique relationship through the purview of friendship provides us with a fuller and more colorful portrait of Spanish–Indian relations during the eighteenth century. It also cues us in on the innovative ways in which colonial inequalities were tempered, manipulated, and frequently redefined by symbolic gestures of amity and goodwill. Civil society was ultimately born amid these ambiguities, contradictions, and ironies.

The Melancholy of Friendship

Ten days after the outbreak of violence, Governor Ortiz Parrilla penned a cautious and nuanced letter to the viceroy of New Spain, Juan Francisco Güemes y Horcasitas, in which he did four main things: (1) present his explanation for the general violence that had disrupted the Pimería under his watch and detail his plan for resolving the situation; (2) justify his admiration for Luis Oacpicagigua, whom he had praised on a number of occasions as a loyal subject to the Crown and his most honorable and trustworthy companion; (3) lay bare his regret and sadness at the loss of this highly valued associate; and (4) place the blame for the rebellion squarely on his Jesuit nemeses, in the process absolving Oacpicagigua of any direct responsibility.

In his account, Ortiz Parrilla named the culprits of the rebellion as Pimas from the Pimería Alta. This news was particularly unnerving because, as he explained, the Pimas had been peaceful and loyal subjects of the Crown, having "served the king and fatherland" with great devotion. For close to a century, since the last major Indian conspiracy in 1686, the Pimas had been the constant source of Spanish admiration and praise.[29] Spanish leaders (military, civil, and religious) had for decades carefully handpicked indigenous leaders for important posts as *gobernadores* (governors), *capitanes* (military officers), *alcaldes* (mayors), *fiscales* (attorneys), *topiles* (constables), *temastiáns* (lay assistants to missionary), and military allies against *indios enemigos*, all while relying on them as guardians of peace and stability. To this end, they were commonly given *varas de justicia* (canes of office) that functioned both as symbols of their authority and as visible signs of their commitment to civil society. The revolt was therefore "strange and unexpected." More unarming for the Spanish residents of the region, however, was the fact that they had unsuspectingly lived with "the satisfaction and confidence dictated by the unwavering friendship and good intercourse of those natives."[30] It had been this false certainty, declared Juan Manuel Ortiz Cortés, *vecino* of San Ignacio, that had tranquilized their sensibilities to the potential for violence and unrest.[31]

Like many of his kinsmen who served in important administrative posts, Oacpicagigua, much like Canito had previously been, was highly regarded as an indio amigo and agent of the Crown. He, for instance, aided Spaniards in conducting campaigns against indios enemigos; headed various *juntas de guerra* (war councils); willingly "gave away" many of his personal possessions to Spanish acquaintances; served as a circuit court judge for Pima missions; successfully reduced and congregated various pueblos and *rancherías* in order that they be introduced to the Christian doctrine and receive baptism "so [that they] follow the law of God and begin to live like people"; chastised and punished his own tribesmen for transgressions against imperial objectives; and routinely remitted Indian prisoners to Ortiz Parrilla "so that they may be placed in irons."[32] In his letter, Ortiz Parrilla argued that Oacpicagigua undertook these commitments not for pay but rather to honor God and king. From the start it seems that Ortiz Parrilla was saying all the right things in an effort to absolve himself and his indigenous companion from any direct responsibility for the rebellion.

Ortiz Parrilla went on to write that Oacpicagigua was "loved" by all the *gente de razón* because he interacted with them "very socially, affectionately, politically, and so very liberally as to fall into prodigal excess," giving away many of his possessions when expedient. Oacpicagigua's subsequent betrayal was deeply lamented by these same men, for never had the Crown had such a "loyal and devoted" subject who, "without cultivation, had surpassed and distinguished himself with so many natural talents worthy of recommendation." For these reasons, Ortiz Parrilla argued, the event responsible for bringing about such a striking change in him must have been of great significance, for "I can assure your Excellency that in his lineage and nature he was the most servile and loyal subject that His Majesty had in all these reduced nations."[33]

The governor explained to the viceroy that Oacpicagigua had become his most "trusted" companion during the various campaigns against indios enemigos (namely, the Seris and Apaches).[34] During these campaigns this "exceptional Indian" had behaved with great zeal: "The fatigues he suffered . . . the ardent spirit with which he encouraged [his men] to their labors, and the generous heart with which he happily exposed himself to the dangers were plain for me to see."[35] Oacpicagigua kept his kinsmen in such a state of obedience to the Crown and to the region's Spanish residents that the Pimería had "never been more faithful and peaceful than in these last years." "This same capitán," wrote the governor, "has been a bulwark in those lands for resisting the hostilities of the fierce Apaches, against whom he has carried out various campaigns, penetrating as far as their own lands with numerous armed troops maintained at his own expense."[36] In this way, Oacpicagigua was following in the tradition of Spanish *adelatados* who reconnoitered unknown territory at their own expense and in return expected to receive appropriate recompense in the form of honorific titles and lucrative positions of authority.

Like most highly functional go-betweens throughout the Americas, Oacpicagigua belonged to both the Indian and Spanish worlds and yet permanently resided in neither. But because of this, he came to understand his precarious social position within the Indian–Spanish borderlands quite well, navigating with great skill the intricacies of cooperation, negotiation, and violence.[37] Just as over the span of several centuries Spaniards throughout much of New Spain developed a keen understanding of their Indian subjects, so too did Indians gain an acute awareness of the Spanish colonial system and of Spanish hopes, dreams, and, subsequently, delusions. Oacpicagigua made ample use of this intimate information, utilizing it to retain authority over his *nación* (nation) while simultaneously remaining complicit to and benefiting from the colonial superstructure.[38] An ample comparison could be drawn to the indigenous elites (*kurakas*) of Peru who, as Yanna Yannakakis has postulated, allowed for a certain degree of abuse and exploitation to their communities, but were not "colonial exploiters behind a native veneer"; rather, they "faced consequences from below, making them accountable to local people in ways that Spaniards were not."[39] In a very real way, then, Oacpicagigua was like those *kurakas* of Peru: a typical frontier "marginal man, caught between the tribal way of life and a complex society that offered many opportunities at the cost of accepting some frightening risks."[40] And yet he is only one of many other similar figures who emerge from the pages of the past as devoted indigenous agents of empire. What specific factors kept some of these colonial agents firmly loyal and others constantly straddling the tightrope of opportunism, teetering between rebellion and cooperation, remains a complex question. It is rather certain, however, that established friendships had much to do with this internal dialogue.

In return for his bravery and loyalty during his operations against indios enemigos, in particular the Seris, the visitor general Joseph Rafael Rodríguez Gallardo granted Oacpicagigua the title of *capitán general*, presenting him with a "fine staff of authority" as a reward for how well he had "comported himself." These staffs of authority were commonly handed out to indigenous leaders as tokens of respect and friendship, conferring onto its bearer social status, distinction, power, and authority over his own community. They were also indicative of an assumed loyalty on the part of the recipient. In many ways, they were strikingly similar to friendship medals handed out to indigenous leaders by American frontiersmen a century later (see figure 3 in chapter 4). Immediately after the 1750 campaign against the Seris, Oacpicagigua asked Ortiz Parrilla to confirm his title, which had been given to him by Gallardo. Said the governor, "When the campaign concluded, they were ordered to withdraw [and] he asked me that I confirm the title that the aforementioned señor visitador had given him. To which supplication I complied, entreating him, I [mean to] say bestowing [upon him] another."[41] According to Henry Dobyns, "Oacpicagigua was rewarded by the civil-military authorities with the title of Captain General of the Northern Pimas, a [Spanish] uniform, and evidently considerable respect."[42] In effect, this title made the Native leader the recognized commander of a one-hundred-man Indian presidio on the Gila.[43]

In a very practical way Oacpicagigua needed his title to remain official. After all, the visitor's stay was only temporary. Oacpicagigua clearly understood this, so by asking the governor to confirm his recently acquired authority, he was making sure his title remained active after Gallardo's departure. But in making this request, Oacpicagigua was also priming the colonial tightrope by astutely conveying his deference and loyalty to Ortiz Parrilla. Conversely, by confirming Oacpicagigua's title, Ortiz Parrilla was presented with an important opportunity to display his patronage and largesse (read: friendship, as Gil-Osle argues),[44] reinforcing his own superior position in Sonoran society. One scholar has argued that Ortiz Parrilla confirmed Oacpicagigua's title simply because he needed the Native leader to conduct future campaigns against the Apaches and simply wished to curry favor with him.[45] While this argument conveys an important element of the story, it oversimplifies the highly symbolic nature of this exchange, glossing over the intricate layers of sophistication and subtle strategizing inherent in colonial relationships of power. If read from the standpoint of their burgeoning friendship, these seemingly rigid layers of power and influence begin to reveal a shrewd subscript of intentionality and manipulation, which can only be gleaned from a close textual reading of their relationship. Unfortunately, by overriding the opinion of the *juez politico* (local judge)—Don Joseph de Olave, who seems to have disliked Oacpicagigua and considered him unworthy of his position—and by not first consulting with the missionary fathers regarding the high title conferred to one of their charges, Ortiz Parrilla made himself partially responsible for the rebellion.[46] Blaming Ortiz Parrilla for the actions of Oacpicagigua was clearly politically motivated, for had it not been the father visitor who had initially granted him this title?

Although Ortiz Parrilla found the "false friendship" of the Pimas distressing, the tone of his letter reached its emotional climax when he described his grief at Oacpicagigua's deception. His greatest affliction, according to this carefully crafted portion of the letter, was that Oacpicagigua had betrayed him, not only by insulting his confidence and patronage, but also by offending God and the Spanish Crown. How, he wondered, could someone who had been granted such distinctions, respect, and freedom be so ungrateful and disloyal? This rather bland condemnation was tempered by melancholic admiration. "It brings tears to my eyes," he wrote, "when I contemplate the honor, fidelity, and effort with which this famous Indian has conducted himself on the many occasions in which he has been able to provide evident examples of grand loyalty."[47]

In many instances, expressions of emotion in official administrative documents by men of significant status such as Ortiz Parrilla represented a staged literary performance that neither emasculated the writer nor made him weak or irrational.[48] Its function as political theater was to convey subtle messages about power and authority. Just as certain cultures use funerary rituals as designated places where the expression of emotion is socially accepted, so too did such a practice exist among the Spanish who inhabited a highly lettered society—the act of letter writing being a ritual onto itself where emotional rhetoric became appropriate while giving magnitude to its political message.[49] As Rebecca Earle and David Weber have argued (the former focusing on personal love letters, the latter on diplomatic language), these sorts of fashionable displays of emotion were simply the product of an eighteenth-century enlightened sensibility prevalent throughout the Hispanic world.[50] While not exactly a love letter, Ortiz Parrilla's letter contained elements of admiration and respect that likened it to an emotional display of love for a friend. For Andrea Noble, "the act of public weeping was an ambiguous and versatile mode of social communication, where to shed tears, or to withhold them, has the potential to express a wide range of emotions—anger, fear, happiness, shame, and so on—which can reveal much about how individuals and groups relate to one another."[51]

The unrestrained sentiment expressed in this letter, particularly in the idea that the governor shed tears for Oacpicagigua, can thus be read in three somewhat interrelated ways: as a product of the more sentimental Age of Reason; as a policy by which "military officers who governed frontier zones often courted autonomous Indians with gifts, generous terms of trade, and friendly alliances even as they strengthened their own military position"; and as a savvy political act of contrition for his supposed ineptness at holding an Indian in such high regard, for it only became necessary to justify this relationship after it had seemingly faltered. By expressing his distress, concern, and sadness to the viceroy and by repeatedly conveying the fact that the revolt was "unexpected and strange," he was absolving himself of the acts committed by the Pima insurgents.[52] But by lavishing such extensive praise on Oacpicagigua while simultaneously making the Jesuit fathers' behavior the main cause of the revolt, he was skillfully justifying his decision for validating Oacpicagigua's title as *capitán general* of the Pimas and for embracing him as an associate and friend. In all this, it was the Jesuits who bore the brunt of Ortiz Parrilla's frustration, as the final section of this chapter reveals.

In the mental world of Ortiz Parrilla, flattery, patronage, and emotion became the chief expressions of his fondness for a friend. Just as Johannes Dantiscus celebrated his friendship with Hernán Cortés by writing a Latin poem in his honor, Ortiz Parrilla was vividly celebrating the achievements of an Indian through a more acceptable medium: the administrative report.[53] Obviously, Ortiz Parrilla could not, in true Renaissance fashion, ever compare Oacpicagigua to an Achilles or an Alexander, for that would have upset the fragile ideological universe both men inhabited. Judging by the melancholic tone of the letter, the governor was grieved at the loss of his most loyal companion. But given the social constraints of eighteenth-century New Spain, how did this friendship come about in the first place? I propose that the harsh experiences of frontier life shared by both men—continuous war with indios enemigos and humiliation endured at the hands of Jesuit missionaries—became the primary veins through which this unique friendship flowed.

War, Violence, and the Symbolic Language of Friendship

In 1750 Ortiz Parrilla ordered all available Spanish soldiers (seventy-five at the time) and indigenous allies to take part in a targeted military campaign against the Seris, whose martial resolve had stayed the economic development of the Sonoran frontier.[54] Bordering the western portion of the province, the Seris had taken refuge on Tiburón Island, their accustomed stronghold off the eastern coast of Baja California, following a short-lived revolt the previous year.[55] In his *Descripción de la provincia de Sonora*, German priest Ignacio Pfefferkorn outlined the military event:

> In 1750 the governor of the province decided to obtain peace for distressed Sonora by the complete extermination of the Seris. To accomplish this he summoned all the soldiers under his command and called for the assistance of the Spaniards living in the province. He also assembled a large number of warlike Pimas who he anticipated would be of the greatest skill, equal to that of the Seris, in climbing steep and rugged mountains. With his army thus assembled, he advanced upon the Cerro Prieto and ordered his soldiers to climb the rocks and attack the enemy. But then he saw in dismay that more than half of his strength was useless, since the American Spaniards are almost always on horseback, they are very poor pedestrians, and become helpless when they are forced to abandon their horses. So the Pimas [led by Oacpicagigua] had to advance alone on the Seris. And they did it with such vigor and bravery that they terrified their enemies.[56]

This so-called war of extermination exposed the inherent weakness of mounted Spanish soldiers against more versatile Seri warriors who were fighting on their own terrain. At the same time, it also enhanced Oacpicagigua's military value, highlighting his leadership abilities and his authority over the four hundred Indian troops he brought to the battle. As a number of scholars have pointed out, through hunting and warfare Natives "gained personal prestige and established a role for themselves in the social and political lives of their communities."[57] This particular event, however, marked one of the most important episodes in their friendship, "endearing Oacpicagigua to Ortiz Parrilla."[58] It was after this particular campaign against the Seris that Ortiz Parrilla confirmed Oacpicagigua's title as *capitán general* of the Pimería Alta.

Oacpicagigua's loyalty to the Spanish authorities of the Pimería was similarly displayed when on a subsequent campaign against the Apaches, undertaken with the help of an unspecified *norteño* (northern) tribe, Oacpicagigua confronted its Native captain, who went by the curious pseudonym of Caballo ("horse"), for having coveted several recently confiscated horses for himself. Since these horses did not belong to Captain Caballo, Oacpicagigua ordered that they be returned to their rightful owners, presumably Spanish settlers or soldiers. Oacpicagigua reproached Caballo, telling him:

> You do not make a good captain nor servant to the King because according to what you have done, it appears that you only came with the goal of appropriating for yourself these goods, without determining [whether] to leave with your people in search of the enemies as I did with my [people], risking my life, and not being fair what you attempt, I advise you that you should return the horses because if you do not, I will inform the Captain of Terrenate [a Spaniard] and the lieutenant of the jurisdiction.[59]

Two decades later, the Reglamento of 1772 would make it official policy that captured livestock and horses taken from indios enemigos be returned to their rightful Spanish or criollo owners.[60] As an agent of empire, Oacpicagigua's critique of Caballo reflected a strong conviction that a good captain should always behave in accordance with the greater interests of the Crown. Incensed by Oacpicagigua's reprimand, Captain Caballo made "various threats and challenges in contempt of the captain of Terrenate and his soldiers, and even gave signs of wanting to revolt [against Spaniards] with his people."[61] Alarmed by the captain's threats, Oacpicagigua promptly gave an account of this incident to Lieutenant Don Antonio Gutiérrez and to the military *alférez* (official), Don Joseph Ignacio de Salazar, in anticipation that they pass along the information to the visitor general, Don Rodríguez Gallardo.[62] The *visitador*, once informed of this event, promptly dispatched the captain of Fronteras, Don Francisco Bustamante, to investigate the accusation.

During the interrogation, Oacpicagigua, who was in the presence of Busta-mente, sternly reproached Caballo about his desire to revolt and for his trans-gressions against the imperial Crown.[63] This portion of Oacpicagigua's testi-mony raises many thought-provoking questions. If, as later Jesuit testimony maintained, Oacpicagigua had designs to revolt against the Spanish prior to the Seri campaign of 1750 and was therefore of like mind with Caballo, why was he so eager to report the captain's rebellious intentions? Why, if Oacpicagigua's 1751 rebellion was really about Spanish maltreatment, as many scholars have argued, did he not simply join Captain Caballo in a unified front against Span-ish oppression? Finally, what was the basis of Oacpicagigua's desire to return the horses to their rightful Spanish owners? If the goal of subjugated people is, as James C. Scott has suggested, to find ways to hinder the colonial process by not consenting to dominance, why then did the Native leader feel so compelled to return to the Spaniards the very means by which to sustain their economy of violence, in turn ensuring the subjugation of his own community?[64]

As *capitán general* of the Pimas, Oacpicagigua had been granted important concessions such as the rights to ride a horse, wear Spanish clothing, wield Spanish weapons, and drink chocolate.[65] By publicly castigating Caballo, it became evident to everyone, especially to the governor, that Oacpicagigua's commitment to the success of the province and to their friendship was sin-cere. But was it really? Since preserving the Spanish superstructure effectively upheld his position of authority and status among the multiethnic residents of the Pimería, was his desire to hold on to power the main motivation behind this vocal, overdramatized public performance? Was access to power and status a more significant reason why he was so willing to accept a certain level of systemic oppression against his kinsmen, regularly contributing to the imple-mentation of their subjugation? Are these the "freighting risks" Oacpicagigua was trapped into accepting?[66]

War is rarely unemotional. Because of this fact, during the various cam-paigns that both men carried out together against indios enemigos there emerged an element of devotion and empathy that unified them as more than mere allies or strategic partners. This is made clear at various points in Ortiz Parrilla's letter to the viceroy. This emotional appendage may be compared to the passionate attachment of men fighting in the trenches, which George Mosse has argued was the cause for the emergence of the German "cult of friendship" in the years after the First World War.[67] But unlike the men who fought in the trenches, this was a friendship among *un*equals. As such, it carried a set of expectations (outlined in chapter 2) unique to eighteenth-century Sonora and the Spanish borderlands. Further, since friendship has no identifiable and universally recognized language of its own, its performance, particularly as it related to the act of conducting warfare against a common enemy, represented an open form of communication that could be read in a manner similar to that of a love letter. Raphael Brewster Folsom, for instance, has argued that due to the linguistic diversity of the northern frontier, it was often difficult for its residents to clearly communicate their intentions, making violence a sort of *lingua franca* and thus "the clearest way to make a point."[68] Lance Blyth has similarly noted that violence was the primary option, and may have been the only means, for both settler and Native communities to establish, sustain, or alter relations with one another.[69] More importantly, the symbolic language of friendship as it was expressed in warfare created unique opportunities for warriors of unequal *calidiad* (quality) to engage in various types of negotiations with one another while still adhering to the social expectations of the frontier.[70] Violence thus represented a form of dialogue that was chockfull of meaning and purpose.

The way Ortiz Parrilla read and interpreted Oacpicagigua's conviction was reflected in his letter to the viceroy with such phrases as "the fatigues he suffered during the enterprise," "the ardent spirit with which he encouraged [his men] to their labors," and "the generous heart with which he happily exposed himself to the dangers."[71] The emotional value of the wars in which Oacpicagigua and Ortiz Parrilla fought side by side united them as somewhat unlikely colleagues and served as the emotional glue in their friendship. This highly performative method of communication made a colonial world that was full of ambiguity and uncertainty both visible and decipherable. It underscored the fact, as Pekka Hämäläinen writes, that "Indian-White frontiers were messy, eclectic contact points where all protagonists were transformed—regardless of whether the power dynamics between them were evenly or unevenly balanced."[72] Both Oacpicagigua and Ortiz Parrilla skillfully maneuvered through such transformative events, war being but one, using friendship as their common currency.

Scholars of early colonial U.S. history have written about the importance of friendship, especially for those who lived on the margins of their societies. For these men, strategic friendships opened up channels of power that were otherwise inaccessible.[73] Up-and-coming lawyers, notes Anya Jabour, sought to form close friendships with more established southern attorneys in order to improve their chances of making it. Isolated at the edges of empire, they "often fostered a more enduring intimacy" through public displays of affection such as hugging, embracing, and caressing.[74] Though Oacpicagigua and Ortiz Parrilla were men also living at the margins of their own respective societies, and though Oacpicagigua and Ortiz Parrilla were of similar social status in relation to their respective charges, their unequal *calidad* made it impossible to exhibit public (though not necessarily private) emotional connections of intimacy. Their friendship endured precisely because their social inequality was publicly maintained. Privately, however, their friendship functioned at a more intimate level. According to Oacpicagigua, when in private the governor was fond of putting his arm around him, often taking him into his quarters to speak privately. Along borderlands, societal rules of intimacy were never solidly fixed—they often inhabited uncertain ground, which made it difficult to distinguish and enforce ideas of *calidad*. Nevertheless, while the governor embraced Oacpicagigua's pragmatic commitment to the colonial project, extolling his "honorable" qualities in his letter to the viceroy, Jesuit missionaries, intent on maintaining a strict behavioral hierarchy with themselves as the sole purveyors of morality and legitimacy, judged Oacpicagigua's behavior by a very different set of social standards.

Humiliation, Moral Order, and the Challenges of Public Amity

The second variant that connected Oacpicagigua and Ortiz Parrilla in friendship was their mutual animosity toward certain Jesuit missionaries.[75] When the Black Robes first arrived in Sonora during the second half of the seventeenth century, many possessed the rather noble ideal of creating a Christian kingdom at the furthest edges of the known world. However, much like the Franciscans who arrived in New Mexico during roughly this same time their missionary vigor rapidly soured amid the harsh realities of frontier life.[76] By the time Ignacio Keller and others of his missionary ilk arrived in Sonora a century later, support for the mission enterprise had begun to decline and a new more practical missionary ethos had taken root.[77] By the early 1700s missionaries no longer obeyed the rules and precepts of their Order; instead, they "criticize[d] their inconsistency, impracticality, and uselessness in the ever more complex frontier society."[78] Additionally, the idea of martyrdom, so influential and invigorating in the days of Pérez de Ribas and Eusebio Kino, had given way to a more systemic and rational approach to colonization by the mid-eighteenth century.[79] This shift was the product of a number of larger political, economic, and ideological changes that were imposed by Bourbon reformers and by the swelling numbers of Spanish settlers who were threatening their economic supremacy. Their new worldview placed a greater emphasis on resettling Indians near mission sites, not so much to convert them as in previous decades—though this was still a priority—but for the express purpose of extracting their labor and in the process "civilizing" them.[80]

Though Indians remained exempt from tribute payments, they were required to work mission lands through *repartimiento* (forced labor recruitment) at least two days a week in order to produce a variety of goods that were sold to Spanish settlers. But settlers and soldiers also had an urgent need for Indian labor and viewed the missions as an obstacle to economic development. Missionaries, for instance, often ignored official requests for Indian labor in the mines and haciendas, undercutting them whenever possible.[81] The stage was thus set for a series of epic clashes that, as David Yetman has noted, created opportunities for Natives savvy enough to exploit them.[82] Through various methods of their own—some brutal, others unctuous—all three Spanish groups (settlers, soldiers, and missionaries), aware of the potential for these internal fractures to be exploited by Natives, sought as best they could to control for this likelihood. Without a doubt, the most pressing conundrum all three groups faced on a daily basis was whether their Indian charges were really as loyal as they professed to be. How much of what Indians said was sincere, and what percentage was carefully constructed lies? As we saw in the previous chapter, the ability for Natives and Spaniards to tell elaborate but convincing fictions was not only essential to survival, but it created important opportunities for those willing and able to take advantage of them. These concerns kept many a Spaniard up at night. As keepers of moral order, it was largely left to missionaries to institute a strict program for regulating the ethos and behavior of the multiethnic peoples of Sonora. The emphasis on keeping a firm hold over the Natives and of their moral sensibilities intensified during the early eighteenth century as a new brand of secular governors—men such as Manuel Bernal Huidobro (appointed in 1732)—sought to challenge Jesuits for control over the region's Native inhabitants. The public friendship between Oacpicagigua and Ortiz Parrilla thus posed a direct challenge to their waning authority.

In general, the Jesuits loathed the governor for criticizing their lack of missionary zeal and for publicly condemning the exploitation of their Indian charges. Ortiz Parrilla, for instance, openly denounced Father Joseph Garrucho, missionary of Guevavi, for having whipped innocent and "loyal" Pimas and for having kidnapped Native children for his own financial interests.[83] Ortiz Parrilla also accused the Jesuits of "spreading rumors about him and of directing 'stupid criticisms' toward his administration."[84] The governor was in turn heavily criticized by several Jesuits for having "excessively flattered" the indigenous residents of the Pimería, which according to the Jesuit fathers had rendered them unmanageable and hostile.[85] According to Father Gaspar Stiger, during the 1750 campaign against the Seris, Ortiz Parrilla promised the Pimas all of the land up to the Colorado River as reward for their participation—a promise that, if carried out, would have jeopardized Jesuit temporal authority over future missions in that region. Stiger concluded that because of the governor's excessive praise and promises following this campaign, the Pimas returned to their missions with a willful arrogance and overbearing sense of entitlement.[86]

Worse still, on several occasions Ortiz Parrilla publicly proclaimed Oacpicagigua to have behaved with integrity and "reason," which, as he noted in his letter to the viceroy, was the principal reason for having granted him such prestige.[87] This social designation essentially elevated Oacpicagigua's *calidad*, converting him into a *persona de razón* (person of reason).[88] That an Indian on the Sonoran frontier could be considered a *persona de razón* remained a contested proposition throughout much of the colonial period. While some administrators and missionaries aspired to turn Indians into "rational men," others didn't think this was possible, thus highlighting the paradoxes of colonial administration and by extension compelling us to reexamine established categories of agency, social caste, and power. In this particular time and place, however, it was Ortiz Parrilla's elevation of an Indian above his social caste that accounted for much of the anger Jesuit missionaries harbored toward him. Several Jesuits— Fathers Jacobo Sedelmayr, Ignacio Keller, Juan Nentvig, Carlos de Rojas, and Joseph Garrucho—maintained that because of the governor's relationship with Oacpicagigua, the Pima leader had become excessively proud and had begun telling his own people to disobey them, relaying to his kinsmen that such directives to disregard Jesuit orders came from Ortiz Parrilla.[89] Such accusations explain why Fathers Keller and Sedelmayr willfully ignored Ortiz Parrilla's various administrative letters with regularity, occasionally tossing them into the fire.[90] In an effort to discredit the governor, they claimed that he had not earned his position of authority; rather, they somewhat condescendingly held that his post as governor of Sonora had been granted to him only because his uncle belonged to the court of Madrid. Jesuit contempt of Ortiz Parrilla hit a high point after the revolt. As far as they were concerned, it was his friendship with the rebellion's leader that made the uprising possible in the first place. Father Visitor de Rojas put it in plain terms: Ortiz Parrilla "only fenced with and bloodied the pen, letting off the carnivorous Pima wolves and sacrificing the innocent missionary lambs."[91]

In a similar vein, Sonora's missionaries believed that Oacpicagigua "was a bad sort, vain and ambitious," and that he was the "sole creation" of Ortiz Parrilla, who in poor judgment had given him "extraordinary civil and military protection," which caused him to disobey them and, as many Jesuits claimed, to become an agent of the devil.[92] Juan Nentvig likened him to a sorcerer, arguing that Oacpicagigua alone, given his egotism and inconstancy, was "enough to stir up an entire nation."[93] Oacpicagigua's relationship with the aforementioned missionaries was no less acrimonious. During an early campaign against the Apaches, Oacpicagigua stopped in Guevavi, where Father Garrucho initially "welcomed the famous Luis, treated him as if he were a vecino, and entertained the Indian in his own quarters."[94] But as the friendship between the governor and Oacpicagigua matured, the relationships among Oacpicagigua, Garrucho, and several of the other missionaries began to sour. Oacpicagigua, many of them came to believe, had become uncontrollable because of the political backing and support he received from the governor. And because of this, he began to flagrantly disobey missionary orders. In one specific instance, Oacpicagigua took it upon himself to "unmarry" two Indians from Guevavi (the very town where previously he had been treated with great respect) who had recently been married through the Church. This aggressive act defied Father Garrucho's authority over his flock, generating resentment on the part of the missionary.[95]

A significant portion of Oacpicagigua's testimony addressed the humiliation he suffered at the hands of several missionaries. One incident in particular weighed heavy on him. Accompanied by his two sons and Sergeant Luis Batiutuc, Oacpicagigua had stopped at Santa María Soamca to confer with Father Keller regarding the location of Captain Don Santiago Atel, who had recently departed on a campaign against the Apaches and whom Oacpicagigua was eager to join. Having greeted the missionary with the customary honorifics, Oacpicagigua handed Keller a letter from Ortiz Parrilla with instructions regarding the campaign: "I bring here a letter from the lord governor in which his lordship orders me to accompany Captain Don Santiago with whatever people he might request of me to go on this campaign. . . . I have come to carry out what my governor orders."[96] Incensed by Oacpicagigua's imposing demeanor, and perhaps upset that Oacpicagigua was going to deprive him of workers for the military campaign, Keller threatened to throw the governor's letter into the fire as he had done on previous occasions.

Keller then chastised Oacpicagigua for wearing Spanish clothing and wielding Spanish weapons. According to Oacpicagigua's testimony, which was narrated by Ortiz Parrilla (an important factor in deciphering Oacpicagigua's testimony), he wrote that he arrived "to the house of the father, dressed with the apparel and arms that Spanish soldiers used, which he was accustomed to wearing as a captain." In this same document Oacpicagigua noted that he had purchased these clothes from Spaniards, whom he called his *noraguas* or *compadres*. Though Oacpicagigua was accustomed to possessing Spanish clothing and other military artifacts as *capitán general*, Keller believed that they effectively clouded his social position as an indigenous person. Throughout much of Peru, *kurakas* commonly donned Spanish hats, stockings, and shoes in order to highlight their superior social status over other Natives.[97] While beneficial to some extent, such evocative practices elicited vehement scorn and abuse from Spanish and Indian communities alike. Indians, like the seventeenth-century chronicler Felipe Guamán Poma de Ayala, loathed Indian men who dressed as Spaniards for seemingly abandoning their native culture.[98] Spaniards equally remained uneasy about the larger social implications of Natives dressing and acting as Spaniards. Colonial anxieties about proper dress and behavior drove Keller to snap: "What clothing is it that you wear, do you not know that this clothing corresponds to Spaniards? Go throw away all this and cover [yourself] with a loincloth."[99] This outright objection to Natives adopting a Spanish demeanor in dress and style was largely the product of an uncertain and hostile frontier environment. Had not the Spanish Ordinances of 1573 clearly stipulated that Natives were to be taught to "live in a civilized manner, clothed and wearing shoes; given the use of bread and wine and oil and many other essentials of life such as food, silk, linen, horses, cattle, tools and weapons, and all the rest that Spain has; and instructed in trades and skills"?[100]

Eager to cut Oacpicagigua down to size and remind him of his appropriate place amid the social hierarchy, Keller followed up by calling him a "Chichimec dog whose proper attire was a coyote skin and a loincloth, and whose normal pastime was chasing rabbits and rodents in the hills."[101] Cheryl English Martin has argued that in frontier societies where personal reputation was paramount to one's status, insults and slander often "sparked violent confrontations."[102] Particularly injurious as an insult was the term *perro* (dog), as it created an association between Oacpicagigua's supposedly uncontrollable animallike behavior and a lack of reason. Keller's cutting diatribe effectively negated Oacpicagigua's growing social status among his charges and among the various segments of the Spanish community, thereby threatening his position of power.

Pointing to some quivers, Keller directed him toward his "proper" social role: "These are your weapons and the ones that you should carry, doing what the rest of the Indians [do], which is maintaining themselves with mule deer, rabbits, deer, rats, and wild sheep." Aware of the situation before him, Oacpicagigua humbly acquiesced, responding, "I will do what your reverence orders me, taking off all this that is [not adhered] to my flesh."[103] Because appearance and behavior were so important in colonial society, Oacpicagigua's nonconformity in relation to his indigenous identity presented Keller, intent on maintaining a strict social and moral hierarchy, with a vexing conundrum. Here, the "colonizer's dilemma" comes sharply into focus. Oacpicagigua was needed by religious and secular officials as an agent of empire; thus, it was important that he adopt the intellectual worldview and ethos of Spanish governance. But by becoming *too* Spanish in dress, behavior and thought, he was also challenging Jesuit moral legitimacy and their right to selectively dole out power and authority to those atop the social hierarchy. This overbearing preoccupation with status explains why the Jesuits vehemently opposed Oacpicagigua's habit of publicly drinking chocolate, since this behavior supposedly belonged to those of European ancestry. On several occasions leading up to his confrontation with Keller, Oacpicagigua had been refused chocolate. According to his testimony, this lack of social acknowledgment enraged him, adding fuel to his anger and possibly becoming a major factor in his decision to revolt.

There is no indication that Ortiz Parrilla opposed Oacpicagigua's choice of drink, clothing, or weapons. In fact, as noted earlier, the governor authorized his right to wear Spanish clothing, and on at least one occasion Oacpicagigua asked Ortiz Parrilla to send him some clothing to wear, for which he thanked him profusely.[104] By requesting Spanish clothing from the governor, Oacpicagigua was once again skillfully reaffirming his status as *capitán*, for only as *capitán general* was he justified in wearing Spanish clothing, wielding Spanish weapons, and drinking chocolate. Such symbolic acts were a major source of their mutual respect for one another. Conversely, they were the main cause of missionary resentment.

Following Oacpicagigua's comment that he would do as Keller asked and take off his Spanish clothing, Keller grew even more irate, now challenging

Oacpicagigua's masculinity: "To me, you are effeminate and neither do you serve for anything." With this final comment Keller mockingly minimized Oacpicagigua's role as *capitán general* of the Pimería Alta. Oacpicagigua tried to defend himself from the missionary's verbal thrashing, but to no avail. Nor was Keller the only missionary to treat Oacpicagigua with such flagrant contempt. Father Jacobo Sedelmayr also lambasted Oacpicagigua on several occasions prior to his meeting with Keller. The most significant of these events occurred when during a meeting he verbally chastised Oacpicagigua for "becoming fond of the señor governador."[105] He then threw a letter Ortiz Parrilla had sent him in the Pima leader's face, admonishing him for living his life as a Spaniard.[106] It was Ortiz Parrilla to whom Oacpicagigua sought redress following his affront with Keller, not only because he felt comfortable and secure expressing his grievances to him, but also because they shared a degree of contempt toward the missionary. In a testimony taken soon after the uprising, Joachin de Raum, a *vecino*, stated that he heard Oacpicagigua complain that during the incident with Keller the priest made him understand that "he no longer had command or authority in his pueblos."[107] John Kessell adds, "Whatever really took place at Soamca that day, it was enough to offend Luis [Oacpicagigua], who now abandoned the campaign and went home nursing black thoughts."[108]

In his letter to the viceroy, Ortiz Parrilla noted that the missionaries' dismissal of Oacpicagigua's authority, and particularly the incident with Keller, was the chief reason behind the revolt. It is also certain, he wrote, "that with this last affliction [Keller's chastisement] he [Oacpicagigua] was reminded of all the injuries that the fathers had done to him . . . his heart had been sadden by such incidences, and because of this, he immediately took off his weapons and solder insignias, selling all of them to the Spaniards."[109] The symbolic act of removing signs of Spanish power from his person was a radical break from his previous practice of embracing them as tokens of authority. Anthropologists who study material culture such as Sophie Woodward have explained that "as material culture, clothing is not seen as simply reflecting given aspects of the self but, through its particular material propensities, is co-constitutive of facets such as identity, sexuality and social role."[110] For Rebecca Earle, this social effect is also evident in the various lawsuits where "individuals seeking to establish their status might appeal not to the genealogies of their ancestors, but rather to the clothing that they typically wore."[111] So long as Oacpicagigua donned Spanish clothing and wielded Spanish weapons, his social status and responsibilities, especially in terms of his friendship with the governor, were visible to everyone, forcing him to perform accordingly. Once he discarded these Spanish material objects, however, his loyalty and responsibility toward Spaniards in general, and the governor in particular, were severed.

The bitterness that missionaries harbored toward Oacpicagigua also extended to the men under his command. On one occasion, following the incident with Keller, Father Garrucho instructed Oacpicagigua to remit back to him runaway Indians who had sought asylum in Sáric. Oacpicagigua, though still dismayed from his encounter with Keller, sent one of his sergeants, Joseph de la Cruz, who was also his nephew, to escort the runaway Indians back to Garrucho. Unfortunately, Garrucho was in no mood to engage with de la Cruz. Upon de la Cruz's return to Guevavi, Father Garrucho chastised and whipped him, taking away his *vara de justicia* (cane of justice/authority), which had been authorized by Oacpicagigua and confirmed by Ortiz Parrilla. So, when Oacpicagigua learned that Father Garrucho had taken away his nephew's *vara*, he immediately asked Ortiz Parrilla that it be restored. According to the governor, following this incident, Oacpicagigua was said to have uttered that "the fathers have already thrown me on my back, they already look at me as nothing, and they have scorned me." Oacpicagigua's loss of influence and authority among the Jesuits caused him to declare that "now I am not worth anything, now I am a tiny, effeminate coyote and a Chichimeco."[112] It was perhaps at this point, with all that had happened up to then, that the tribal leader who so dutifully straddled the colonial tightrope between violence and accommodation fell decisively on the side of rebellion.

For the Jesuits, there was no clearer sign of Oacpicagigua's long-standing deceit than his subsequent uprising. To them the Pima Revolt of 1751 was wholly illegitimate, since it could only have been born out of revenge or blind rage. Indeed, Oacpicagigua's rebellion only reaffirmed their initial assessment of him—his outward Spanish behavior and dress was a shallow façade for his real intentions, which resided within him for several years prior to the revolt. In testimony taken three years after the uprising, Father Juan Nentvig stated that long before the 1751 revolt, Oacpicagigua had already lost touch with his Christian principles and was reverting to paganism by sponsoring drinking parties in the mountains.[113] Ortiz Cortés similarly testified that Oacpicagigua had summoned Luis del Pitic, his sergeant, who had declared and confessed to Ortiz Cortés that upon return from the campaign in Tiburón, Oacpicagigua had already started to talk about rebellion.[114] In fact, Pitic stated that Oacpicagigua was intent on killing the governor the moment he had the chance, stabbing him in the back as he was dismounting his horse. Like Nentvig and Cortés, Father

Miguel Quijano directed a similar accusation against Oacpicagigua. Quijano reported that when Oacpicagigua returned from his campaign against the Seris in 1750, he changed his name back to Bacquiopa, which meant "enemy of the Adobe houses."[115]

Such accusations, made years after the revolt, show that Fathers Nentvig and Quijano sought to minimize any attempt to make Oacpicagigua's rebellion a "just war," as the governor had proposed. This designation would have given credibility and justification to Oacpicagigua's actions. The effort made to defame Oacpicagigua was especially necessary considering that he was seen as a credible threat to their authority, which rested on their ability to keep their charges in a submissive, infantilized position. To have an Indian leader adhering to Western norms of valor, masculinity, justice, and friendship and being aided by a recluse governor did not fare well for their spiritual and moral supremacy over Sonora.

Ortiz Parrilla saw Oacpicagigua's actions very differently. For him, while he also believed that revenge was the main issue that had motivated Oacpicagigua toward rebellion, missionary cruelty toward him and his kinsmen had left Oacpicagigua with no choice other than violence. Oacpicagigua, argued Ortiz Parrilla, was simply acting out of a sense of compulsory justice. Ortiz Parrilla must have mulled over in his mind, notes John Kessell, whether his trust of Oacpicagigua "had been so plainly misplaced, or was this basically good and loyal vassal of the Spanish king fighting a just war against his Jesuit oppressors?"[116] How could Ortiz Parrilla fault Oacpicagigua for the revolt when several Jesuit priests continuously overstepped their boundaries?[117] Father Juan Nentvig was a case in point. Ortiz Parrilla accused the priest of several egregious offenses, which included illegitimately appropriating Oacpicagigua's lands, ordering him to give fifty lashes to his own lieutenant (Pedro Chihuahua), and lambasting Oacpicagigua both for living in concubinage and for living like a Spaniard.[118] When all was said and done, despite Ortiz Parrilla's distress over what he saw as a betrayal of their friendship, when Oacpicagigua was brought to San Ignacio the following year to be interrogated, the governor welcomed him "as if he were some famous captain of the ancient Romans."[119]

Conclusion

In an effort to justify his decision for having granted and validated Oacpicagigua's authority, Ortiz Parrilla went to great lengths to explain to the viceroy the circumstances behind his relationship with the leader of the 1751 Pima Revolt, expressing in a melancholic tone his favorable opinion of the Pima leader. According to the governor, when Oacpicagigua went to war with the Seris in 1750, he not only behaved with honor and deference, but he also performed laudable acts of bravery, masculinity, and justice, all of which brought them closer as friends. This strategic friendship coalesced through two central avenues: war and humiliation. The experiences both men shared in war laid a solid emotive foundation for their relationship, while the disrespect they suffered at the hands of the missionaries reinforced their friendship through the shared feeling of humiliation. For his part, Oacpicagigua had skillfully conformed to the expectations of proper behavior in regard to his friendship with the governor, through whom he was able to gain access to the Spanish social system and win Spanish confidence, material rewards, status, and ultimately the title of *capitán general* of the Pimería Alta. However, when Jesuit opposition to Oacpicagigua's growing authority—and, in particular, his behaving and dressing as a Spaniard—challenged his ability to gain and negotiate power among the various ethnic and social sectors of the Pimería, Oacpicagigua organized the 1751 Pima Revolt.

Oacpicagigua and Ortiz Parrilla's friendship emerges from the pages of the governor's letter to the viceroy as well as in the investigation that followed the rebellion. Instead of going after the Pima rebel with martial might, the governor limited his actions to diplomacy and reconnaissance, sending a peace commission to reason with him, ultimately offering him amnesty. On March 18, 1752, after months of negotiations with Oacpicagigua—who had set as conditions for peace Keller's banishment from the Pimería and the return of several Pima servants who had been taken by Father Garrucho—the rebel leader accepted his Spanish friend's offer of amnesty and surrendered to Captain Joseph Díaz del Carpio. The remaining holdouts likewise threw down their weapons and descended from their mountain hideouts to reaffirm their submission, loyalty, and friendship to the king.

The interrogations that the governor conducted after the revolt also reveal his closeness with Oacpicagigua, whom he attempted to shield from any direct responsibility for the revolt. According to the testimony of *vecino* Juan Manuel Ortiz Cortés taken by Father Joseph de Utrera in 1754, Cortéz was asked by Ortiz Parrilla to interpret for Oacpicagigua, but to ensure that Oacpicagigua did not say anything incriminating so that he could emerge from the testimony unscathed.[120] This testimony, argued Father Utrera, was to focus exclusively on the behavior of the Jesuit fathers, who from his perspective were innocent of inciting the Pima toward rebellion. It should be noted that by this time (1754) Ortiz Parrilla was no longer governor of Sonora, and it was in Ortiz Cortés's best interest that his testimony take issue with the former governor and absolve the Jesuits of any fault. Ortiz Cortés continued, "[Ortiz Parrilla said] that Luis was a poor little thing, and that it was necessary to free him." He was "convinced that the intent of the lord governor was to find the fathers guilty and [to hold] Luis blameless, since he was his making."[121]

During the months and years following the revolt, efforts to determine the cause of the rebellion resulted in the compilation of three separate sets of testimonies. In the first set, obtained and supervised by Ortiz Parrilla, the blame for the revolt was placed squarely on the Jesuits, with the allegation that their maltreatment of the Pimas in general and of Oacpicagigua in particular had been the root cause for the violence. Two years later, Don Pablo de Arce y Arroyo, Ortiz Parrilla's replacement as governor, ordered a new set of testimonies to be taken from many of the original declarants. The change of interrogator led to major modifications in the original testimonies, with the new set revealing that many of the original declarants had been coerced to testify against the Jesuits, often under threat of punishment. In a dramatic reversal, many of the original declarants who had blamed the Jesuits for the revolt now stated that it was Ortiz Parrilla's fault for "showering excessive praise on Luis [Oacpicagigua] after the Indian leader had fought well against the Seris."[122] As a result, they claimed, Oacpicagigua began to feel like he was the owner of the Pimería, and because of this, he began to plot his rebellion. And if we are to believe Father Miguel Quijano's 1751 testimony, Oacpicagigua even changed his name to Bacquiopa, or "Enemy of the Adobe Houses."

The third and final set of testimonies was taken by the Jesuit father visitor General Joseph Utrera. Predictably, the missionary found the revolt to have been the result of two central factors: the innate character of frontier Indians, who were by nature prone to such violent behavior, and the excessive praise and authority given to an Indian by Ortiz Parrilla. Seven Pima Indians questioned in this last set of testimonies all gave pro-Jesuit testimonies. In 1758, the official investigation of the rebellion was finally concluded, and the Jesuit missionaries were absolved of any responsibility for the revolt. Despite having evaded prison time for his part in the rebellion, once Ortiz Parrilla's tenure ended, Oacpicagigua was imprisoned for allegedly trying to instigate another revolt. After a failed suicide attempt, he died in 1755 in an Horcasitas prison cell.

Roberto Solmón has written that "the Pima Revolt failed because it was too closely identified with the personality of Luis Oacpicagigua. . . . [H]e was caught in the middle of an evolutionary society."[123] His control over many of the Natives under his command, and his relationship with the Jesuits, had been significantly influenced by his friendship with Ortiz Parrilla. Nevertheless, what remains most impressive is that both men, coming from different ends of the social spectrum, were able to forge such close ties of amity. Though remarkable, their friendship should not be surprising, nor unique for that matter—these types of contradictory and ironic relationships characterized life on the frontier. "The strands of Spanish, Mexican, and Indian life" writes Solmón, "became tightly interwoven in a fabric of unique and partly cynical relationships."[124] It was important for both these men, "marginal men" in their own right, to find creative ways to traverse the convoluted ideological and cultural world of the frontier. Friendship facilitated this process as it offered both Oacpicagigua and Ortiz Parrilla a socially prescribed context through which they could interpret, perform, and manipulate colonial relationships of power. It equipped both men with an ideological, behavioral, and emotional mechanism with which to maneuver through the Pimería's interethnic social spaces: Ortiz Parrilla maintained the impression of social order through Oacpicagigua, while Oacpicagigua negotiated Spanish privilege and influence through Ortiz Parrilla, simultaneously increasing his own authority. Friendship became a strategic tool for navigating this tricky social dynamic.

Conclusion

In 1517, a Spanish expedition led by Francisco Hernández de Córdoba (d. 1517) left Cuba in search of glory and gold. Three weeks later, having endured a number of harrowing days at sea, Córdoba and his crew finally came within sight of land. The following day, ten Mayan canoes approached the Spanish ship showing little fear of their mysterious visitors and exhibiting to what the Spanish seemed like unmistakable signs of friendship. They cordially exchanged greetings. The Indians were then given glass beads and other trinkets, which they graciously accepted. Wrongly assuming that their initial encounter had forged something of a détente, and potentially a friendship, the Spaniards went ashore the following day, the Indians "still smiling and affable."[1] Their tentative rapport was strengthened when the Indian cacique "beckoned them towards the town, saying something that sounded like *'cones catoche, cones catoche,'* which the Spaniards guessed meant 'come to our houses.'"[2] Both the initial exchange of goodwill and the generous invitation into their homes had convinced the Spanish that the Natives were good natured and wished to establish ties of friendship with them. Not being entirely sure, however, they kept their weapons close. This would prove a wise move, for no sooner had they entered the town they called *El Gran Cairo* then they were ambushed by Indian warriors donning cotton armor and wielding bows and arrows. On that fateful day the Spanish learned a painful lesson in the obscure nuances of conquest, for "amid this complex interplay of power and negotiation lay deceptive displays of friendship."[3]

This story, which opens Inga Clendinnen's aptly titled *Ambivalent Conquests*, thoroughly captivated my imagination as a graduate student, inadvertently introducing me to my future dissertation topic, of which this book is the end product. The intricate days-long performance displayed by the indigenous peoples of the Yucatan highlights all that this book has sought to lay bare. Essentially, that friendships, especially within the colonial context, were almost always convoluted, uncertain, nuanced, contradictory, and performed. As the product of a social environment that was resonant with death, violence, and despair but also rich with opportunity, friendships had many uses, some sincere and principled, others sinister and unsavory. To that same end, friendships, depending on the social circumstances in which they were forged, were compelled to embrace the gradations and contradictions of idealism, logic, rhetoric, or emotion—oftentimes, all four.

Given that the Spanish encounter with the Maya occurred along a frontier zone, I was convinced that there was something unique about these ill-defined areas that fostered a particularly engaged and volatile form of friendship. As a research associate at the Office of Ethnohistorical Research at the Arizona State Museum, I spent many hours reading through colonial-era documents trying to figure out if this was indeed the case. Over time, I grew increasingly worried, for no one document gave me what I was looking for—a clear, unobstructed view of colonial-era friendship. On the verge of abandoning my dissertation topic altogether, I came to the realization that perhaps I was looking at it all wrong. Why would I expect to find perfect, ideal examples of friendship in an environment that was itself nebulous and uncertain? Perhaps I needed to take a closer look; perhaps I needed to turn the concept on its side, inspect it from the inside out. Perhaps, I needed to acquaint myself with its various disguises.

The story I found lurking beneath the seemingly endless colonial façade of paper—the currency of empire—was a fascinating one, one that if told in a way that highlighted the paradoxes of colonial society would be useful for understanding not only the Spanish frontier but the whole of colonial encounters across time and space. As I have shown in this book, friendship was as much a tool of conquest and exploitation as it was an instrument of empowerment and survival. Europeans, as I model in chapters 1, 2, and 4, used the coded and moralizing language of friendship to reinforce proper behavioral norms among their colonial subjects. This colonial language was found everywhere from legal and planning codes to criminal documents and travel diaries. As these documents underscored, Europeans expected Natives to embrace those specific values that would ultimately result in a civil society—politics, Christianity, loyalty, and, most importantly, friendship. Theirs was also a joint venture. Soldiers, settlers, missionaries, and administrators—all in their own way and for vastly different purposes, and sometimes cross-purposes—worked toward the common goal of civilizing Natives.

Natives, however, far from being unassuming victims of colonialism, waded through the inherent ironies and contradictions of the colonial order so as to produce a version of friendship that promoted their best interest—and they did it with a resolution and exactness worthy of admiration. Just as the Natives of the Yucatan understood that by utilizing the symbolic and emotional properties of friendship they could enter into relations of power and manipulation with foreigners, so too did the indigenous peoples of Sonora understand the complex opportunities afforded them by engaging in friendships with Europeans. As I illustrate early on in this book, while Spaniards maintained a somewhat rigid description of friendship taken from religious and classical scholars, Natives, almost from the onset, practiced a form of friendship that was purposely ambiguous, the better to negotiate space and political influence. It also helped hide, as I display in chapter 4, one's true intentions, as in instances of revenge or political strategy. But as the colonial era proceeded, Spaniards too came to understand that while ideals were helpful in structuring the colonial order, it was absolutely necessary to engage with nuance and irony, but in a very astute and particular way that kept the balance of power squarely on their side.

In addition to fulfilling the basic necessitates of survival, friendship also had the potential to elevate one's reputation and social standing within the colonial hierarchy. As we witnessed in chapters 3 and 5, befriending the right person or community could open up a number of important doors. Sigüenza sought desperately to earn the friendship of Eusebio Francisco Kino in order to gain full admittance into the "Republic of Science," which, he believed, would help magnify his hard-earned reputation. As he soon discovered, however, attaining the academic endorsement of a well-reputed colleague could leave one exposed to the harsh realities of a negative—and in this case, unreasonable—critique. Similarly, Oacpicagigua sought out the friendship of Ortiz Parrilla for all the benefits it afforded him—namely, status and power. But here too Oacipagigua encountered disappointment when he came to the realization that Ortiz Parrilla's secular authority was little match for the moral weight of the Jesuit fathers. In an effort to take away Oacipagigua's hard-earned status and reestablish a "proper" moral order along the frontier, missionaries insulted and demeaned the Native leader, hoping to put him back in his "rightful" place. Forced to save face, both Sigüenza and Oacipagigua, betrayed by the enigmas of the colonial environment of which they were a product, waged their own uprisings: Sigüenza through the might of the pen and Oacipagigua by means of the arrow. These personal associations, which were almost always contingent on misunderstandings, on the shifting nature of personal feelings, and on the whims of ambition and desire, severely complicate the study of friendship. Where there was a warm and loving friendship one day, there was animosity the next.

Friendship was also quite costly. As I outline in chapters 1 and 2, friendships among Natives demanded a significant financial and political contribution, either through the handing over of revered leaders, through gifts and promises of aid, or by means of elaborate dance ceremonies or community sporting events. These rituals and expectations were essential to Native lifeways, but they could also prove to be a serious burden to those who could not afford them. The same held true for Spaniards who expected their indios amigos to assist them in the daily administration of the colony. In order for this power sharing to work, it was important to give indigenous leaders like Canito access to channels of administrative knowledge. But this was a major gamble since it was unknowable if and when an indio amigo might become an indio enemigo. Such a possibility was always present in the minds of Europeans because it was an extremely dangerous liability for an indio amigo turned indio enemigo to have knowledge of the internal workings of the colonial structure. Nevertheless, that false friendships functioned alongside authentic relations of amity was a reality that was purposely overlooked because, at some level, friendship was a useful social vehicle for all parties involved. But friendship, like most human relationships, needed to be maintained in balance. Friendships between Indians and Spaniards worked only so long as the pros outweighed the cons. Once this balance was tipped too far in either direction, friendship turned into a major hindrance that was often only remedied through violence.

Along the Sonoran frontier, friendships were thus conceived at both the macro (group) and micro (individual) levels. In this hostile landscape, befriending Indians at the macro level involved a delicate balance of both indoctrination and patronage. The development of more individualized personal friendships, however, was in large measure the organic outgrowth of political, military, and economic circumstances in addition to the psychological detachment from centers of viceregal power.[4] By looking at friendship from both ideological and practical viewpoints, I have shown the ways in which the history of ideas informed the cultural negotiation of space, status, and power. As David Weber reminds us, "In complex societies several standards of conduct can exist side by side . . . only by understanding the existence of contradictory and competing values and practices and the changes wrought by time and circumstances can one move beyond caricatures to full portraits of society."[5] That is exactly what this book has in some small part attempted to do.

NOTES

Introduction

1. Eberhard Hermes, trans. and ed., *The "Disciplina Clericalis" of Petrus Alfonsi* (Berkeley: University of California Press, 1977), 106. Quoted in Marilyn Stone, *Marriage and Friendship in Medieval Spain: Social Relations According to the Fourth Partida of Alfonso X* (New York: Peter Lang, 1990), 115. This story is part of a larger genre of "test of friendship" tales found in medieval literary collections.

2. A May 2012 article from the *Atlantic Monthly* titled "Is Facebook Making Us More Lonely?" makes the claim that friendships via Facebook are severing traditional and more meaningful forms of fellowship, replacing them with ersatz and transitory versions. This claim was reiterated in a September 2017 piece from *The Atlantic* titled "Have Smartphones Destroyed a Generation?" In *Community and Society (Gemeinshaft and gesselschaft)*, Ferdinand Tönnies argued that friendship, a pillar of traditional society, has been severely disrupted by the individualistic ethos inspired by capitalism and industrialization. See Ferdinand Tönnies, *Community and Society*, trans. Charles Loomis, first published in 1887 (Mineola, N.Y.: Dover Publications, 2011).

3. Plutarch (CE 46–120) also believed that friendship was hard and serious work and did not come easily. True friendship was not based on a chance encounter but on years of engagement. Thus, for Plutarch the idea that one man could possess many friends was incomprehensible and foolish. See Plutarch, "How to Profit by One's Enemies. On Having Many Friends. Chance. Virtue and Vice. Letter of Condolence to Apollonius. Advice About Keeping Well. Advice to Bride and Groom. The Dinner of the Seven Wise Men. Superstition," in *Moralia*, vol. 2., trans. Frank Cole Babbitt, Loeb Classic Library (Cambridge, Mass.: Harvard University Press, 1928).

4.   A similar "test of friendship" tale comes from Konrad von Würzburg's *Engelhard* (ca. 1280). In this story, Engelhard's father gave him three apples and advised him to observe the behavior of the men he should give the apples to. Those who eat the apple without so much as offering to share are, according Engelhard's father, untrustworthy and devoid of any honor. However, those who divide it up equally are honorable and worthy of his friendship: "then let him ride along with you and stay with him all the time as a good friend." Of the three men Engelhard offered the apples to, only one man (Dieterich) offered to share. In time, Engelhard came to consider Dieterich, whom he believed was gifted to him by God, to be a dear friend and brother, a second self. Engelhard then thanked God for having sent him a "true" friend.

5.   See H. E. Yuanguo, "Confucius and Aristotle on Friendship: A Comparative Study," *Frontiers of Philosophy in China* 2, no. 2 (April 2007): 291–307.

6.   "Friendship on Earth," MSS *Romances de los Señores de la Nueva España*, fol. 27. Quoted in Miguel León Portilla, *Pre-Columbian Literatures of Mexico*, trans. Grace Lobanov (Norman: University of Oklahoma Press, 1969), 79.

7.   See Michel de Montaigne, *On Friendship*, trans M. A. Screech (New York: Penguin, 1991). There is a ritual among the Cherokee called the "friendship dance" in which two young men publicly proclaim their friendship to onlookers through the ritual of dance. Each dancer slowly, throughout the course of the dance, removes his clothes and replaces them with his companion's. Thus, "each of them publicly received the other as himself, and became pledged to regard and treat him as himself while he lived." See Gregory D. Smithers, "'Our Hands and Hearts Are Joined Together': Friendship, Colonialism, and the Cherokee People in Early America," *Journal of Social History* 50, no. 4 (2017): 617.

8.   See Ruth Murray Underhill, *Singing for Power: The Song Magic of the Papago Indians of Southern Arizona* (Berkeley: University of California Press, 1938); and Donald Bahr, *How Mockingbirds Are: O'odham Ritual Orations* (Albany, N.Y.: SUNY Press, 2011).

9.   See Pekka Hämäläinen, *The Comanche Empire* (New Haven, Conn.: Yale University Press, 2009), 105.

10.   Smithers, "'Our Hands and Hearts Are Joined Together,'" 615.

11.   See Siddhartha Gautama, *Sigalovada Sutra*. For the Buddha there were four basic types of false friends: (1) the selfish friend who only pretends to be your friend because of fear or obligation, (2) the friend who makes false promises, (3) the friend who routinely speaks ill of you behind your back, and (4) the immoral friend who can lead you toward a life of sin and moral decay. Confucius argued that to make friends with those ingratiating in action (individuals whose behavior is immoral and dishonest), pleasant in appearance (friends who seem sincere but are really deceitful), and plausible in speech (individuals who are your friends purely out of self-interest) was to lose. Aristotle similarly warned against lower forms of friendship—namely, advantage-friendship (friendship designed to further one's own selfish interests) and pleasure-friendship (friendship oriented around the

momentary quality of pleasure). See Daniel Hruschka, *Friendship: Development, Ecology, and Evolution of a Relatonship* (Berkeley: University of California Press, 2010), 5.

12.   See Boncompagno Da Signa, *Amicitia and De Malo Senectutis Et Senii*, Dallas Medieval Texts and Translations (Dudley, Mass.: Peeters, 2012).

13.   Ideals in the sense that they constituted normative standards for judging what characterized a true friendship based on a series of emotional and behavioral strictures. Janet Moore Lindman makes a similar argument. She states, "As a historical phenomenon, friendship contains strong currents of both continuity and change over time. Capturing the often subtle but substantive alterations in the practice and significance of friendship is as important as demonstrating those aspects that remained the same." See Janet Moore Lindman, "Histories of Friendship in Early America: An Introduction," *Journal of Social History* 50, no. 4 (2017): 603.

14.   The idea of friendship as a universal condition is not without its detractors. Anthropologist J. Carrier, for instance, argues that at the core of friendship lies sentimentality (love, affection, loyalty). Friendship, for him, cannot exist without sentimentality, which hinges on the idea of personhood. Since the concept of sentiment emanates from the individual self and since not all societies have conceptions of the self, as among Melanesians, then friendship cannot be a universal trait. See J. Carrier, "People Who Can Be Friends: Selves and Social Relationships," in *The Anthropology of Friendship*, ed. Sandra Bell and Simon Coleman (Oxford: Oxford University Press, 1999).

15.   Here we are not talking about civil society as it pertained to the rise of market capitalism and the demand for liberty occasioned by the French and American revolutions. In many respects, my use of the term "civil society," which is modeled on Anthony Pagden's use of the term, may more popularly be called "political society," "civic society," or "civilized society." For the purposes of uniformity I will use "civil society" with the aforementioned caveats. Though Thomas Carothers and William Barndt note that the term "civil society" can be traced back to the ancient Greeks, our modern understanding of civil society has been influenced by two main trends: the work of Antonio Gramsci, who wanted to "portray civil society as a special nucleus of independent political activity" aimed at fighting dictatorship and tyranny during the mid-twentieth century, and the more modern trend operating since the 1990s of political advocacy for democratic institutions in formerly dictatorial regions, NGOs, environmental groups, human rights groups, teachers associations, and sports clubs. Civil society in this modern sense can also include White Power groups, separatist organizations, the National Rifle Association, and the like. See Thomas Carothers and William Barndt, "Civil Society," *Foreign Policy* 117 (Winter 1999–2000): 18–29. Víctor M. Pérez-Díaz outlines two different versions of civil society as they relate to the twentieth century. In the first form, civil society *sensu lato* "denotes a set of sociopolitical institutions including a limited government or state operating under the rule of law; a set of institutions such as markets (or spontaneous extended orders) and associations based on voluntary

agreements among autonomous agents; and a public sphere in which these agents debate among themselves and with the state about matters of public interest and engage in public activities. . . . It is 'civil' inasmuch as its autonomous agents are 'citizens' (as opposed to mere subjects of a despotic ruler or of a ruling caste) and therefore members of a 'civilized' society (as opposed to a barbaric or backwards one). But the point is that they may be citizens *only* because they are autonomous agents, and they may by autonomous vis-à-vis the state *only* because the state has a limited power to enter these agents' reserved domain. . . . Civil society in a more restricted sense [the second form] refers to social institutions such as markets and associations and the public sphere and excludes state institutions proper." See Víctor M. Pérez-Díaz, *The Return of Civil Society: The Emergence of Democratic Spain* (Cambridge, Mass.: Harvard University Press, 1993), 55–56.

16. See Anthony Pagden, *Lords of All the World: Ideologies of Empire in Spain, Britain, and France c. 1500–c.1800* (New Haven, Conn.: Yale University Press, 1995); and Anthony Pagden, *The Fall of Natural Man: The American Indian and the Origins of Comparative Ethnology* (Cambridge: Cambridge University Press, 1982). The version of civil society that I use in this work is modeled on Pagden's definition. For friendship in antiquity, see David Konstan, *Friendship in the Classical World* (Cambridge: Cambridge University Press, 1997); and Horst Hutter, *Politics as Friendship: The Origins of Classical Notions of Politics and the Theory and Practice of Friendship* (Waterloo, Ontario: Wilfrid Laurier University Press, 1978).

17. J. H. Elliott, *Empires of the Atlantic World: Britain and Spain in America, 1492–1830* (New Haven, Conn.: Yale University Press, 2006), 37.

18. For an example of how friendship helped lay the foundations for civil society in Italy, see Peter Miller, "Friendship and Conversation in Seventeenth-Century Venice," *Journal of Modern History* 73, no. 1 (March 2001): 1–31.

19. The Greek polis was composed of the Asty (city) and Chora (hinterland). In New Spain this same model of the city and the rural estate made up the Spanish-American model that became the foundation for the *hacienda* (estate) and the *estancia* (small farm).

20. Richard Morse, "The Urban Development of Colonial Spanish America," in *The Cambridge History of Latin America*, ed. Leslie Bethell (Cambridge: Cambridge University Press, 1984), 2:70.

21. For instance, civilization versus barbarism, *gente de razón* versus *gente sin razón*, *vecino* (citizen of good standing, usually a property owner) versus *gentile* (unconverted Indian). Relationships of power between Spaniards and Indians have been analyzed by a number of scholars in a variety of ways. To my knowledge, *The Intimate Frontier* is the first to analyze power through the purview of friendship.

22. David Weber argues that eighteenth-century missionaries tended to judge Indians more by their behavior than by ethnicity or race. See David Weber, *Bárbaros: Spaniards and Their Savages in the Age of Enlightenment* (New Haven, Conn.: Yale University Press, 2005), 97. *Gente de razón*—literally, "people of reason"—refers to free and rational individuals who were subject to the laws of the jurisdiction but

were not wards of the mission. The term denoted social or economic superiority and was usually reserved for Spaniards and mestizos, though acculturated Indians and mixed-race people could also be considered *gente de razón*. See John Kessell, *Mission of Sorrows: Jesuit Guevavi and the Pimas, 1691–1767* (Tucson: University of Arizona Press, 1970), 51–52; and Thomas Sheridan, *Empire of Sand: The Seri Indians and the Struggle for Spanish Sonora, 1645–1803* (Tucson: University of Arizona Press, 1999), 465.

23.   Henry Kaman, *Empire: How Spain Became a World Power, 1492–1763* (New York: HarperCollins, 2003), 363.

24.   Martin Austin Nesvig, *Promiscuous Power: An Unorthodox History of New Spain* (Austin: University of Texas Press, 2018), 13.

25.   Cynthia Radding, *Landscapes of Power and Identity: Comparative Histories in the Sonoran Desert and the Forests of Amazonia from Colony to Republic* (Durham, N.C.: Duke University Press, 2005).

26.   Susan Deeds, *Defiance and Deference in Mexico's Colonial North: Indians Under Spanish Rule in Nueva Vizcaya* (Austin: University of Texas Press, 2003), 177; Weber, *Bárbaros*, 44.

27.   José Rafael Rodríguez Gallardo, *Informe sobre Sinaloa y Sonora, 1750*, ed. Germán Viveros (Mexico City: Archivo Histórico de Hacienda, 1975), 30. See also David Brading, *The First America: The Spanish Monarchy, Creole Patriots and the Liberal State, 1492–1867* (Cambridge: Cambridge University Press, 1993). Rebecca Earle's *The Return of the Native: Indians and Myth-Makiing in Spanish America, 1810–1930* (Durham, N.C.: Duke University Press, 2007) highlights the emotional and political uses of such anti-Spanish rhetoric in the years after independence, noting that state builders conveniently saw themselves as descendants of the Aztecs, Mayas, and Incas who, through the process of independence, sought to vindicate them from three hundred years of brutal colonial rule.

28.   Daniel Matson and Bernard Fontana, *Friar Bringas Reports to the King: Methods of Indoctrination on the Frontier of New Spain, 1796–97* (Tucson: University of Arizona Press, 1977), 19. See also Weber, *Bárbaros*.

29.   Raphael Brewster Folsom, *The Yaquis and Their Empire: Violence, Spanish Imperial Power, and Native Resilience in Colonial Mexico* (New Haven, Conn.: Yale University Press, 2014).

30.   Vanessa Smith, *Intimate Strangers: Friendship, Exchange, and Pacific Encounters* (Cambridge: Cambridge University Press, 2010), 14.

31.   Seventeenth-century letters and official documents do not follow contemporary laws of grammar; they typically do not include punctuation or paragraph breaks, nor in many cases do they indicate when one scribe is replaced by another—that is left up to the critical eye of the scholar. Typical among many of these documents is the often absurd length of sentences, which can occupy several pages. A single thought can meander through a host of issues—often unrelated—until it reaches its main point several pages later, bestowing onto the scholar a test in the virtue of patience.

32. Cassandra Good, *Founding Friendships: Friendships Between Men and Women in the Early American Republic* (Oxford: Oxford University Press, 2017).

33. See Laura Alejandra Buentura Gómez, *Malas amistades: Infanticidios y relaciones ilícitas en la provincia de Antioquia (Nueva Granada), 1765–1803* (Bogotá: Editorial Universidad del Rosario, 2017); Ana María Atondo Rodríguez, *El amor venal y la condición femenina en el México colonial* (Mexico City: Instituto Nacional de Antropología e Historia, 1992); Amanda Herbert, *Female Alliances: Gender, Identity, and Friendship in Early Modern Britain* (New Haven, Conn.: Yale University Press, 2014); and Maryiln Yalom, *The Social Sex: A History of Female Friendship* (New York: Harper Perennial, 2015).

34. Herbert Eugene Bolton, *The Padre on Horseback: A Sketch of Eusebio Francisco Kino, S. J., Apostle to the Pimas* (San Francisco: Sonora Press, 1932); Herbert Eugene Bolton, *Rim of Christendom: A Biography of Eusebio Francisco Kino, Pacific Coast Pioneer* (New York: Macmillan, 1936); Herbert Eugene Bolton, "The Mission as a Frontier Institution in the Spanish-American Colonies," *American Historical Review* 23, no. 1 (1917): 42–61; John Francis Bannon, *The Spanish Borderland Frontier, 1513–1821* (Albuquerque: University of New Mexico Press, 1974); Edward H. Spicer, *Cycles of Conquest: The Impact of Spain, Mexico, and the United States on Indians of the Southwest, 1533–1960* (Tucson: University of Arizona Press, 1962); Ernest Burrus, *Kino and the Cartography of Northwestern New Spain* (Tucson: Arizona Pioneers' Historical Society, 1965); José Luis Mirafuentes Galván, *La Insurreccion de los series, 1725,* vol. 3 (Mexico City: Archivo general de la nación, 1979); Charles Polzer, *Rules and Precepts of the Jesuit Missions of Northern New Spain* (Tucson: University of Arizona Press, 1976); Peter Masten Dunne, *Pioneer Jesuits in Northern Mexico* (Greenwood Press, 1979); David Weber, *The Spanish Frontier in North America* (New Haven, Conn.: Yale University Press, 1992); John Kessell, *Spain in the Southwest: A Narrative History of Colonial New Mexico, Arizona, Texas, and California* (Norman: University of Oklahoma Press, 2002); Deeds, *Defiance and Deference in Mexico's Colonial North*; Cynthia Radding, *Wandering Peoples: Colonialism, Ethnic Spaces, and Ecological Frontiers in Northwestern Mexico, 1700–1850* (Durham, N.C.: Duke University Press, 1997).

35. See Albert Hurtado, *Intimate Frontiers: Sex, Gender, and Culture in Old California* (Albuquerque: University of New Mexico Press, 1993).

36. Raphael Brewster Folsom makes frequent mention of friendships between Indians and Spaniards, noting that on various occasions Indians welcomed "Europeans into their most sacred rites of friendship, kinship, and alliances." Folsom, *The Yaquis and the Empire,* 70.

37. See, for instance, George Wolfskill and Stanley Palmer, eds., *Essays on Frontiers in World History* (College Station: Texas A&M Press, 1983); A. I. Asiwaju and P. O. Adeniyi, *Borderlands in Africa* (Lagos, Nigeria: University of Lagos Press, 1989); Michiel Baud and Willem Van Schendel, "Toward a Comparative History of Borderlands," *Journal of World History* 8 (Fall 1997): 211–42; Jeremy Adelman and

S. Aron, "From Borderlands to Borders: Empires, Nation-States, and the Peoples in Between in North American History," *American Historical Review* 104 (1999): 814–41; Donna Guy and Tom Sheridan, eds., *Contested Ground: Comparative Frontiers on the Northern and Southern Edges of the Spanish Empire* (Tucson: University of Arizona Press, 1998); Andrew Graybill and Benjamin Johnson, "Introduction: Borders and their Histories in North America," in *Bridging National Borders in North America: Transnational and Comparative Histories*, ed. Andrew Graybill and Benjamin Johnson (Durham, N.C.: Duke University Press, 2010), 1–32; Ramón Gutiérrez and Elliot Young, "Transnationalizing Borderlands History," *Western Historical Quarterly* 41 (Spring 2010): 27–53; and Paul Redman, Cynthia Radding, and Chad Bryant, *Borderlands in World History, 1700–1914* (London: Palgrave Macmillan, 2014).

38. See Miguel León-Portilla, "The Norteño Variety of Mexican Culture: An Ethnohistorical Approach," in *Plural Society in the Southwest*, ed. Edward H. Spicer and Raymond H. Thompson (New York: Interbook, 1972), 77–114; Ana María Alonso, *Thread of Blood: Colonialism, Revolution, and Gender on Mexico's Northern Frontier* (Tucson: University of Arizona Press, 1995); James Brooks, *Captive and Cousins: Slavery, Kinship, and Community in the Southwest Borderlands* (Chapel Hill: University of North Carolina Press, 2002); Thomas Sheridan, *Landscapes of Fraud: Mission Tumacácori, the Baca Float, and the Betrayal of the O'Odham* (Tucson: University of Arizona Press, 2006); Ned Blackhawk, *Violence Over the Land: Indians and Empires in the Early American West* (Cambridge, Mass.: Harvard University Press, 2006); Hämäläinen, *The Comanche Empire*; Lance Blyth, *Chiricahua and Janos: Communities of Violence in the Southwestern Borderlands, 1680–1880* (Lincoln: University of Nebraska Press, 2012); David Yetman, *Conflict in Colonial Sonora: Indians, Priests, and Settlers* (Albuquerque: University of New Mexico Press, 2012).

39. In the *Iliad*, Homer tells the story of Diomedes (an invading Greek) and Glaucus (a Trojan), two men on opposing sides of the Trojan War. During the battle they realized that their grandfathers had actually been guest-friends. The friendship between their grandfathers meant that they too were bound by the same expectations of guest-friendship. Here we have an account of an inherited friendship.

40. See for instance, Alejandro Cañeque, *The Kings Living Image: The Culture and Politics of Viceregal Power in Colonial Mexico* (New York: Routledge, 2004).

41. Evan Killick and Amit Desai, "Valuing Friendship," in *The Ways of Friendship: Anthropological Perspectives*, ed. Amit Desai and Evan Killick (New York: Berhahan, 2010), 1. See also Sandra Bell and Simon Coleman, eds., *The Anthropology of Friendship* (New York: Bloomsbury, 1999).

42. Killick and Desai, "Valuing Friendship," 1. In 1974 anthropologist Elliott Leyton, in his edited volume titled *The Compact: Selected Dimensions of Friendship* (Newfoundland: Institute of Social and Economic Research, Memorial University of Newfoundland, 1975), suggested that Western idealistic notions of friendship could

not be applied to non-Western societies. Social ideals of friendship, he argued, were specific and unique to individual societies.

43.   See Richard Godbeer, *The Overflowing of Friendship: Love Between Men and the Creation of the American Republic* (Baltimore: Johns Hopkins University Press, 2009); and Dale Kent, *Friendship, Love, and Trust in Renaissance Florence* (Cambridge, Mass.: Harvard University Press, 2009).

44.   Killick and Desai, "Valuing Friendship," 1.

45.   See Hugo Nutini, Pedro Carrasco, and James Taggart, eds., *Essays on Mexican Kinship* (Pittsburgh: University of Pittsburgh Press, 1976). In "The Demographic Functions of *Compadrazgo* in Santa María Belén Azitzimititlán and Rural Tlaxcala," Nutini reveals thirty-one types of *compadrazgo* that are sometimes, but not always, determined by friendship.

46.   For an analysis of African friendship patterns in colonial Mexico, see Hermann Bennett, *Africans in Colonial Mexico: Absolutism, Christianity, and Afro-Creole Consciousness, 1570–1640* (Bloomington: Indiana University Press, 2005).

47.   Arthur Rubel, "The Mexican-American Palomilla," *Anthropological Linguistics* 7, no. 4 (1965): 92–97.

48.   In Laredo, Texas, this type of association is referred to as an *amigazco*. In Spain and in Argentina, they are known as *pandillas*.

49.   Sarah Chambers, "Republican Friendship: Manuel Sáenz Writes Women into the Nation, 1835–1856," *Hispanic American Historical Review* 81, no. 2 (May 2001): 230–31.

50.   Rubel, "The Mexican-American Palomilla," 92–97.

51.   See Eric Wolf, "Kinship, Friendship, and Patron-Client Relations in Complex Societies," in *The Social Anthropology of Complex Societies*, ed. Michael Banton (New York: Praeger, 1966); Miguel León de Portilla, *Poesía náhuatl: La de ellos y la mía* (Mexico City: Diana, 2006); George Foster, "The Dyadic Contract: A Model for the Social Structure of a Mexican Peasant Village," *American Anthropologist* 63, no. 6 (1961): 1173–92.

52.   Foster, "Dyadic Contract," 1173.

53.   Foster, "Dyadic Contract," 1178. While the dyadic contract is still used by scholars as a useful framework, contemporary archeologists argue that it depends on the larger social environment as well.

54.   Paul Lazarsfeld and Robert K. Merton, "Friendship as a Social Process: A Substantive and Methodological Analysis," in *Freedom and Control in Modern Society*, ed. Morroe Berger, Theodore Abel, and Charles H. Page (Toronto: Van Nostrand, 1954), 18–66; L. Weiss and M. F. Lowenthal, "Life-Course Perspective on Friendship," in *Four Stages of Life*, ed. Marjorie Fiske Lowenthal, Majda Thurnher, and David Chiriboga (San Francisco: Josey-Bass, 1975), 48–61; J. S. Kon and V. A. Losenkov, "Friendship in Adolescence: Values and Behavior," *Journal of Marriage and the Family* 40 (1978): 143–55.

55.   Plutarch, "On Having Many Friends," in *Moralia*, 96A–B; 97A.

56.   Ray Pahl, *On Friendship* (Cambridge: Cambridge University Press, 2000), 3. See also Gloria Anzaldúa, "(Un)natural Bridges, (Un)safe spaces," in *This Bridge We*

Call Home: Radical Visions for Transformation, ed. Gloria Anzaldúa and Ana Louise King (New York: Routledge, 2002), 1–5.

57. See, for instance, Carol Stearns and Peter Stearns, "Emotionology: Clarifying the History of Emotions and Emotional Standards," *American Historical Association* 90 (October 1985): 813–36; Carol and Peter Stearns, *Anger: The Struggle for Emotional Control in America's History* (Chicago: University of Chicago Press, 1986); John Demos, "Shame and Guilt in Early New England," in *Emotion and Social Change: Towards a New Psychohistory*, ed. Carol and Peter Stearns (Teaneck, N.J.: Holmes and Meier, 1988); William Reddy, *The Navigation of Feeling* (Cambridge: Cambridge University Press, 2001); Barbara Rosenwein, *Emotional Communities in the Middle Ages* (Ithaca, N.Y.: Cornell University Press, 2007).

58. See Johan Huizinga, *The Waning of the Middle Ages: A Study of the Forms of Life, Thought, and Art in France and the Netherlands in the Dawn of the Renaissance* (Edward Arnold and Co., 1924); Norbert Elias, *The Civilizing Process: The History of Manners* (Blackwell Publishing; Revised edition, 2000); Lucien Febvre, "Sensibility in History: How to Reconstitute the Emotional Life of the Past," in *A New Kind of History from the Writings of Lucien Febvre*, ed. Peter Burke, trans. K. Folca (Routledge, 1973).

59. See, for instance, the work of Jonathan Haight on personality traits of Republicans and Democrats and their connections to morality and disgust. See Jonathan Haight, *The Righteous Mind: Why Good People Are Divided by Politics and Religion* (New York: Vintage Books, 2013).

60. Daniel Hruschka, *Friendship: Development, Ecology, and Evolution of a Relationship* (Berkeley: University of California Press, 2010), 18.

61. Jon Elster, *The Cement of Society: A Study of Social Order* (Cambridge: Cambridge University Press, 1989), viii.

62. Octavio Paz, *El orgo philantrópico* (Barcelona: Seix Barral, 1960), 38.

63. Weber, *Bárbaros*, 32–34.

64. Matthew O'Hara describes this concept as including "markers such as occupation, social reputation, and personal networks." See O'Hara, *A Flock Divided: Race, Religion, and Politics in Mexico, 1749–1857* (Durham, N.C.: Duke University Press, 2010), 5.

65. Douglas Cope, *The Limits of Racial Domination: Plebian Society in Colonial Mexico City, 1660–1720* (Madison: University of Wisconsin Press, 1994), 3–5.

66. The scholarship on friendship and sexuality is vast. See, for instance, Caroll Smith Rosenberg, "The Female World of Love and Ritual: Relations Between Women in Nineteenth-Century America," *Signs: Journal of Women in Culture and Society* 1, no. 1 (1975); George L. Mosse, *Nationalism and Sexuality: Respectability and Abnormal Sexuality in Modern Europe* (New York: Howard Fertig, 1985); Lillian Faderman, *Surpassing the Love of Men: Romantic Friendship and Love Between Women from the Renaissance to the Present* (New York: HarperCollins, 2001); Michael Rocke, *Forbidden Friendships: Homosexuality and Male Culture in Renaissance Florence* (Oxford: Oxford University Press, 1996); Katherine O'Donnell and Michael O'Rourke, *Love, Sex, Intimacy and Friendship Between Men, 1550–1800*

(London: Palgrave Macmillan, 2003); Martha Vicinus, *Intimate Friends: Women Who Loved Women, 1778–1928* (Chicago: University of Chicago Press, 2004); William E. Benemann, *Male-Male Intimacy in Early America: Beyond Romantic Friendships* (New York: Routledge, 2006); Sharon Marcus, *Between Women: Friendship, Desire, and Marriage in Victorian England* (Princeton, N.J.: Princeton University Press, 2007); Axel Nissen, *Manly Love: Romantic Friendship in American Fiction* (Chicago: University of Chicago Press, 2009); Kenneth Loiselle, *Brotherly Love: Freemasonry and Male Friendship in Enlightenment France* (Ithaca, N.Y.: Cornell University Press, 2014). Interestingly, the connection between sex and sexuality and friendship has been also taken up by anthropologists who study the animal world; see, for instance, Barbara Smuts, *Sex and Friendship in Baboons* (Chicago: Aldine, 2009).

67. Godbeer, *Overflowing of Friendship*, and Daniel Yaconove, "Abolitionists and the Language of Franternal Love," in *Meanings for Manhood: Constructions of Masculinity in Victorian America*, ed. Mark Carnes and Clyde Griffen (Chicago: University of Chicago Press, 1990).

68. Godbeer, *Overflowing of Friendship*, 5.

69. Ruben Reina, "Two Patterns of Friendship in a Guatemalan Community," *American Anthropologist* 61, no. 1 (February 1959): 44–50.

70. Godbeer, *Overflowing of Friendship*, 4.

71. See C. Stephen Jaeger, *Ennobling Love: In Search of a Lost Sensibility*, Middle Ages Series (Philadelphia: University of Pennsylvania Press: 1999), 15.

72. Ann Twinam, *Public Lives, Public Secrets: Gender, Honor, Sexuality, and Illegitimacy in Colonial Spanish America* (Palo Alto, Calif.: Stanford University Press, 1999); Asuncion Lavrin, *Sexuality and Marriage in Colonial Latin America* (Lincoln: University of Nebraska Press, 1992); Zeb Tortorici, "Against Nature: Sodomy and Homosexuality in Colonial Latin America," *History Compass* 10, no. 2 (2012): 161–78; Zeb Tortorici, "Masturbation, Salvation, and Desire: Connecting Sexuality and Religiosity in Colonial Mexico," *Journal of the History of Sexuality* 16, no. 3 (September 2007): 355–72; Zeb Tortorici, "'Heran Todos Putos': Sodomitical Subcultures and Disordered Desire in Early Colonial Mexico," *Ethnohistory* 54, no. 1 (January 2007): 36–67.

73. Konstan, *Friendship in the Classical World*, 38. "It is important," writes Ivy Schweitzer, "to note that in fifth century B.C.E. Athens, erotic friendship between men coexisted with heterosexual marriage and the fathering of children as a carefully regulated set of pedagogical, pederastic, and social structures that linked young boys of the ruling class to older men who shaped them into citizens. Such strictly complementary erotic relations were meant to lead to a higher spiritual communion and the contemplation of the highest Good through Beauty." See Ivy Schweitzer, *Perfecting Friendship: Politics and Affiliation in Early American Literature* (Chapel Hill: University of North Carolina Press, 2006), 34.

74. Mosse, *Nationalism and Sexuality*, 66. Mosse also notes that in postwar Berlin, "the name 'Friendship' was often used to disguise homosexual or lesbian clubs and journals." Mosse, *Nationalism and Sexuality*, 87.

75. See also Georges Duby and Philippe Aries, eds., *A History of Private Life: Revelations of the Medieval World*, trans. Arthur Goldhammer (Cambridge, Mass.: Belknap Press of Harvard University Press, 1988), 163–67, 238, 240–45.

76. Rebecca Earle, "Letters and Love in Colonial Spanish America," *Americas* 62, no. 1 (July 2005): 17–46.

77. Weber, *Bárbaros*, 101.

78. Godbeer, *Overflowing of Friendship*, 12.

79. Stuart Voss, *On the Periphery of Nineteenth-Century Mexico: Sonora and Sinaloa, 1810–1877* (Tucson: University of Arizona Press, 1982), 2.

80. See Ida Altman, *The War for Mexico's West: Indians and Spaniards in New Galicia, 1524–1550* (Albuquerque: University of New Mexico Press, 2010); Dana Velasco Murillo, *Urban Indians in a Silver City, Zacatecas, Mexico, 1546–1810* (Palo Alto, Calif.: Stanford University Press, 2016); and María Laura Cutrera, *Subordinarlos, someterlos, y sujetarlos al ordern: Rosas y los indios amigos de Buernos Aires entre 1829 y 1855* (Teseo, Argentina: Universidad de San Andrés, 2013).

81. See, for instance, Hämäläinen, *The Comanche Empire*, 123. See also Laws of the Indies, 1513, Ordinance 138.

82. See Thierry Saignes, *Ava y Karai: Ensayos sobre la frontera chiriguano: Siglos XVI–XX* (La Paz, Bolivia: Hisbol, 1990), 131–32. Quoted in Weber, *Bárbaros*, 145.

83. See Laws of the Indies, 1513, Ordinances 136–39.

84. Paul J. Burton, *Friendship and Empire: Roman Diplomacy and Imperialism in the Middle Republic (353–146 BC)* (Cambridge: Cambridge University Press, 2011), 80.

85. Graham Smith, "Introduction. Friendship: An Unanswered Question," *AMITY: A Journal of Friendship Studies* 1, no. 1 (2013): 3.

86. Ann Stoler, "Tense and Tender Ties: The Politics of Comparison in North American History and (Post) Colonial Studies," *The Journal of American History* 88, no. 3 (December 2001): 830, 832.

87. James Scott, *Weapons of the Weak: Everyday Forms of Peasant Resistance* (New Haven, Conn.: Yale University Press, 1987); James Scott, *Domination and the Arts of Resistance* (New Haven, Conn.: Yale University Press, 1992); James Scott, *Seeing Like a State: How Certain Schemes to Improve the Human Condition Have Failed* (New Haven, Conn.: Yale University Press, 1999). See also Robert Darnton, *The Great Cat Massacre and Other Episodes in French Cultural History* (New York: Basic Books, 2009); Sergio Serulnikov, *Subverting Colonial Authority: Challenges to Spanish Rule in Eighteenth-Century Southern Andes* (Durham, N.C.: Duke University Press, 2003). A number of Latin American scholars such as Douglas Cope and Laura Matthew, building on Scott's work, have made similar claims. See Cope, *Limits of Racial Domination*; Laura Matthew, *Memories of Conquest: Becoming Mexican in Colonial Guatemala* (Chapel Hill: University of North Carolina Press, 2012).

88. Both Michel Foucault and Edward Said emphasize language as a central factor in the dissemination of power. See Michel Foucault, *The Order of Things: An Archeology of the Human Sciences* (New York: Vintage, 1994); Edward Said, *Orientalism* (New York: Vintage, 1979).

89. But as Douglas Cope in *The Limits of Racial Domination* reminds us, we should be cautious of fitting plebian behavior into systems of meaning devised by the elite.

90. See Barbara Rosenwein, "Worrying About the Emotions in History," *American Historical Review* 107, no. 3 (2002): 821–45; Barbara Rosenwein, *Emotional Communities in the Early Middle Ages* (Ithaca, N.Y.: Cornell University Press, 2006).

91. Deeds, *Defiance and Deference*, 6.

92. On the connection between warfare, masculinity, and marriage, see Blyth, *Chiricahua and Janos*.

93. See Richard White, *The Middle Ground: Indians, Empires, and Republics in the Great Lakes Region, 1650–1815* (Cambridge: Cambridge University Press, 1991); Weber, *Bárbaros*; Brooks, *Captive and Cousins*; Juliana Barr, *Peace Came in the Form of a Woman: Indians and Spaniards in the Texas Borderlands* (Chapel Hill: University of North Carolina Press, 2007); Hämäläinen, *Comanche Empire*.

94. Graham Allen makes this very point, noting that oftentimes the first problem in approaching the concept of friendship is that there is no agreed-upon criteria for determining what makes a person a friend as opposed to an associate or perhaps an acquaintance. See Graham Allen, *Kinship and Friendship in Modern Britain* (Oxford: Oxford University Press, 1996), 85.

95. Lawrence Stone's classic book *The Family, Sex, and Marriage in England, 1500–1800* (New York: Harper and Row, 1977) focuses on the changes in marriage that occurred over this period of time. One of his main contentions is that companionate marriage began by the eighteenth century to place a focus on emotion as a necessary precursor to marriage. Love and friendship were thus integral elements in this new conceptualization of marriage. By the mid-nineteenth century men and women who wrote to their spouses opened their letters with "my dearest friend" or "my other self." In contemporary parlance, you often hear husbands call their wives their better halves. Earlier scholars had made similar claims. Take, for example, Plutarch, who in his *Moralia* (CE 100) argued that the friendship between husband and wife was of the highest order, and Thomas Aquinas, who in his *Summa Theologiae* (1265–74) wrote that friendship between a man and his wife belonged to the natural order of things.

96. See Alexander Wendt, *Social Theory of International Politics* (Cambridge: Cambridge University Press, 1999), 298–306; Preston King and Graham Smith, *Friendship in Politics: Theorizing Amity in and Between States* (New York: Routledge, 2008).

97. This example is taken from Hruschka, *Friendship*, 17, where he writes: "In the presence of a Wandeki friend, the phrase [described above] means something quite the opposite—unbridled affection and happiness at seeing a companion after a long separation."

98.   Cheryl English Martin has argued that commonly used insults in colonial Chihuahua such as *cabrón* or *cornudo* (both of which meant cuckold) frequently led to violent encounters and in some cases lawsuits, especially if the protagonists were social unequals. In other instances among male friends, however, these insults also reflected a deep endearment or admiration, as argued by Slavoj Žižek (see note 99). See Cheryl English Martin, "Popular Speech and Social Order in Northern Mexico, 1650–1830," *Comparative Studies in Society and History* 32, no. 2 (April 1990): 305–24.

99.   See Slavoj Žižek, "Humanity Is OK, but 99% of People Are Boring Idiots," *The Guardian*, June 10, 2012.

100. Ancient and classical thinkers believed masculine friendships to be superior to those of women. Greek and Roman ideals of friendship were supremely masculine. This notion is reflected in philosophy, in literature, and "in the homey generalizations of the 'person on the street,'" as Paul Wright has argued. See Paul Wright, "Men's Friendships, Women's Friendships and the Alleged Inferiority of the Latter," *Sex Roles* 8, no. 1 (January 1982): 2. But sociologists Alan Booth and Elaine Hess maintain quite the opposite, noting that friendships between women tend to be of a richer and more sincere quality than those of men. See Alan Booth and Elaine Hess, "Cross-Sex Friendships," *Journal of Marriage and the Family* 36, no. 1 (1974): 38–47. See also Patricia McDougall and Shelley Hymel, "Same-Gender Versus Cross-Gender Friendship Conceptions Similar or Different?" *Merrill-Palmer Quarterly* 53, no. 3, Special Issue: Gender and Friendships (July 2007): 347–80. While I do not directly address differences or similarities in the practice of friendship between men and women, I do look at the symbiotic relationship between masculinity and friendship.

101. Barr, *Peace Came in the Form of a Woman*.

102. See, for instance, Earle, "Letters and Love in Colonial Latin America," 17–46. See also William French, *A Peaceful and Working People: Manners, Morals, and Class Formation in Northern Mexico* (Albuquerque: University of New Mexico Press, 1996); William French, *The Heart in the Glass Jar: Love Letters, Bodies and the Law in Mexico* (Lincoln: University of Nebraska Press, 2015).

103. See J. Carrier, "People Who Can Be Friends: Selves and Social Relationships," in Bell and Coleman, *The Anthropology of Friendship*; Victor Manuel Macías-Gonzalez, "Masculine Friendships, Sentiment, and Homoerotics in Nineteenth-Century Mexico: The Correspondence of José María Calderón y Tapia, 1820s–1850s," *Journal of the History of Sexuality* 16, no. 3 (September 2007): 422. Cicero in his *Laelius de Amicitia* also wrote that friendship is impossible without virtue.

104. See Howard Wirada, *The Soul of Latin America: The Cultural and Political Tradition* (New Haven, Conn.: Yale University Press, 2003); Godbeer, *Overflowing of Friendship*, 18.

105. See David Brading, *The First America: The Spanish Monarchy, Creole Patriots and the Liberal State, 1492–1867* (Cambridge: Cambridge University Press, 1993); Jorge Cañizares-Esguerra, *How to Write the History of the History of the New World:*

Histories, Epistemologies, and Identities in the Eighteenth-Century Atlantic World (Palo Alto, Calif.: Stanford University Press, 2001).

106. See Jorge Cañizares-Esguerra, "New World, New Stars: Patriotic Astrology and the Invention of Indian and Creole Bodies in Colonial Spanish America, 1600–1650," *The American Historical Review* 104, no.1 (February 1999): 33–68.

107. Norbert Elias, in his classic study of medieval Europe, addresses a similar form of behavior modification. See Norbert Elias, *The Civilizing Process: Sociogenic and Psychogenic Investigations* (Hoboken, N.J.: Blackwell, 2000).

Chapter One

1. Ivy Schweitzer, "Making Equals: Classical Philia and Women's Friendship," *Feminist Studies* 42, no. 2 (2016): 340. There are some caveats to this assertion, however. Shelomo Goitein, for instance, maintains that in pre-Islamic Arabia friendship was of little import. Though highly valued, friendships were less important than the bonds of blood and kinship. This orientation, however, changed drastically with Muhammad and his followers, who utilized the hand clasp to signify their friendships. From that point on, Goitein writes, "spiritual bonds of the greatest variety became the base of sustained personal relationships transcending family attachments." See Shelomo Goitein, "Formal Friendship in the Medieval Near East," *Proceedings of the American Philosophical Society* 115, no. 6 (December 1971): 485–86. Anthropologist Daniel Hruscska, however, notes that friendship or friendship-like relations have been found by ethnographers "on all inhabited continents and among groups at all levels of social complexity." See Daniel Hruschka, *Friendship: Development, Ecology, and Evolution of a Relatonship* (Berkeley: University of California Press, 2010), 52.

2. See Irving Leonard, *Baroque Times in Old Mexico: Seventeenth Century Persons, Places, and Practices* (Ann Arbor: University of Michigan Press, 1959); Howard Wirada, *The Soul of Latin America: The Cultural and Political Tradition* (New Haven, Conn.: Yale University Press, 2003). For an overview of friendship practices in the English colonies, see Richard Godbeer, *The Overflowing of Friendship: Love Between Men and the Creation of the American Republic* (Baltimore: Johns Hopkins University Press, 2009).

3. Peter Watson, *Ideas: A History of Thought and Invention from Fire to Freud* (New York: HarperCollins, 2005), 88. The *Epic of Gilgamesh* was discovered by Hormuzd Rassam in 1853 and was first translated in the 1870s by George Smith. The earliest fragments of Sumerian Gilgamesh poems date to around 2000 BCE. These individual poems were later incorporated into the full epic known as the "standard version." The version of the epic outlined here was edited and expanded by Sin-lequi-unninni in the middle Babylonian period (1300–1000 BCE). See N. K. Sandars, trans., *The Epic of Gilgamesh* (New York: Penguin, 1972).

4. Sandars, *The Epic of Gilgamesh*.

5.   Sandars, *The Epic of Gilgamesh*. Quoted in Georges Contenau, *Everyday Life in Babylon and Assyria* (London: Edward Arnold, 1954), 204.

6.   *Philia*, as it was understood by the Greeks, did not simply mean a relationship between two people. It encompassed a wide range of social relationships from friendship among family members to acquaintances among travelers. At its core was the notion of the good life and the idea that one must help friends and harm enemies.

7.   *The Iliad*, Caroline Alexander, trans. (Ecco, 2015). Quoted in David Konstan, *Friendship in the Classical World* (Cambridge: Cambridge University Press, 1997), 41.

8.   J. C. Shairp, "Friendship in Ancient Poetry," *The North American Review* 139, no. 336 (November 1984): 461.

9.   María del Carmen Martínez Martínez, "Francisco López de Gómara y Hernán Cortéz: Nuevos testimonios de la relación del cronista con los marqueses del Valle de Oaxaca," *Annuario de Estudios Americanos* 67, no. 1 (January–June 2010): 267–302. Similarly, Fray Gerónimo de Mendieta described Cortés as the new Moses who had opened up the way to the promised land. Mendieta also erroneously believed that Cortés and Martin Luther were born in the same year.

10.   David Brading, *The First America: The Spanish Monarchy, Creole Patriots and the Liberal State, 1492–1867* (Cambridge: Cambridge University Press, 1993), 49.

11.   Joseph Campbell, *The Hero with a Thousand Faces* (1949; repr. Princeton, N.J.: Princeton University Press, 1973).

12.   Schweitzer, "Making Equals," 345.

13.   Schweitzer, "Making Equals," 337.

14.   In the Near East, *xenia*, or "guest-friendships," were known as *rafīq*, which also meant "travel companions."

15.   Konstan, *Friendship in the Classical World*, 4.

16.   H. E. Yuanguo, "Confucius and Aristotle on Friendship: A Comparative Study," *Frontiers of Philosophy in China* 2, no. 2 (April 2007): 294.

17.   Yuanguo, "Confucius and Aristotle on Friendship," 295. See also Shelomo D. Goitein, "Formal Friendship in the Medieval Near East," *Proceedings of the American Philosophical Society* 115, no. 6 (December 1971): 484.

18.   Goitein, "Formal Friendship in the Medieval Near East," 487.

19.   Elsie Clews Parsons, "Ceremonial Friendship at Zuñi," *American Anthropologist* 19, no. 1 (March 1917): 1-8.

20.   Parsons notes that this was common in cases where older men befriended much younger men—Jim was eight at the time. However, in most other cases as when the participants were of equal age, permission was not necessary. See Parsons, "Ceremonial Friendship at Zuñi," 2.

21.   Parsons, "Ceremonial Friendship at Zuñi," 2.

22.   Parsons, "Ceremonial Friendship at Zuñi," 2.

23.   Ruben Reina, "Two Patterns of Friendship in a Guatemalan Community," *American Anthropologist* 61, no. 1 (February 1959): 44–50.

24.   Parsons, "Ceremonial Friendship at Zuñi," 4.

25. For an analysis of the importance of women's friendships in democratic societies, see Sibyl A. Schwarzenbach, "On Civic Friendship," *Ethics* 107, no. 1 (October 1996): 97–128.

26. Elsie Clews Parsons, "Friendship, A Social Category," *American Journal of Sociology* 21, no. 2 (September 1915): 232.

27. 1 Samuel 18:1, in *Holy Bible*, King James Version. See Goitein, "Formal Friendship in the Middle Near East," 484–89. Of some interest in this particular case is the fact that the friendship between Jonathan and David was denoted by the word *berlt*, which meant "covenant," the same word the Bible uses to designate the bond between a husband and his wife.

28. An interesting variation of a friendship dance involves the Ute's Bear Dance in which, through the ritual of dance, friendships are solidified between the human and animal worlds. See Verner C. Reed, "The Bear Dance," *The American Anthropologist* 9 (July 1896): 237–43.

29. Gregory D. Smithers, "'Our Hands and Hearts Are Joined Together': Friendship, Colonialism, and the Cherokee People in Early America," *Journal of Social History* 50, no. 4 (2017): 617.

30. Goitein, "Formal Friendship in the Medieval Near East," 486.

31. Socrates never directly wrote anything about friendship. His ideas about the topic are filtered through the writings of Plato and can be found in his *Lysis*.

32. Shairp, "Friendship in Ancient Poetry," 457. Socrates, Plato, and Aristotle are only a few of the various Greek thinkers who wrote about friendship. Others included Pythagoras, the pre-Socratics, Xenephon, Epicurus, Zeno, and Panaetius.

33. For an analysis of the connection between friendship and civil society, see Peter Miller, "Friendship and Conversation in Seventeenth-Century Venice," *Journal of Modern History* 73, no. 1 (March 2001): 1–31.

34. See Plato's *Lysis* 214 b-d, in Plato, *Complete Works*, trans. H. N. Fowler (Cambridge, Mass.: Harvard University Press, 1914). Quoted in Barbara Cain, ed., *Friendship: A History* (New York: Routledge, 2009), 16.

35. See Plato's *Laws*, trans. with notes and and interpretative essay by Thomas Pangle (Chicago: University of Chicago Press, 1979), 836b, 837a, 837b, 837e, 640b. Quoted in Cain, *Friendship*, 18.

36. Yuanguo, "Confucius and Aristotle on Friendship," 298.

37. Sibyl A. Schwarzenbach, "On Civic Friendship," *Ethics* 107, no. 1 (October 1996): 100.

38. Aristotle, *Nichomachean Ethics: Translated with Introduction, Notes, and Glossary*, trans. Terence Irwin (Indianapolis: Hackett Publishing, 1999), 1155b17–1156a10. Quoted in Jonathan Barnes, ed., *The Complete Works of Aristotle*, vol. 2 (Princeton, N.J.: Princeton University Press, 1984), 1827.

39. Aristotle, *Magna Moralia*, in *Metaphysics*, vol. 2, trans. Hugh Tredenick and G. Cyril Armstrong (Cambridge, Mass.: Harvard University Press, 1935), 2.15.7.

40. Anthony Pagden, "The Diffusion of Aristotle's Moral Philosophy in Spain, ca. 1400–1600," *Taditio* 31 (1975): 287–313; Anthony Pagden, *The Fall of Natural Man:*

The American Indian and the Origins of Comparative Ethnology (Cambridge: Cambridge University Press, 1982).

41. During the Hellenic period Alexander the Great's generals separated the Greek world into four kingdoms, spreading Greek culture throughout the Mediterranean world. Of particular importance was the philosophy of Epicureanism, which promoted the achievement of happiness through the indulging of friendship.

42. Cicero, "De amicita," 6.20. Quoted in Caroline White, *Christian Friendship in the Fourth Century* (Cambridge: Cambridge University Press, 1992), 32.

43. Cicero, "De amicita," 7.23. Quoted in Constant J. Mews, "Cicero on Friendship," in Barbara Caine, ed., *Friendship: A History* (Routledge, 2009), 70. "The man who keeps his eye on a true friend, keeps it, so to speak, on a model of himself." See also Shairp, "Friendship in Ancient Poetry," 466; and Schweitzer, "Making Equals," 344.

44. Cicero, "De amicita," 7.23. Quoted in Schweitzer, "Making Equals," 342.

45. See Seneca, *Ad Lucilium epistulae morales*, ed. and trans. Richard M. Gummere (London: Heiemann, 1917–25); and Seneca, *Letters from a Stoic: Epistulae morales ad Lucilium*, trans. Robin Campbell (Harmondsworth, U.K.: Penguin, 1969).

46. Ahmad ibn-Muhammad Miskawah, *Tahdhīb al-Akhlāq* (*The Refinement of Character*), trans. Constantine K. Zurayk (Beirut: American University of Beirut, 1968). See also Goitein, "Formal Friendship in the Medieval Near East," 486. Miskawah's ruminations on friendship can be found in his Fifth Discourse titled "Love and Friendship."

47. The work of the Church Fathers helped develop the monastic ideal of friendship, something that later Jesuits would incorporate into their own programs of instruction. This shift was a result of the encounter between classical elitism and Christian universalism.

48. John 15:12–15, in *Holy Bible*, King James Version. Quoted in Schweitzer, "Making Equals," 349.

49. Cain, *Friendship*, xi.

50. For an analysis of the ideas on spiritual friendship written by Bernard of Clairvaux and Aelred of Rievaulx, see James Macintosh Houston, ed., *The Love of God and Spiritual Friendship* (Portland, Ore.: Multnomah Press, 1983). This trend carries on into the seventeenth century. In one of Father Eusebio Kino's early letters to the Duchess of Aveiro (1680), he concludes the letter in the following manner: "I repeatedly commend myself to the good prayers of your Excellency and express my highest regards. I pray that you be given all heaven-sent happiness and prosperity with which the divine goodness and might of Our Lord is wont to bless His friends." Ernest Burrus, ed., *Kino Writes to the Duchess: Letters of Eusebio Francisco Kino. S. J. to the Duchess of Aveiro* (Rome: Jesuit Historical Institute, 1965), 69. The original manuscript is kept at the Huntington Library (HM 9996).

51. See Albrecht Classen, "Friendship in the Middle Ages: A Ciceronian Concept in Konrad von Würzburg's Engelhard (ca. 1280)," *Mittellateinisches Jahrbuch* 41, no. 2 (2006): 228; Liz Carmichael, "Monastic Friendship and Aelred of Rievaulx 'Shall I Say—God Is Friendship'?," in Liz Carmichael, *Friendship: Interpreting Christian Love* (New York: T&T Clark, 2004).

52. Carmichael, "Monastic Friendship and Aelred of Rievaulx"; Peter Atkinson, *Friendship and the Body of Christ* (London: SPCK, 2004).

53. See Boncompagno Da Signa, *Amicitia and De Malo Senectutis Et Senii*, Dallas Medieval Texts and Translations (Dudley, Mass.: Peeters, 2012). See also Michael Dunne, "Good Friends or Bad Friends: The Amicitia of Boncompagno da Signa," in *Amor amicitiae: On the Love That Is Friendship: Essays in Medieval Thought and Beyond in Honor of Rev. Professor James McEvoy*, ed. Thomas A. Kelly and Phillip W. Rosemann (Dudley, Mass.: Peeters, 2004); 147–66; and Constant J. Mews and Neville Chiavaroli, "The Latin West," in Cain, *Friendship*, 91.

54. Classen, "Friendship in the Middle Ages," 228.

55. Classen, "Friendship in the Middle Ages," 229.

56. For a translated version of Cicero's *De Inventione*, see H. M. Hubbell, *Cicero: De Inventione, De Optimo Genere Oratorum, Topica* (Ashok: Free Books Online), accessed April 9, 2019, https://archive.org/details/in.ernet.dli.2015.189092.

57. Rebecca Earle, "Letters and Love in Colonial Latin America," *Americas* 62, no. 1 (July 2005): 33.

58. Reginald Hyatte, *The Arts of Friendship: The Idealization of Friendship in Medieval and Early Renaissance Literature* (New York: Kolon, 1994), 2.

59. Alfonso X, *Las siete partidas del Rey Don Alfonso el Sabio*, Tomo III (Madrid: Emprenta Real, 1807), Google Books Online; Florentina del Mar, *La Amistad en la Literatura Española* (Madrid: Editorial Alambra, 1944), 16.

60. Alfonso X, *Las siete partidas*, 145. Title 27 reads: "Del debdo qe han los homes entre si por razon de amistad." Law 1 reads: "Qué cosa es Amistad"; law 2: "A qué tiene pro la amistad"; law 3: "Cómo se debe home aprovechar des consejo del amigo, et qual home debe seer escogido por esto"; law 4: "Quántas maneras son las amistad"; law 5: "Como debe seet guardada la amistad entre los amigos"; law 6: "Cómo el home debe amar á su amigo"; and finally law 7: "Por quáles razones se desata el amistad."

61. Marilyn Stone, *Marriage and Friendship in Medieval Spain* (New York: Peter Lang, 1990), 117.

62. Stone, *Marriage and Friendship in Medieval Spain*, 120.

63. Alfonso, *Las siete partidas*, 7.3.5. Quoted in Stone, *Marriage and Friendship in Medieval Spain*, 122.

64. Stone, *Marriage and Friendship in Medieval Spain*, 119.

65. Anthony Pagden, "The Diffusion of Aristotle's Moral Philosophy in Spain, ca. 1400–1600," *Traditio* 31 (1975): 294.

66. Pagden, "Diffusion of Aristotle's Moral Philosophy in Spain," 294.

67. J. H. Elliott, *Empires of the Atlantic World: Britain and Spain in America, 1492–1830* (New Haven, Conn.: Yale University Press, 2006), 131.

68. Sabatino G. Maglione, "Amity and Enmity in Cervantes's *La Numancia*," *Hispania* 83, no. 2 (May 2000): 179.

69. Pagden, "Diffusion of Aristotle's Moral Philosophy in Spain," 289.

70. Pagden, "Diffusion of Aristotle's Moral Philosophy in Spain," 289.

71. Pagden, "Diffusion of Aristotle's Moral Philosophy in Spain," 209.

72. Maglione, "Amity and Enmity in Cervantes's *La Numancia*," 179.

73. Matthew A. Wyszynski, "Friendship in Garcilaso's Second Eclogue: Thematic Unity and Philosophical Inquiry," *Hispanic Review* 68, no. 4 (Autumn 2000): 397–414.

74. Maglione, "Amity and Enmity in Cervantes's La Numancia," 180.

75. This story is found in Part One, Book Four, of *Don Quixote de la Mancha*. *Don Quixote* was published in two parts between 1605 and 1615.

76. Maglione, "Amity and Enmity in Cervantes's *La Numancia*," 180.

77. Alfonso de Molina, *Vocabvlario en lengva castellana y Mexicana* (Mexico: Antonio de Spinosa, 1571).

78. "Friendship on Earth," MSS *Romances de los Señores de la Nueva España*, fol. 27. Quoted in Miguel León Portilla, *Pre-Columbian Literatures of Mexico*, trans. Grace Lobanov (Norman: University of Oklahoma Press, 1969), 79.

79. "Song of Brotherhood." Quoted in Portilla, *Pre-Columbian Literatures of Mexico*, 80.

80. "Temilotzin's Poem." Quoted in Portilla, *Pre-Columbian Literatures of Mexico*, 81.

81. Poem quoted in Portilla, *Pre-Columbian Literatures of Mexico*, 82.

82. Variations included *amigo en parte onesta, amigo en esta manera, amigo pequeño, amigable cosa, amigo de mujer, amiga de varon, amiga de otra mujer, amiga pequeña, amigar bazer amigos, amigable cosa, amigable como amoroso, amistad, amistad beniuolencia*. See the Real Academia Española at http://ntlle.rae.es/ntlle/SrvltGUILoginNtlle.

83. Real Academia Española.

84. Real Academia Española.

85. Del Mar, *La Amistad en la Literatura Española*.

86. Irving A. Leonard, "Spanish Ship-Board Reading in the Sixteenth Century," *Hispania* 32, no.1 (February 1949): 53–58.

87. Jorge Gracia, foreword to *The History of Philosophy in Colonial Mexico*, by Mauricio Beuchot, O. P., trans. Elizabeth Millán (Washington, D.C.: Catholic University of America Press, 1998), xxi.

88. Brading, *First America*, 5.

89. Gracia, "Foreword," in Beuchot, *History of Philosophy*, xxiii.

90. Pagden, *Fall of Natural Man*, 20. See also Colin M. MacLachlan, *Spain's Empire in the New World: The Role of Ideas in Institutional and Social Change* (Berkeley: University of California Press, 1988), 1.

91. See Wiarda, *Soul of Latin America*, 47. See also Walter Ullmann, *A History of Political Thought: The Middle Ages* (Middlesex, U.K.: Penguin, 1970), 21.

92. Pagden, *Fall of Natural Man*, 20–21.

93. See Francis Fukuyama, *The End of History and the Last Man* (New York: Free Press, 2006).

94. As Colin MacLachlan notes, this colonial discussion was focused chiefly on modes of labor. See MacLachlan, *Spain's Empire in the New World*, 45–66. See also Brading, *First America*; Jorge Cañizares-Esguerra, *How to Write the History of the History of*

the New World: Histories, Epistemologies, and Identities in the Eighteenth-Century Atlantic World (Palo Alto, Calif.: Stanford University Press, 2001).

95.   J. H. Elliott, *Empires of the Atlantic World: Britain and Spain in America, 1492–1830* (New Haven, Conn.: Yale University Press, 2006), 130.

96.   See Jorge Cañizares-Esguerra, "New World, New Stars: Patriotic Astrology and the Invention of Indian and Creole Bodies in Colonial Spanish America, 1600–1650," *The American Historical Review* 104, no. 1 (February 1999): 33–68.

97.   Luna Nájera, "Myth and Prophesy in Juan Ginés de Sepúlveda's Crusading 'Exhortación,'" *Bulletin for Spanish and Portuguese Historical Studies* 35, no. 1 (December 2010): 48–68.

98.   Juan Ginés de Sepúlveda, *Tratado sobre las justas causas de la guerra contra los indios*, ed. Manuel García-Pelayo (Mexico: 1941; repr. 1971), 101, 105. See also Brading, *First America*, 86.

99.   Brading, *First America*, 89.

100. Beuchot, *History of Philosophy*, 28.

101. Bartolomé de Las Casas, *Brevísima relación de la destrucción de las Indias* (1542). For a reprint of this work, see Bartolomé de Las Casas, *Tratados*, 2 vols., ed. Lewis Hanke et al. (Mexico, 1965).

102. See Luis de Granada, *Breve tratado en que se declara de la manera que se podría proponer la doctrina de nuestra santa fe y religión cristiana á los nuevos fieles* (*A Brief Treatise Which Declares the Manner by Which the Doctrine of Our Holy Faith and Christian Religion Can Be Propounded to New Believers*). Quoted in Don Paul Abbott, *Rhetoric in the New World: Rhetorical Theory and Practice in Colonial Spanish America* (University of South Carolina Press, 1996), 14.

103. In particular, Vasco de Quiroga, bishop of Michoacán, was so inspired by More's *Utopia* that he established his famous pueblo-hospitals of Santa Fe along the shores of Lake Pátzcuaro in the communitarian manner outlined by More.

104. Schweitzer, *Perfecting Friendship: Politics and Affiliation in Early American Literature* (Chapel Hill: University of North Carolina Press, 2006), 16.

105. Schweitzer, *Perfecting Friendship*, 16.

106. Alejandro Cañeque, "The Emotions of Power," in *Emotions and Daily Life in Colonial Mexico*, ed. Javier Villa-Flores and Sonya Lipsett-Rivera (Albuquerque: University of New Mexico Press, 2014), 97.

107. See, for instance, Sabine MacCormack, *On the Wings of Time: Rome, the Incas, Spain, and Peru* (Princeton, N.J.: Princeton University Press, 2009).

108. David Weber, *Bárbaros: Spaniards and Their Savages in the Age of Enlightenment* (New Haven, Conn.: Yale University Press, 2005), 17.

109. Pérez de Ribas, *Triumphs*, 440.

110. José de Acosta, *De Procuranda Indorum Salute* (Mexico City: Consejo Superior de Investigacion cientificas, 1987).

111. Francisco de Paula Sanz, *Viaje por el virreinato de Río de la Plata: El camino del Tabaco*, ed. Daisy Rípodas Ardanz (Buenos Aires: Centro de Estudios Interdisci-

plinarios de Hispanoamérica Colonial, Librería Editorial Platero S.R.L., 1977), 81. See also Weber, *Bárbaros*, 17.

112. Matthew D. O'Hara, *A Flock Divided: Race, Religion, and Politics in Mexico, 1749–1857* (Durham, N.C.: Duke University Press, 2010), 64.

113. Anthony Pagden, *Lords of All the World* (New Haven, Conn.: Yale University Press, 1995), 31.

114. Axel I. Mundigo and Dora Crouch, "The City Planning Ordinances of the Laws of the Indies Revisited. Part 1: Their Philosophy and Implications," *The New Town Planning Review* 48, no. 3 (July 1977): 248.

115. Mundigo and Crouch, "City Planning Ordinances of the Laws of the Indies Revisited," 257.

116. Mundigo and Crouch, "City Planning Ordinances of the Laws of the Indies Revisited," 258.

117. Niccolò Machiavelli's *The Prince* was published in 1513, the same year of the Laws of the Indies. I am uncertain about what impact this influential book had on the later 1523 and 1573 amendments.

118. Bernardo de Vargas Machuca, *Milicia y descripción de las Indias, por el Capitan don Bernardo de Vargas Machuca, Cauallero Castellano, natural de la villa de Simancas* (Madrid, 1599), Google Books Online.

119. Machuca, *Milicia y descripción*. Quoted in Richard Morse, "The Urban Development of Colonial Spanish America," in Leslie Bethal, ed., *The Cambridge History of Latin America*, ed. Leslie Bethal, vol. 2 (Cambridge: Cambridge University Press, 1984), 75.

120. Elliott, *Empires of the Atlantic World*, 31.

121. Machuca, *Milicia y descripción*. Quoted in Morse, "Urban Development of Colonial Spanish America," 75.

122. Morse, "Urban Development of Colonial Spanish America," 76.

123. David Yetman, *Conflict in Colonial Sonora: Indians, Priests, and Settlers* (Albuquerque: University of New Mexico Press, 2012), 27.

124. Edward Spicer, *Cycles of Conquest: The Impact of Spain, Mexico, and the United States on Indians of the Southwest, 1533–1960* (1962; repr. Tucson: University of Arizona Press, 2015), 332.

125. Weber, *Bárbaros*, 8.

126. Cañeque, "Emotions of Power," 97.

127. Agustín de Castro, *Conclusiones politicas del Príncipe, y sus virtudes . . . : Question principal, quien deua a quien más amor, el Príncipe a los vassallos, o los vassallos al Principe?* (Madrid, en la Imprenta Real, 1638).

128. Alfonso X, *Las siete partidas*, 2.10.2. Quoted in Colin M. MacLachlan, *Spain's Empire in the New World: The Role of Ideas in Institutional and Social Change* (Berkeley: University of California Press, 1988), 9. See also del Mar, *La amistad en la literatura Española*; Stone, *Marriage and Friendship in Medieval Spain*.

129. See Desiderius Erasmus, *The Education of a Christian Prince*, trans. Lester K. Born (New York, 1936), 175. Quoted in MacLachlan, *Spain's Empire in the New World*, 6.

130. Quoted in MacLachlan, *Spain's Empire in the New World*, 6.

131. Juan Pablo Gil-Osle, "Early Modern Illusions of Perfect Male Friendship: The Case of Cervantes's 'El curioso impertenente,'" *Bulletin of the Cervantes Society of America* 29, no. 1 (Spring 2009): 105.

132. Miguel Lastaria, *Documentos para la historia Argentina, Tomo III, Colonias Orientales del rio Paraguay ó de la Plata* (Buenos Aires: Compañia sud-americana de billetes de banco, 1804), 452.

133. Lastaria, *Documentos para la historia de Argentina*, 396.

134. Lastaria, *Documentos para la historia de Argentina*, 388.

135. Lastaria, *Documentos para la Historia de Argentina*. Quoted in Weber, *Bárbaros*, 15.

136. The documentary record is replete with references to indios amigos as Indians who maintain loyalty to Spaniards while simultaneously engaging in acts of war against their enemies.

137. Elliott, *Empires of the Atlantic World*, 131.

138. Daniel Matson and Bernard Fontana, *Friar Bringas Reports to the King: Methods of Indoctrination on the Frontier of New Spain, 1796–97* (Tucson: University of Arizona Press, 1977), 2.

139. As Elizabeth A. H. John notes, "All that amity among Frenchmen and Indians on the plains seemed to Governor Vélez Cachupín to threaten the very existence of New Mexico." See Elizabeth A. H. John, *Storms Brewed in Other Men's Worlds: The Confrontation of Indians, Spaniards, and French in the Southwest, 1540–1795*, 2nd ed. (Norman: University of Oklahoma Press, 1996), 319.

140. See Eric R. Wolf, "Kinship, Friendship, and Patron-Client Relations in Complex Societies," in *The Social Anthropology of Complex Societies*, ed. Michael Banton (New York: Frederick A. Praeger, 1966): 1–20.

141. See Alejandro Cañeque, *The King's Living Image: The Culture and Politics of Viceregal Power in Colonial Mexico* (New York: Routledge, 2004); Clarence Haring, *The Spanish Empire in America* (New York: Oxford University Press, 1947); Michael C. Meyer, William L. Sherman, and Susan M. Deeds, *The Course of Mexican History*, 9th ed. (Oxford: Oxford University Press, 2011), 117.

142. See Robert Wright, *Non-Zero: The Logic of Human Destiny* (New York: Vintage Books, 2001).

143. José Joaquín Fernández de Lizardi, *El periquillo sarniento*. Quoted in Nancy Vogeley, "Defining the Colonial Reader: El Periquillo Sarniento," *PMLA* 102, no. 5 (October 1987): 794.

Chapter Two

1. J. H. Elliott, *Empires of the Atlantic World: Britain and Spain in America, 1492–1830* (New Haven, Conn.: Yale University Press, 2006), 130.

2.   Gerónimo de Mendieta, *Historia eclesiástica indiana*. Quoted in John L. Phelan, *The Millennial Kingdom of the Franciscans in the New World: A Study of the Writings of Gerónimo de Mendieta (1525–1604)* (Berkeley: University of California Press, 1956), 82.

3.   J. H. Elliot's *The Old World and the New* provides a useful deconstruction for how the New World was understood, articulated, and assimilated into the European imagination. See J. H. Elliot, *The Old World and the New, 1492–1650* (Cambridge: Cambridge University Press, 1992). Here Adam refers to the first man according to the bible.

4.   Quoted in Peter Winn, *The Changing Face of Latin America and the Caribbean* (Berkeley: University of California Press, 2006), 41.

5.   Charles Truxillo, "Hispanic Catholicism in New Spain and New Mexico with Special References to Mora," *Center for Regional Studies* 108 (Summer 1999):2. See also Mario Gongora, *Studies in the Colonial History of Spanish America* (Cambridge: Cambridge University Press, 1975).

6.   Truxillo, "Hispanic Catholicism in New Spain," 2.

7.   Truxillo, "Hispanic Catholicism in New Spain," 2. See also Luis Weckman, *The Medieval Heritage of Mexico* (New York: Fordham University Press, 1992).

8.   Henry Kamen, *Empire: How Spain Became a World Power, 1492–1763* (New York: HarperCollins, 2003), 255.

9.   *Estremeño* refers to someone from the region of Estremadura, Spain.

10.   Scholars have generally acknowledged that most of the indios amigos who accompanied Coronado were Tlaxcallans. David Snow does not, however, see the evidence for this assertion. See David Snow, *New Mexico's First Colonists: The 1597–1600 Enlistment for New Mexico under Juan Oñate, Adelantado and Gobernador* (Albuquerque: Hispanic Genealogical Research Center of New Mexico, 2010).

11.   Kamen, *Empire*, 245.

12.   Elinore Barrett, *Conquest and Catastrophe: Changing Rio Grande Pueblo Settlement Patterns in the Sixteenth and Seventeenth Centuries* (Albuquerque: University of New Mexico Press, 2002), 6.

13.   Carroll Riley, *The Kachina and the Cross: Indians and Spaniards in the Early Southwest* (Salt Lake City: University of Utah Press, 1999), 46.

14.   For more on Oñate, see George P. Hammond and Agapito Rey, eds., *Don Juan de Oñate: Colonizer of New Mexico, 1595–1628* (Santa Fe: Patalacio, 1927; repr., Albuquerque: University of New Mexico Press, 1953); Marc Simmons, *The Last Conquistador: Juan de Oñate and the Settling of the Far Southwest* (Norman: University of Oklahoma Press, 1991).

15.   Relación que envió Don Juan de Oñate de algunas jornadas. Quoted in Herbert E. Bolton, *Spanish Exploration in the Southwest, 1542–1706* (New York: Barnes and Noble, 1908), 234–38.

16.   Kamen, *Empire*, 254.

17. Ramón Eduardo Ruiz, *Triumphs and Tragedy: A History of the Mexican People* (New York: W. W. Norton, 1993), 74. By 1600, silver ore accounted for upwards of 80 percent of exports to Spain and the Far East.

18. For a discussion of the ethnic and economic development of this colonial city, see Dana Velasco Murillo, *Urban Indians in a Silver City: Zacatecas, Mexico, 1546–1810* (Palo Alto, Calif.: Stanford University Press, 2016). See also Gilbert Cruz, *Let There Be Towns: Spanish Municipal Origins in the American Southwest, 1610–1810* (College Station: Texas A&M University, 1996).

19. Cruz, *Let There Be Towns*, 13.

20. James Rodney Hastings, "People of Reason and Others: The Colonization of Sonora to 1767," *Arizona and the West* 3, no. 4 (Winter 1961): 331.

21. Thomas Sheridan, "The Limits of Power: The Political Ecology of the Spanish Empire in Greater Southwest," *Antiquity* 66, no. 250 (March 1992): 159.

22. Stuart F. Voss, *On the Periphery of Nineteenth-Century Mexico: Sonora and Sinaloa, 1818–1877* (Tucson: University of Arizona Press, 1982), 6.

23. There were two main types of mining in northern New Spain. The first type was vein-mining, which required substantial capital to cut shafts, timber to reinforce the shafts, and sufficient resources to maintain and feed a permanent labor force. The second type was placer-mining, which essentially required *bateas* (hard wooden bowls) to pan for gold along the river beds.

24. Sheridan, "The Limits of Power," 159.

25. See James F. Brooks, *Captives and Cousins: Slavery, Kinship, and Community in the Southwest Borderlands* (Chapel Hill: University of North Carolina Press, 2002).

26. Harry Prescot Johnson, "Diego Martínez Hurdaide: Defender of the Northwestern Frontier of New Spain," *Pacific Historical Review* 11, no. 2 (June 1942): 171.

27. Prescot Johnson, "Diego Martínez Hurdaide," 171.

28. Andrés Pérez de Ribas, *History of the Triumphs of Our Holy Faith Amongst the Most Barbarous and Fierce Peoples of the New World*, trans. Daniel T. Reff, Maureen Ahern, and Richard Danford (Tucson: The University of Arizona Press, 1999). Quoted in Raphael Brewster Folsom, *The Yaquis and the Empire: Violence, Spanish Imperial Power, and Native Resilience in Colonial Mexico* (New Haven, Conn.: Yale University Press, 2014), 44.

29. Folsom, *Yaquis and the Empire*, 44.

30. Pérez de Ribas, *Triumphs*, 361.

31. Pérez de Ribas, *Triumphs*, 362.

32. Diego Martínez de Hurdaide, letter to *gobernador* concerning Indian affairs in Sinaloa, San Felipe, February 27, 1616. Archivo General de la Nación, Mexico, Historia, legajo 0316.

33. Pérez de Ribas, *Triumphs*, 338.

34. Pérez de Ribas, *Triumphs*, 360.

35. Pérez de Ribas, *Triumphs*, 360.

36. Evelyn Hu-DeHart, *Yaqui: Resistance and Survival* (Madison: University of Wisconsin Press, 1984), 5.

37. Pérez de Ribas, *Triumphs*. Quoted in David Brading, *The First America: The Spanish Monarchy, Creole Patriots, and the Liberal State, 1492–1867* (Cambridge: Cambridge University Press, 1991), 177.

38. Pérez de Ribas, *Triumphs*, 360.

39. Folsom, *Yaquis and the Empire*, 52.

40. Juan María de Salvatierra, *Relación itineraria de Juan María Salvatierra*, 1701. Archivo General de la Nación, Mexico, Historia, legajo 21. "Que años ha venian acompañando bayle que estos llaman Mico, algunos cuchillos. Es á saber, que vá corriendo ese bayle hasta la última punta de Californias, ó S. Lucas, y no se sabe á donde empieza por lo tocante á tierras del Norte, y corre con cabecitas de paxaros; y animalitos, y plumas varias de paxaros, que dá cada tierra, y si hay otra curiosidad viene corriendo con las prendas del Mico. De suerte, que las rancherias del Norte caminan una, ó dos jornadas, y entregan estas prendas del Mico á otras rancherias mas abajo que reciben los huespedes presentandoles muchas bateas grandes como fuentes de sus semillas, y baylan las prendas unos, y otros con solemnidad, y despues se buelven los primeros á sus tierras, y los segundos de este mesmo modo corren con el Mico mas abajo, y son recibidos con la mesma solemnidad, y asi corren de mano en mano hasta el remate de la tierra; conociendose y confirmandose las amistades, y aplacandose los pleytos de unas naciones con otras."

41. David Yetman, "Pedro de Perea and the Colonization of Sonora," *Journal of the Southwest* 53, no.1 (Spring 2011): 36.

42. Yetman, "Pedro de Perea," 36.

43. David Yetman, *Conflict in Colonial Sonora: Indians, Priests, and Settlers* (Albuquerque: University of New Mexico Press, 2012), 2.

44. Yetman, *Conflict in Colonial Sonora*, 2.

45. Anthony Pagden, *Lords of All the World: Ideologies of Empire in Spain, Britain, and France c. 1500–c.1800* (New Haven, Conn.: Yale University Press, 1995), 95.

46. Voss, *On the Periphery of Nineteenth-Century Mexico*, 12.

47. Sheridan, "The Limits of Power," 158.

48. Ignaz Pfefferkorn, *Sonora: A Description of a Province*, trans. Theodore E. Treutlein (Tucson: University of Arizona Press, 2016).

49. For more on the Pima, see Bernard Fontana, "The O'odham," in *The Pimería Alta Missions and More*, ed. James Officer, Mardith Schuetz-Miller, and Jorge Olvega (Tucson, Ariz.: Southwest Mission Research Center, 1996). Today Pima typically only refers to the Akimel O'odham living along the Gila River near Phoenix.

50. Brading, *First America*, 177.

51. Voss, *On the Periphery of Nineteenth-Century Mexico*, 9.

52. María Laura Cutrera, *Subordinarlos, someterlos y sujetarlos al orden: Rosas y los indios amigos de Buenos Aires entre 1829 y 1855* (Buenos Aires: Tesea, 2014); Silvia Ratto, *Indios y Cristianos: Entre la guerra y la paz en las fronteras* (Buenos Aires: Sudamericana, 2007).

53. Andrea Ruíz Esquide, *Los indios amigos en la frontera Araucana* (Santiago: Impreso de Chile, 1993).

54.   Abelardo Levaggi, "Una institución chilena transplantada al Rio de la Plata: El Capitán de Amigos," *Revista de Estudios Histórico-Juridicos* 13 (1989): 100.

55.   Ida Altman, *The War for Mexico's West: Indians and Spaniards in New Galicia, 1524–1550* (Albuquerque: University of New Mexico Press, 2010).

56.   John Douglas and William Graves, "New Mexico and the Pimería Alta: A Brief Introduction to the Colonial Period in the American Southwest," in *New Mexico and the Pimería Alta: A Brief Introduction to the Colonia Period in the American Southwest*, ed. John Douglas and William Graves (Boulder: University Press of Colorado, 2017), 17.

57.   In another study, Rebecca Earle argues that the rhetoric of the "the loyal Indian" was used by royalist officers during the Wars of Independence in an effort to counter republican claims that Indians had borne the brunt of Spain's backward policies. If this were true, they contented, why were so many Indians fighting against separation from Spain? See Rebecca Earle, "Creole Patriotism and the Myth of the 'Loyal Indian,'" *Past and Present* 172 (August 2001): 125–45.

58.   See, for instance, Jay Kinsbruner, *The Colonial Spanish-American City: Urban Life in the Age of Atlantic Capitalism* (Austin: University of Texas Press, 2005); and Angel Rama, *The Lettered City*, trans. John Charles Chasteen (Durham, N.C.: Duke University Press, 1996).

59.   Mark Simmons, *Witchcraft in the Southwest: Spanish and Indian Supernaturalism on the Rio Grande* (Lincoln: University of Nebraska Press, 1974), 14.

60.   Camila Louerio Diaz, "Jesuit Maps and Political Discourse," *Americas* 69, no. 1 (July 2012).

61.   See Juliana Barr, "Geographies of Power: Mapping Indian Borders in the 'Borderlands' of the Early Southwest," *William and Mary Quarterly* 68, no. 1 (January 2011): 5–46.

62.   For a full rendition of this story, see López de Gómara, *Historia General de las Indias* (Biblioteca Virtual Universal, 2003).

63.   See Robert Ricard, *The Spiritual Conquest of Mexico* (Berkeley: University of California Press, 1966).

64.   Fray Gerónimo de Mendieta, *Historia eclesiástica Indiana*, ed., Joaquín Garcia Icazbalceta (Alicante: Biblioteca Virtual Miguel de Cervantes, 1999). Missionaries saw the Indians as blind to the word of God. This idea is taken from the parable in Luke 14, in which a man (God) gave a supper and invited everyone in the town. He sent out invitations to the townsfolk by way of a messenger (missionaries, the king, and the pope). All those invited began to make excuses for their failure to attend the supper. The first man stated that he had just bought a farm and needed to look over it; the second man responded that he had just purchased five pairs of oxen and needed to attend to those matters; a third said that he had just married and was unable to come. The man holding the supper (God) fell into a rage and so sent word that the poor, the cripples, the blind, and the lame should be compelled to come. But even after this, there was still

room. Then the man said, "Go out into the highways and the hedgerows, and give them no choice but to come in, that my house may be filled. I tell you, none of those who were first invited shall taste of my supper" (Luke 14:23). According to Gerónimo de Mendieta, the first invitation corresponded to the traits of the "perfidious" Jews, the second to the "false" Muslims, and the final invitation to the "blindness" of the Gentiles. The man's servants who had been sent out to bring the people to the supper were the missionaries. See John Leddy Phelan, *The Millennial Kingdom of the Franciscans in the New World* (Berkeley: University of California Press, 1970), 7–11.

65. Elliott, *Empires of the Atlantic World*, 130.

66. For a history of the Franciscans in the New World, see David Rex Galindo, *To Sin No More: Franciscans and Conversion in the Hispanic World, 1683–1830* (Palo Alto, Calif.: Stanford University Press, 2018).

67. Brading, *First America*, 176.

68. Folsom, *Yaquis and the Empire*, 50.

69. See Brading, *First America*; David Brading, *Mexican Phoenix: Our Lady of Guadalupe: Image and Tradition Across Five Centuries* (Cambridge: Cambridge University Press, 2003); Jacques Lafaye, *Quetzalcóatl and Guadalupe: The Formation of Mexican National Consciousness, 1531–1813* (Chicago: University of Chicago Press, 1974).

70. Folsom, *Yaquis and the Empire*, 47. The Jesuit Order was first authorized by a papal bull of Paul III, which was dated September 27, 1540.

71. These inroads were usually made along river systems—for example, the Río Sinaloa, Río Fuerte, Río Sonora, and Río Mayo.

72. John Augustine Donohue, S. J., *After Kino: Jesuit Missions in Northwestern New Spain, 1711–1767* (Rome: Jesuit Historical Institute, 1969), 8. One of the best sources detailing the early history of the Jesuits in northern New Spain during this period is Andrés Pérez de Ribas's *Historia de los Triumphos de nuestra Santa Fé entre Gentes las más bárbaras y fieras ddel Nuevo Orbe; Conquistados por los Soldados de la Milicia de la Compañia de Jesús en las Missiones de Nueva España* (Madrid: A. de Paredes, 1645). Pérez de Ribas first traveled to the New World in 1602 at the age of twenty-seven, completing his studies as a novice in Mexico City before departing to the college in Tepotzotlán two years later to assume his duties as rector and master of novices. In 1626 he took on the title as rector of the Colegio Máximo in Mexico City. After a five-year stint as superior of the Casa Profesa, a position he accepted in 1632, Ribas became the supreme head of the Jesuit Order in New Spain.

73. Voss, *On the Periphery of Nineteenth-Century Mexico* (Tucson: University of Arizona Press, 1982), 3.

74. Herbert Eugene Bolton, *Rim of Christendom: A Biography of Eusebio Francisco Kino, Pacific Coast Pioneer* (New York: Macmillan Company, 1936), 7.

75. William B. Taylor notes that not until after the 1960s did the study of such secondary groups come to the fore. See William B. Taylor, "Between Global Process and Local Knowledge: An Inquiry into Early Latin American Social History, 1500–

1900," in *Reliving the Past: The Worlds of Social History*, ed. Olivier Zunz (Chapel Hill: University of North Carolina Press, 1985), 115–190.

76. Brandon Bayne, "A Passionate Pacification: Sacrifice and Suffering in the Jesuit Missions of Northwestern New Spain, 1594–1767" (PhD diss., Harvard Theological Seminary, 2012), 25.

77. Bayne, "Passionate Pacification," 25.

78. Bayne, "Passionate Pacification," 26.

79. Bayne, "Passionate Pacification," 26.

80. Luis de Granada, *Ecclesiasticae rhetoricae*, bk. 3. Quoted in Abbott, *Rhetoric in the New World*, 12.

81. Abbott, *Rhetoric in the New World*, 16.

82. Folsom, *Yaquis and the Empire*, 51.

83. Pagden, *Lords of All the World*, 31.

84. Elliott, *Empires of the Atlantic World*, 38.

85. This statement is found at the conclusion of the first set of arguments that Aristotle develops in the second chapter of Book One of the *Politics* (Pol. I, 2, 1252a24–1253a3). Quoted in Anthony Pagden, *The Fall of Natural Man: The American Indian and the Origins of Comparative Ethnology* (Cambridge: Cambridge University Press, 1982), 21.

86. Virgil, *The Aeneid*, 6.1151–54. Quoted in Frederick Holland Dewey, trans., *The Aeneid: Interlinear Translation* (Wildside Press, 2008), 312.

87. David Weber, *Bárbaros: Spaniards and Their Savages in the Age of Enlightenment* (New Haven, Conn.: Yale University Press, 2005), 2.

88. Yetman, *Conflict in Colonial Sonora*. 142.

89. Voss, *On the Periphery of Nineteenth-Century Mexico*, 4.

90. Richard Morse, "The Urban Development of Colonial Spanish America," in *The Cambridge History of Latin America*, ed. Leslie Bethal, vol. 2 (Cambridge: Cambridge University Press, 1984), 84.

91. Pagden, *Lords of All the World*, 18.

92. Pagden, *Lords of All the World*, 18.

93. Domingo Faustino Sarmiento, *Facundo: Or, Civilization and Barbarism* (1845; repr. New York: Penguin, 1998).

94. Yetman, *Conflict in Colonial Sonora*, 42.

95. According to Charles Polzer, a *reducción* "applies to an incipient community where the Indians had been gathered together for more efficient and effective administration, both spiritual and temporal. The intention behind forming *reducciónes* was to 'lead the Indian back' form the mountains and woods into a community where he could better learn the rudiments of Christian belief and the elementary forms of Spanish social and political organization." See Charles Polzer, *Rules and Precepts of the Jesuit Missions of Northwestern New Spain* (Tucson: University of Arizona Press, 1976), 7. In this regard, Michael Meyer's work on water scarcity is valuable in that is shows how the struggle for this essential commodity shaped land prices, military defense, and ideological perspectives.

96. Polzer, *Rules and Precepts*, 10.

97. Kamen, *Empire*, 270.

98. See Vanessa Smith, *Intimate Strangers: Friendship, Exchange and Pacific Encounters* (Cambridge: Cambridge University Press, 2010).

99. Kino, *Favores Celestiales*, in *Kino's Historical Memoir of Pimería Alta: A Contemporary Account of the Beginnings of California, Sonora, and Arizona*, ed. and trans. Herbert Eugene Bolton, published for the first time from the original manuscript in the Archives of Mexico (New York: AMS Press, 1976).

100. Kino, *Favores Celestiales*, 93.

101. Kino, *Favores Celestiales*, 93.

102. Kino, *Favores Celestiales*, 112.

103. Kino, *Favores Celestiales*, 126.

104. Salvatierra, *Relación itineraria de Juan María Salvatierra*, 1701. Archivo General de la Nación, Mexico, Historia, legajo 21.

105. Jacobo Sedelmayr, 1748, Holliday Collection, Arizona Pioneers' Historical Society, Reel no: J-07-C-03.

106. Jacobo Sedelmayr, 1748, Holliday Collection, Arizona Pioneers' Historical Society, Reel no: J-07-C-03.

107. Diego Bringas, in *Friar Bringas Reports to the King: Methods of Indoctrination on the Frontier of New Spain, 1796–97*, ed. Daniel S. Matson and Bernard L. Fontana, Documentary Relations of the Southwest: The Franciscan Relat (Tucson: University of Arizona Press, 1977), 25.

108. Bringas, in *Friar Bringas Reports to the King*, 26.

109. Sonora lay several weeks journey from the political seat of the province, which prior to 1630 was Durango. After this date the seat of political power was moved to Parral, which was still a three-week journey.

110. Charles Polzer has argued that isolation was one of the biggest factors in determining the guidelines for missionary work along the frontier, and as a result it became a central theme in the early writings of Sonora's Jesuit population. See Polzer, *Rules and Precepts*. In Michael Meyer's *Water in the Hispanic Southwest*, Meyer addresses the disservice Spaniards committed by relocating Indians into *reducciónes* away from places that the Indians had strategically chosen due to water availability. He argues that in part these *reducciónes* were developed because of the Spanish tendency for urbanity. See Michael Meyer, *Water in the Hispanic Southwest: A Social and Legal History, 1550–1850* (Tucson: University of Arizona Press, 1996).

Chapter Three

1. Irving A. Leonard, *Baroque Times in Old Mexico: Seventeenth-Century Persons, Places, and Practices* (Ann Arbor: University of Michigan Press, 1959), 206.

2. Kino to the Duchess of Aviero, November 15, 1680, in *Kino Writes to the Duchess: Letters of Eusebio Francisco Kino, S. J., to the Duchess of Aveiro*, ed. Ernest Burrus (Rome: Jesuit Historical Institute, 1965), 82. Kino notes that his interest in China

was awakened after having read the life and martyrdom of Reverend Father Charles Spinola. The Duchess of Aviero was well known as a patroness of missions in Asia.

3. Kino to the Duchess of Aviero, November 15, 1680, in Burrus, *Kino Writes to the Duchess*, 82.

4. Irving A. Leonard, *Don Carlos de Sigüenza y Góngora: A Mexican Savant of the Seventeenth Century* (Berkeley: University of California Press, 1929), 56.

5. Sigüenza never became a Jesuit, as he was expelled from the Order in 1667.

6. Anna More, "Cosmopolitanism and Scientific Reason in New Spain: Carlos de Sigüenza y Góngora and the Dispute over the 1680 Comet," in *Science in the Spanish and Portuguese Empires, 1500–1800*, ed. Daniela Bleichmar, Paula de Vos, Kristin Huffine, and Kevin Sheehan (Palo Alto, Calif.: Stanford University Press, 2009), 120. Spanish Creoles were Spaniards born in the New World.

7. See More, "Cosmopolitanism and Scientific Reason in New Spain," for a discussion of this imaginary republic.

8. More, "Cosmopolitanism and Scientific Reason in New Spain," 116.

9. See Erika Rummel, "Professional Friendships Among Humanist: Collaboration or Conspiracy?," in *Laudem Caroli: Renaissance and Reformation Studies for Charles G. Nauert*, ed. Charles Garfield Nauert and James V. Mehl (Kirksville, Mo.: Thomas Jefferson University Press, 1998), 35–44.

10. Rummel's article focuses on three issues: disguised sponsorship, open attempts by an individual to obtain patronage or render services to a fellow scholar, and cases of multiple sponsorship involving letter-writing campaigns. See Rummel, "Professional Friendships Among Humanist."

11. Eobanus Hesus, quoted in Rummel, "Professional Friendships Among Humanist," 37.

12. Rummel, "Professonal Friendships among Humanists," 38.

13. See, for instance, Dmitri M. Bondarenko, "The Second Axial Age and Metamorphoses of Religious Consciousness in the 'Christian World,'" *Journal of Globalization Studies* 2, no. 1 (May 2011): 113–36.

14. Leonard, *Baroque Times in Old Mexico*, 30.

15. Leonard, *Baroque Times in Old Mexico*, 213.

16. Leonard, *Baroque Times in Old Mexico*, 213.

17. Leonard, *Baroque Times in Old Mexico*, 214.

18. The comet was seen over the Spanish sky between November and February. Kino was in Cádiz at the time.

19. Ellen Shaffer, "Father Eusebio Francisco Kino and the Comet of 1680–1681," *Historical Society of Southern California Quarterly* 34, no. 1 (March 1952): 57.

20. Leonard, *Baroque Times in Old Mexico*, 209.

21. See Leonard, *Baroque Times in Old Mexico*, 213.

22. José Rojas Garcidueñas, *Don Carlos de Sigüenza y Góngora, erudito barroco* (Mexico City: Ediciones Xochitl, 1945), 50.

23. Don Carlos de Sigüenza y Góngora, quoted in Shaffer, "Father Eusebio Francisco Kino and the Comet of 1680–1681," 58.

24. On the ideas of Athanasius Kircher, see John E. Fletcher, "Astronomy in the Life and Correspondence of Athanasius Kircher," *Isis* 61, no. 1 (Spring 1970): 52–67. Quoted in Shaffer, "Father Eusebio Francisco Kino and the Comet of 1680–1681," 60.

25. *Exposicion astronomica de el cometa, que el ano de 1680, por los meses de Noviembre y Diziembre, y este ano de 1681 por los meses de Enero y Febrero, se ha visto en todo el mundo, y le ha observado en Ciudad de Cadiz el P. Eusebio Francisco Kino, de la Comnpania de Jesus, con licencia en Mexico por Francisco Rodriguez Luperci* (Biblioteca Virtual Miguel de Cervantes). The book itself is divided into ten chapters, titled as follows: Chapter I, *Que linage de creatura sea el Cometa*; Chapter II, *Que el Cometa no fue más que uno, y de el tiempo que duró*; Chapter III, *Del movimiento, y lugar del Cometa*; Chapter IV, *Del lugar verdadero y aparente del Cometa, y de su Paralaxi*; Chapter V, *Que tanto disto el Cometa del tierra, según se saca y deduce de los principios paralácticos*; Chapter VI, *Que el Cometa no fue elementar, sino celeste donde se comprueba con nuevos argumetos, la exorbitante distancia que a via de nosotros a el, numerados sus leguas según el computo Español*; Chapter VII, *De la similtud cotexo y comparación del Cometa de 1680 y 1681 con el del ano de 1665 y 1665*; Chapter VIII, *De la magnitud y corpulencia del Cometa, y de la longitud de su cauda, reducida su candidad a legus Españolas*; Chapter IX, *De la atmosphera del cuerpo del Cometa, y de que fuerte se forma su cauda, per se varie y fenezca*; Chapter X, *De lo que prognostica Cometa de 1680 y 1681 o que anuncio prospero o infeliz amague*.

26. Burrus, *Kino Writes to the Duchess*, 9.

27. Eusebio Kino, letter to Luis Espinosa, 1680. Quoted in Burrus, *Kino Writes to the Duchess*, 97.

28. Eusebio Kino, letter to Luis Espinosa, 1680. Quoted in Burrus, *Kino Writes to the Duchess*, 97. His measurements were thus, "I estimate its distance from the earth at 3,000 leagues or more, and the length of its train at 5,444 leagues, which is more than thrice the earth's radius." 97.

29. More, "Cosmopolitanism and Scientific Reason in New Spain," 118.

30. Natalie Zemon Davis, "Beyond the Market: Books as Gifts in Sixteenth-Century France: The Prothero Lecture," *Transactions of the Royal Historical Society*, Fifth Series 33 (1983): 86.

31. Sigüenza, *Libra astronómica y filosófica*, ed. José Goas (Mexico, 1954). Quoted in More, "Cosmopolitanism and Scientific Reason in New Spain," 126.

32. Leonard, *Baroque Times in Old Mexico*, 207.

33. Kino, *Exposición astronómica*. Quoted in Leonard, *Baroque Times in Old Mexico*, 207.

34. Sigüenza, *Libra asronómica*. Quoted in Moore, "Cosmopolitanism and Scientific Reason in New Spain," 121.

35. Sigüenza, *Libra astronómica*. Quoted in Moore, "Cosmopolitanism and Scientific Reason in New Spain," 122.

36. Francis L. Ramos, *Identity, Ritual, and Power in Colonial Puebla* (Tucson: University of Arizona Press, 2012), 136.

37. David Brading, *The First America: The Spanish Monarchy, Creole Patriots and the Liberal State 1492–1867* (Cambridge: Cambridge University Press, 1993), 367.

38.   Sigüenza, *Libra astronómica.* Quoted in Moore, "Cosmopolitanism and Scientific Reason in New Spain," 123.

39.   Leonard, *Baroque Times in Old Mexico,* 210.

40.   Brading, *First America,* 368.

41.   Sigüenza, *Libra astronómica.* Quoted in Shaffer, "Father Eusebio Francisco Kino and the Comet of 1680–1681," 65.

42.   Sigüenza, *Libra astronómica.* Quoted in Brading, *First America,* 367.

43.   Sigüenza, *Libra astronómica.* Quoted in Leonard, *Baroque Times in Old Mexico,* 206.

44.   Sigüenza, *Libra astronómica.* Quoted in Leonard, *Baroque Times in Old Mexico,* 208.

45.   Interestingly, Bolton's hagiographic account of Kino makes no mention of this event. Instead, Bolton notes that "before leaving Mexico, Kino prepared himself for his scientific task by studying California geography, borrowing maps for the purpose from the viceroy's palace and taking them to the Colegio Máximo de San Pedro y Pablo to copy." See Herbert Eugene Bolton, *The Padre on Horseback: A Sketch of Eusebio Francisco Kino, Apostle to the Pimas* (San Francisco: Sonora Press, 1932), 33.

46.   Shaffer, "Father Eusebio Francisco Kino and the Comet of 1680–1681," 66.

47.   More, "Cosmopolitanism and Scientific Reason in New Spain," 120.

48.   Anthony Grafton, "A Sketch Map of a Lost Continent: The Republic of Letters," *Republics of Letters* 1, no. 1 (July 2009): 14.

49.   Sigüenza, *Libra astronómica.* Quoted in Shaffer, "Father Eusebio Francisco Kino and the Comet of 1680–1681," 66.

50.   More, "Cosmopolitanism and Scientific Reason," 122.

51.   Shaffer, "Father Eusebio Francisco Kino and the Comet of 1680–1681," 67.

52.   The scholarship on Kino is extensive. See for instance, Boniface Bolognani, *Pioneer Padre: A Biography of Eusebio Francisco Kino, S. J., Missionary, Discoverer, Scientist* (Sherbrooke, Quebec: Editions Paulines, 1968); Bolton, *Padre on Horseback*; Herbert Eugene Bolton, *Rim of Christendom: A Biography of Eusebio Francisco Kino, Pacific Coast Pioneer* (New York: Macmillan, 1936); Ernest J. Burrus, *Kino and Manje: Explorers of Sonora and Arizona* (Rome: Jesuit Historical Institute, 1971); Ben Clevenger, *Far Side of the Sea: The Story of Kino and Manje in the Pimería* (Tucson: Jesuit Fathers of Southern Arizona, 2003); Jane Candia Coleman, *The White Dove* (Glendo, Wyo.: High Plains Press, 2007); Fay Jackson Smith, John L. Kessell, and Francis J. Fox, *Father Kino in Arizona* (Phoenix: Arizona Historical Foundation, 1966); Frank C. Lockwood, *With Padre Kino on the Trail* (Tucson: University of Arizona, 1934); Jorge H. Olvera, *Finding Father Kino: The Discovery of the Remains of Father Eusebio Francisco Kino, S. J.* (Tucson, Ariz.: Southwestern Mission Research Center, 1998); Charles W. Polzer, *Kino, a Legacy: His Life, His Works, His Missions, His Monuments* (Tucson: Jesuit Fathers of Southern Arizona, 1998); Rufus Kay Wyllys, *Pioneer Padre: The Life and Times of Eusebio Francisco Kino* (Dallas: Southwest Press, 1935).

53.   Kino's mission at Dolores was constructed near the Indian village of Cosari.

54.   Bolton, *Padre on Horseback.*

55. Herbert Eugene Bolton, ed., *Kino's Historical Memoir of Pimería Alta* (Berkeley: University of California Press, 1948), 22.

56. See Ernest J. Burrus, "Kino, Historian's Historian," *Arizona and the West* 4, no. 2 (Summer 1962): 146.

57. Burrus, "Kino, Historian's Historian," 151.

58. Kino, *Favores Celestiales*, reprinted in Bolton, *Historical Memoir*, 43.

59. Quoted in Charles Polzer, *Rules and Precepts of the Jesuit Missions of Northwestern New Spain* (Tucson: The University of Arizona Press, 1976), 45.

60. Polzer, *Rules and Precepts*, 45.

61. Polzer, *Rules and Precepts*, 45.

62. Polzer, *Rules and Precepts*, 54.

63. Polzer, *Rules and Precepts*, 49.

64. Luis de Verlarde, quoted in Bolton, *Historical Memoir*, 63.

65. Francisco Xavier Saeta, quoted in Bolton, *Historical Memoir*, 134.

66. Manuel Gonzáles, quoted in Francisco Xavier de Mora, S. J., Juan de Palacios, S. J., and Gabriel Gómez Padilla, *Kino, ¿Frustrado alguacil y mal misionero?: Informe de Francisco Xavier de Mora SJ al provincial Juan de Palacios, Arizpe, 28 de Mayo de 1698*, trans. Gabriel Gómez Padilla (Guadalajara: Universidad de Guadalajara, 2004). At the time of Kino's arrival in the Pimería, Gonzáles was the visitor general. Kino speaks fondly of the father visitor. See Kino, *Favores Celestiales*, reprinted in Bolton, *Historical Memoir*.

67. Padre Francisco Xavier de Mora, Arizipe, March 30, 1709. Arch. Hist. Hacienda, México. Temp. legajo 0325, no. 078. Microfilm copy in the Office of Ethnohistorical Research, Arizona State Museum, University of Arizona, Tucson.

68. By this time Polici had received reports from several soldiers about Kino's actions in the Pimería. See, for instance, Relación de Capitan Cristobal Martin Bernal al padre visitador horacio polici, 1697. AZTM. Jesuit Hist. Inst. Amer. Div., Tucson , Ariz. Mf. J-02-D-09.

69. Letter from Francisco Xavier de Mora to the viceroy, October 3, 1696. Western Americana Collection, Beinecke Rare Book and Manuscript Library, Yale University. WA MSS S-1515 Xa5. For a reproduction of the letter, see Padilla, *Kino, ¿Frustrado alguacil y mal misionero?*.

70. Letter from Francisco Xavier de Mora to the viceroy, October 3, 1696.

71. Eusebio Kino, response to Francisco Xavier de Mora to viceroy, October 7, 1696. Western Americana Collection, Beinecke Rare Book and Manuscript Library, Yale University.

72. Eusebio Kino, *Favores Celestiales*. Also quoted in Kino, *Favores celestiales*, reprinted in Bolton, *Historical Memoir*, 98.

73. Polzer, *Rules and Precepts*, 54.

Chapter Four

1. Letter from Don Francisco del Castillo Betanuer, July 19, 1686. Archivo Histórico del Hidalgo de Parral, Chihuahua, México. Microfilm copy in the University of

Arizona Main Library, film 0318, reel 1686B, fr. 758–803, Tucson. Santa Cruz de Quíburi was a Sobaipuri settlement located along the San Pedro River valley. See Map 1. The Janos, Jocomes, and Sumas were located to the northeast in the region of Chihuahua. According to Forbes, the Janos and Sumas may have been the same people. In any case, they occupied the same area, just south of modern-day El Paso, Texas. After the 1680s the Janos and Jocomoes were located in the Chiricahua Mountains of southeastern Arizona. David Weber wrote: "Throughout the vast lands just below the present United States-Mexican border, exploited natives, many of them mission Indians such as Janos, Sumas, Conchos, Tobosos, Julimes, and Pimas, ravaged missions and settlements and fled from Spanish oppression." See David Weber, *The Spanish Frontier in North America* (New Haven, Conn.: Yale University Press, 1992), 137.

2. Pérez de Ribas's *Triumphs of the Holy Faith* provides several instances in which he personally took it upon himself to befriend individual Indians. See Andrés Pérez de Ribas, *History of the Triumphs of Our Holy Faith Amongst the Most Barbarous and Fierce Peoples of the New World*, trans. Daniel T. Reff, Maureen Ahern, and Richard Danford (Tucson: The University of Arizona Press, 1999).

3. Raphael Brewster Folsom, *The Yaquis and Their Empire: Violence, Spanish Imperial Power, and Native Resilience in Colonial Mexico* (New Haven, Conn.: Yale University Press, 2014), 52.

4. Antonio Ruiz de Montoya, *Conquista spiritual hecha por los religiosos de la compañia de Jesús en las provincias del Paraguay, Paraná, Uruguay, y Tape*, first published in 1639, 2nd ed. (Bilbao, 1892). David Brading, *The First America: The Spanish Monarchy, Creole Patriots and the Liberal State, 1492–1867* (Cambridge: Cambridge University Press, 1993), 172.

5. Martin Nesvig argues, however, that the Inquisition may not have been as all-powerful as earlier works have led us to believe. See Martin Austin Nesvig, *Promiscuous Power: An Unorthodox History of New Spain* (Austin: University of Texas Press, 2018).

6. Brading, *First America*, 171.

7. David Weber, *Bárbaros: Spaniards and Their Savages in the Age of Enlightenment* (New Haven, Conn.: Yale University Press, 2006), 142.

8. Charles Cutter, *The Legal Culture of Northern New Spain, 1700–1810* (Albuquerque: University of New Mexico Press, 1995). In his *History of the Triumphs*, Andrés Pérez de Ribas outlined many of the reasons why the Yaqui Indians named Lautaro and Babilonio sought to persuade their people to engage in war with the Spanish. See Andrés Pérez de Ribas, *History of the Triumphs of Our Holy Faith Amongst the Most Barbarous and Fierce Peoples of the New World*, trans. Daniel T. Reff, Maureen Ahern, and Richard Danford (Tucson: University of Arizona Press, 1999), 339.

9. Sylvia Sellers-García, *Distance and Documents at the Spanish Empire's Periphery* (Palo Alto, Calif.: Stanford University Press, 2014), 26.

10. Though Spanish was considered the language of empire, most Iberians spoke regional languages such as Catalan, Basque, and Gaelic. Few outside Castile

understood formal Spanish. Even in the New World, for much of the colonial period Spanish was in the minority as most people spoke their native languages from America, Europe, and Africa.

11. As Stuart Voss writes, during the colonial period Sonora's geographical isolation and royal disinterest meant that Sonorans were largely left to fix their own problems. Stuart Voss, *On the Periphery of Nineteenth-Century Mexico: Sonora and Sinaloa, 1810–1877* (Tucson: University of Arizona Press, 1982).

12. Zeb Tortorici, "Visceral Archives of the Body: Consuming the Dead, Digesting the Divine," *Journal of Gay and Lesbian Studies* 20, no. 4 (2014): 409.

13. See Natalie Zemon Davis, *Fiction in the Archives: Pardon Tales and Their Tellers in Sixteenth-Century France* (Palo Alto, Calif.: Stanford University Press, 1987).

14. Don Antonio Barba Figueroa, Auto de Torment, November 7. "Criminal contra y Yndio llamado Canuto [*sic*] por haber sido traidor á la Real Corona, 1686." Archivo Histórico del Hidalgo de Parral, Chihuahua, México. Microfilm copy in the University of Arizona Main Library, film 0318, reel 1686B, fr. 758–803, Tucson. "Canito y el yndio llamado el coyote le dixo dho' Gobernador de cocospora en [manchado:tr] an en fe de amigos entre los españoles ben y rreconoçen lo que para entre dhos' españóles y luego ban y dan quentta a dhas' nasiones Jocomes y Janos de la prebençion."

15. P. E. Digeser provides a useful framework for distinguishing between variations in the use of term *friendship*. He writes, "Ordinary language allows us to distinguish between 'acting friendly' and 'being friends' and between 'befriending' someone (that is providing assistance and support) and 'being a friend.' . . . Using phrases such as 'acting friendly', 'befriending someone', 'being a friend to' do not require either mutuality or feeling of friendship. Instead, these terms are purely or largely behavioral in that they can be successfully deployed with a variety or absence of feelings." See P. E. Digeser, "Friendship Between States," *British Journal of Political Science*, 39, no. 2 (April 2009): 327n9.

16. Weber, *Bárbaros*, 39.

17. See Javier Villa-Flores, "Reframing a 'Dark Passion': Bourbon Morality, Gambling, and the Royal Lottery in New Spain," in *Emotions and Daily Life in Colonial Mexico*, ed. Javier Villa-Flores and Sonya Lipsett-Rivera (Albuquerque: University of New Mexico Press, 2014), 164. See also Norbert Elias, *The Civilizing Process: Sociogenic and Psychogenic Investigations*, rev. ed., trans. Edmund Jephcott (Oxford: Oxford University Press, 2000).

18. Virginia Company Charter, 1609. Quoted in Anthony Pagden, *Lords of All the World* (New Haven, Conn.: Yale University Press, 1995), 35.

19. Alfredo Jiménez, "Who Controls the King?," in *Choice, Persuasion, and Coercion: Social Control on Spain's North American Frontiers*, ed. Jesús de la Teja and Ross Frank (Albuquerque: University of New Mexico Press, 2005), 20.

20. Jiménez, "Who Controls the King?," 20. In *The Civilizing Process*, Elias makes a similar claim. He argues, for instance, that once the constant wars and feuds of the Middle Ages receded, the battle became internalized; thus, "an individualized pattern of near-automatic habits is established and consolidated within [the human

being], a specific 'super ego,' which endeavors to control, transform, or suppress his affects in keeping with the social structure." Elias, *The Civilizing Process*, 375.

21. Susan Deeds, "Subverting the Social Order: Gender, Power, and Magic in Nueva Vizcaya," in Teja and Frank, *Choice, Persuasion, and Coercion*, 113.

22. Barbara Rosenwein, *Emotional Communities in the Early Middle Ages* (Ithaca, N.Y.: Cornell University Press, 2006), 2.

23. Rosenwein, *Emotional Communities*, 2.

24. Alejandro Cañeque, "The Emotions of Power: Love, Anger, and Fear, or How to Rule the Spanish Empire," in Villa-Flores and Lipsett-Rivera, *Emotions and Daily Life in Colonial Mexico*, 97. See also Jiménez, "Who Controls the King?," 5.

25. See Ramon Gutierrez, *When Jesus Came the Corn Mothers Went Away: Marriage, Sexuality, and Power in New Mexico, 1500–1846* (Palo Alto, Calif.: Stanford University Press, 1991); Patricia Seed, *To Love, Honor, and Obey in Colonial Mexico: Conflicts over Marriage Choice, 1574–1821* (Palo Alto, Calif.: Stanford University Press, 1992); Albert Hurtado, *Intimate Frontiers: Sex, Gender, and Culture in Old California* (Albuquerque: University of New Mexico Press, 1999); and Douglas Cope, *The Limits of Racial Domination: Plebian Society in Colonial Mexico City, 1660–1720* (Madison: University of Wisconsin Press, 1994).

26. See Robert Alun Jones, *Émile Durkheim: An Introduction to Four Major Works* (Thousand Oaks, Calif.: SAGE Publications, 1986), 82–114.

27. See, for instance, Louis M. Burkhart, "The Destruction of Jerusalem as Colonial Nahuatl Historical Drama," in *The Conquest All Over Again: Nahuas and Zapotecs Thinking, Writing, and Painting Spanish Colonialism*, ed. Susan Schroeder (Portland, Ore.: Sussex Academic Press, 2011): 74–100.

28. See, for instance, Serge Gruzinski, *The Mestizo Mind: The Intellectual Dynamics of Colonization and Globalization* (New York: Routledge, 2002).

29. Jiménez, "Who Controls the King?," 3. See also Laura E. Matthew and Michel R. Oudijk, eds., *Indigenous Conquistadors Indian Conquistadors: Indigenous Allies in the Conquest of Mesoamerica* (Tulsa: University of Oklahoma Press, 2014).

30. Charles Truxillo, "Hispanic Catholicism in New Spain and New Mexico with Special Reference to Mora," *Center for Regional Studies* 108 (Summer 1999): 7.

31. William French, *The Heart in a Glass Jar: Love Letters, Bodies, and the Law in Mexico* (Lincoln: Nebraska University Press, 2015), 37.

32. Alejandro Cañeque argues that for elite Spaniards living in Mexico City the rules of proper etiquette created "mental maps" for how people should and shouldn't behave in public. See Alejandro Cañeque, *The King's Living Image: The Culture and Politics of Viceregal Power in Colonial Mexico* (New York: Routledge, 2004), 138.

33. See Paul J. Burton, *Friendship and Empire: Roman Diplomacy and Imperialism in the Middle Republic (353–146 BC)* (Cambridge: Cambridge University Press, 2011), 78; Craig A. Williams, *Reading Roman Friendship* (Cambridge: Cambridge University Pres 2012).

34. Sonya Lipsett-Rivera, *Gender and the Negotiation of Daily Life in Mexico, 1750–1856* (Lincoln: University of Nebraska Press, 2012), 31–67.

35. Lipsett-Rivera, *Gender and the Negotiation of Daily Life*, 33.

36. Gaston Bachelard, *The Poetics of Space*, trans. Maira Jolas (New York: Orien Press, 1964).

37. James Taylor Carson notes that we should "view the native landscape as both a cultural and moral space." See James Taylor Carson, "Ethnogeography and the Native American Past," *Ethnohistory* 49, no. 4 (Fall 2002): 783.

38. Folsom, *Yaquis and the Empire*, 7.

39. Joanne Rappaport and Tom Cummings, *Beyond the Lettered City: Indigenous Literacies in the Andes* (Durham, N.C.: Duke University Press, 2012), 188.

40. According to Cynthia Radding, the colonial pact represented a complex of "political ties between the Spanish Crown and Indian communities through which communities asserted certain basic claims to their means of livelihood and to a degree of local autonomy for their internal governance." See Cynthia Radding, *Wandering Peoples: Colonialism, Ethnic Spaces, and Ecological Frontiers in Northwestern Mexico, 1700–1850* (Durham, N.C.: Duke University Press, 1997), 52–53.

41. See, for instance, David Yetman's discussion on shifting social alliances in *Conflict in Colonial Sonora: Indians, Priests, and Settlers* (Albuquerque: University of New Mexico Press, 2012), 1–2.

42. For a scholarly discussion on the potential causes of the Pueblo Revolt, see David J. Weber, ed., *What Caused the Pueblo Revolt of 1680?* (Boston: Bedford/St. Martin's, 1999).

43. The Spanish would reconquer New Mexico in 1692. For a general overview of the Pueblo Revolt, see Andrew L. Knaut, *The Pueblo Revolt of 1680: Conquest and Resistance in Seventeenth-Century New Mexico* (Norman: University of Oklahoma Press, 1995).

44. Yetman, *Conflict in Colonial Sonora*, 80.

45. Ned Blackhawk, *Violence Over the Land: Indians and Empires in the Early American West* (Cambridge, Mass.: Harvard University Press, 2006). 32.

46. Deeds, "Subverting the Social Order," 103.

47. Ellen Shaffer, "Father Eusebio Francisco Kino and the Comet of 1680–1681," *The Historical Society of Southern California Quarterly* 34, no. 1 (March 1952): 60.

48. Yetman, *Conflict in Colonial Sonora*, 95.

49. Luis Navarro Garcia, *Sonora y Sinaloa en el Siglo XVII* (Sevilla: Consejo Superior de Investigaciones Cientificas, 1967), 265.

50. Yetman, *Conflict in Colonial Sonora*, 90.

51. Ann Laura Stoler, *Along the Archival Grain: Epistemic Anxieties and Colonial Common Sense* (Princeton, N.J.: Princeton University Press, 2010), 20.

52. Yetman, *Conflict in Colonial Sonora*, 81.

53. Thomas Sheridan, "The Limits of Power: The Political Ecology of the Spanish Empire in Greater Southwest," *Antiquity* 66, no. 250 (March 1992): 161.

54. Lance Blyth, *Chiricahua and Janos: Communities of Violence in the Southwestern Borderlands, 1680–1880* (Lincoln: University of Nebraska Press, 2015), 24–55.

55. Don Antonio Barba Figueroa, Auto de Torment, November 7. "Criminal contra y Yndio llamado Canuto [*sic*] por haber sido traidor á la Real Corona, 1686." Archivo Histórico del Hidalgo de Parral, Chihuahua, México. Microfilm copy in the University of Arizona Main Library, film 0318, reel 1686B, fr. 758–803, Tucson. "<V>n hindio llamado el coyote y otro llamado el malaya y asimesmo, otro que comunmente llaman el canitto son los que conmueben y amparan a los Janos y Jocomes y les dan el modo y forma de urtar la caballada a los españo les y asimesmo dho' Canito y el yndio llamado el coyote le dixo dho' Gobernador de cocospora en [manchado:tr] an en fe de amigos entre los españoles ben y rreconoçen lo que para entre dhos' españóles y luego ban y dan quentta a dhas' nasiones Jocomes y Janos de la prebençion . . ." The translations for this essay were the product of a collaborative effort, which took place at the Office of Ethnohistorical Research at the Arizona State Museum from 2010 to 2012. The analysis and interpretation of these documents are my own. Any errors or inaccuracies of words or phrases are also my own.

56. Bernal Díaz del Castillo writes about the deceptive nature of the Indians during the conquest of Mexico who practiced deceptive displays of friendship to leer the Spaniards close, only to promptly ambush them. See Bernal Díaz del Castillo, *Historia verdadera de la conquista de la Nueva España* (1576).

57. For examples of these types of resistance strategies, see James Scott, *Weapons of the Weak: Everyday Forms of Peasant Resistance* (New Haven, Conn.: Yale University Press, 1987).

58. It is important to recognize that the actual Indian voice is difficult to ascertain since most declarations are provided by means of a Spanish interpreter and written down by Spanish scribes.

59. Don Antonio Barba Figueroa, Auto de Torment, November 7. "Criminal contra y Yndio llamado Canuto [*sic*] por haber sido traidor á la Real Corona, 1686." Archivo Histórico del Hidalgo de Parral, Chihuahua, México. Microfilm copy in the University of Arizona Main Library, film 0318, reel 1686B, fr. 758–803, Tucson. "Comun., m.te llaman pio pio. y muy afecto. y amigo de los españoles Segun. es publico. y ñotorio . . . y que luego enpezo el canito ablar en castilla con ellos y que los abrazo y que este testigo no entendio lo que les dezia porque les abla<u>a en castilla. . . . En otraôcaz.on estubieron. en la Rancheria de los ajos. en la cassa donde bi<u>e dho yndio Canito y el con ellos. y les cojia. La mano y trata<u>a Como amigos y familiares Suios."

60. See Paul Burton, *Friendship and Empire: Roman Diplomacy and Imperialism in the Middle Republic (353–146 BC)* (Cambridge: Cambridge University Press, 2011).

61. Burton, *Friendship and Empire*, 41, 97–98.

62. Ivy Schweitzer, *Perfecting Friendship: Politics and Affiliation in Early American Literature* (Chapel Hill: University of North Carolina Press, 2006), 18.

63. Teurícache was located to the south of Corodéguache (also known as Fronteras), which was located along the Río Moctezuma. On Map 1, Fronteras is located to

the far right. Because of extreme isolation, Teurícache was later relocated. This is why it is not identified on Map 1.

64. Don Antonio Barba Figueroa, Auto de Torment, November 7. Criminal contra y Yndio llamado Canuto [*sic*] por haber sido traidor á la Real Corona, 1686." Archivo Histórico del Hidalgo de Parral, Chihuahua, México. Microfilm copy in the University of Arizona Main Library, film 0318, reel 1686B, fr. 758–803, Tucson. "Dixo q' lo que dise dho yndio Jeentil es que le a oydo desiir a un yndio Jentil que comun mente llaman el canito que para que hera el en el mundo si no bengaba la muerte que dio a su hermano la Justicia de los españoles y asimesmo declara dho yndio Jentil Segun los dise el interprete q' a oydo desir a los mismos parientes del dho' yndio canito que para la bengança de la muerte de su hermano les desia su pariente el Canito Se aria amigo de los Sumas Jocomes y Janos para con su ayuda destruir y acabar la caballada de los españoles ynposibilitandolos para que no tubiesen con q' poder aserles guerra y biendolos a pie el Con todos sus amigos los confederados y amistados con el daran a los españoles y matarlos."

65. Don Antonio Barba Figueroa, Auto de Torment, November 7. "Criminal contra y Yndio llamado Canuto [*sic*] por haber sido traidor á la Real Corona, 1686." Archivo Histórico del Hidalgo de Parral, Chihuahua, México. Microfilm copy in the University of Arizona Main Library, film 0318, reel 1686B, fr. 758–803, Tucson. "Los yndios janos jocomes y sumas les querian dar en su rancheria para matarlos y que ellos de miedo largaron sus millpas y se les perdieron y demas de eso an dubo Vesitando otr [manchado:os ??] endo a los pimas que donde esta<u>an los janos y jocomes y que ellos le respondian que no lo sa<u>ian que el que hablaba con ellos como su amigo sabria donde esta<u>an a lo cual les decia que ya los españoles estaban enojados con ellos y que iban a darles y matarlos juntos con los soldados y que esto abra ocho dias que se lo decia a los pimas y que sa<u>e muy bien que el go<u>ernador de los janos y jocomes Vino a el parajeque llaman del oso y alli se hiso amigo con el canito y los dos determina ron que el dho' go<u>ernador de los janos pasase a las demas rancherias de los pimas y se hisiese amigo con todos los go<u>ernadores de ellas para lo cual despacharon <V>n yndio pima a a<u>isarles y que este declarante y demas go<u>ernadores pimas . . ."

66. Francisco Pacheco Zevallos, September 20. "Criminal contra y Yndio llamado Canuto [*sic*] por haber sido traidor á la Real Corona, 1686." Archivo Histórico del Hidalgo de Parral, Chihuahua, México. Microfilm copy in the University of Arizona Main Library, film 0318, reel 1686B, fr. 758–803, Tucson. "Fuele preguntado Como en la ocaz.on que los seis indios Re<u>elados que binieron a su cassa les dijo a los de su naz.on mandando [manchado:los?] Como Cappn gen.l que Era ysiesen amistades Condhos yndios Re<u>eldes."

67. Don Antonio Barba Figueroa, Auto de Torment, November 7. "Criminal contra y Yndio llamado Canuto [*sic*] por haber sido traidor á la Real Corona, 1686." Archivo Histórico del Hidalgo de Parral, Chihuahua, México. Microfilm copy in the University of Arizona Main Library, film 0318, reel 1686B, fr. 758–803, Tucson.

68. Alonso de Villadiego Vascuña y Montoya, *Instrucción política y práctica judicial* (Madrid: Imprenta Juan de Ariztia, 1720), Google Books Online, 87, art. 322.

69. See Anton Daughters, "Torture in Colonial Spain's Northwestern Frontier: The Case of Joseph Romero 'Canito,' 1686," *Journal of the Southwest* 56, no. 2 (Summer 2014): 233–52.

70. Fracisco Pacheco Zevallos, "Criminal contra y Yndio llamado Canuto [*sic*] por haber sido traidor á la Real Corona, 1686." Archivo Histórico del Hidalgo de Parral, Chihuahua, México. Microfilm copy in the University of Arizona Main Library, film 0318, reel 1686B, fr. 758–803, Tucson. "Dixo aViendole dado tormento en <V>n dedo Pulgar que es Verdad que quando estubo con los janos jocomes Y Sumas despues de a<u>erles dado el rrecaudo que tiene declarado de parte de los Capess Jossephy Rom [manchado:o] de Vi<u>ar y juan fernandez de la fuente se enojaron Con el dhos yndios y que de miedo que les tubo les dijo que jurtasen la Ca<u>allada que pudiesen de os españoles y que no les dixo otra Cosa y Responde. Ffuele preguntado que como a tenido En el puesto de los ajos seis yndios de dhas' nasiones Re<u>eladas y trato de haserse amigo con ellos como se hizo y pretendio Como capitan general que era que todos los de su naçion hisiesen amistades con dhos' Yndios janos."

71. Don Antonio Barba Figueroa, Auto de Torment, November 7. "Criminal contra y Yndio llamado Canuto [*sic*] por haber sido traidor á la Real Corona, 1686." Archivo Histórico del Hidalgo de Parral, Chihuahua, México. Microfilm copy in the University of Arizona Main Library, film 0318, reel 1686B, fr. 758–803, Tucson. "Dixo que es Verdad que todos Sus parientes an pretendido matar a este confesante porque no les a consentido hacer las amistades con dhos xanos y xocomess Y que tenian tratado que en matandolo se arian todos amigos para matar a los españoless."

72. Don Antonio Barba Figueroa, Auto de Torment, November 7. "Criminal contra y Yndio llamado Canuto [*sic*] por haber sido traidor á la Real Corona, 1686." Archivo Histórico del Hidalgo de Parral, Chihuahua, México. Microfilm copy in the University of Arizona Main Library, film 0318, reel 1686B, fr. 758–803, Tucson. "Fuele preguntado. Como niega la <u>erdad pues abra tienpo de Dos años que en su cassa admitio por amigos a los yndios Re<u>elados Contra la rl Corona las naciones Sumas Jocomes y Janas y les dio tierras para que senbrese Diga la <u>erdad."

73. Don Antonio Barba Figueroa, Auto de Torment, November 7. "Criminal contra y Yndio llamado Canuto [*sic*] por haber sido traidor á la Real Corona, 1686." Archivo Histórico del Hidalgo de Parral, Chihuahua, México. Microfilm copy in the University of Arizona Main Library, film 0318, reel 1686B, fr. 758–803, Tucson. "Los pimas son Amigos de los españoles."

74. Canito seems to have become a Christian during his interrogation. During the early stages of the trial he is labeled a heathen.

75. Don Antonio Barba Figueroa, Auto de Torment, November 7. "Criminal contra y Yndio llamado Canuto [*sic*] por haber sido traidor á la Real Corona, 1686." Archivo Histórico del Hidalgo de Parral, Chihuahua, México. Microfilm copy in

the University of Arizona Main Library, film 0318, reel 1686B, fr. 758–803, Tucson. "Condena<u>a y Conden [manchado:e] al dho Yndio de nacion Pima nombrado Joseph rromo a Tormentto y Tormenttos para que en ellos declare la Verdad del Casso Y attentto a que en este Valle no ay potro En dondé podersselos dar Solo Tormentto de Torttura En las piernas mas abaxo de las espinillas Con dos palos atra<u>esados y aber el rematte de ellos Unos Cor deles por [donde?] Senpne Un palo y le ba dando las bueltas que el dar dispone."

76. Don Antonio Barba Figueroa, Auto de Torment, November 7. "Criminal contra y Yndio llamado Canuto [*sic*] por haber sido traidor á la Real Corona, 1686." Archivo Histórico del Hidalgo de Parral, Chihuahua, México. Microfilm copy in the University of Arizona Main Library, film 0318, reel 1686B, fr. 758–803, Tucson.

77. Don Antonio Barba Figueroa, Auto de Torment, November 7. "Criminal contra y Yndio llamado Canuto [*sic*] por haber sido traidor á la Real Corona, 1686." Archivo Histórico del Hidalgo de Parral, Chihuahua, México. Microfilm copy in the University of Arizona Main Library, film 0318, reel 1686B, fr. 758–803, Tucson. "Yque solo este Confesantte queria mal a los españoles como lle<u>a Confesado p que a<u>ian a Horcado a dho su hermano y que el diablo lo traia engañado."

78. Jorge Cañizares-Esguerra, *Puritan Conquistadors: Iberianizing the Atlantic, 1550–1700* (Palo Alto, Calif.: Stanford University Press, 2006).

79. Don Antonio Barba Figueroa, Auto de Torment, November 7. "Criminal contra y Yndio llamado Canuto [*sic*] por haber sido traidor á la Real Corona, 1686." Archivo Histórico del Hidalgo de Parral, Chihuahua, México. Microfilm copy in the University of Arizona Main Library, film 0318, reel 1686B, fr. 758–803, Tucson.

80. Andrew L. Knaut, *The Pueblo Revolt of 1680: Conquest and Resistance in Seventeenth-Century New Mexico* (Norman: University of Oklahoma Press, 1995), 177.

81. Don Antonio Barba Figueroa, Auto de Torment, November 14. "Criminal contra y Yndio llamado Canuto [*sic*] por haber sido traidor á la Real Corona, 1686." Archivo Histórico del Hidalgo de Parral, Chihuahua, México. Microfilm copy in the University of Arizona Main Library, film 0318, reel 1686B, fr. 758–803, Tucson. "Por esta rrazon y las que por mi eschrito lle<u>o alegadas Vmd mediante Justizia se a de ser<u>ir de mandar por de ningun balor de todas las aqusaziones contra el dho joseph rromo."

82. Don Antonio Barba Figueroa, Auto de Torment, November 14. "Criminal contra y Yndio llamado Canuto [*sic*] por haber sido traidor á la Real Corona, 1686." Archivo Histórico del Hidalgo de Parral, Chihuahua, México. Microfilm copy in the University of Arizona Main Library, film 0318, reel 1686B, fr. 758–803, Tucson. "En el Rl y minas de San joseph de Parral en Catorze de Junio de mill y Seissos y ochenta y siette ã. El s.r Gen.l Don joseph de neira y quiroga Ca<u>o del horden. de Santiago Go<u>.or y cappn Generalde este R.no de la nue<u>a <U>izcaya, Dijo, que por q, to El Gen.l Don Antonio Bar<u>a de Figueroa, Alcalde mayor. Y Capp.n a guerra, Y th.e de go<u>.or en la pro<u>.a de sonora. fulmino Caussa Criminal, Prinzipiada, Por franCo pacheco ze<u>allos. Su teniente, contra <V>n

Yndio de Nazion pima, llamado, Joseph Romo, Y por otro nombre, El Canito Capp.n General que fue en el tiempo de su jentilidad, de dha nazion Sobre, a<u>er Dado Passo. A los yndios Re<u>elados A la Rl corona, de las naziones. Sumas. Jocomes y Janos. Con El pretesto de que <U>engasen. la muerte de <V>n hermano Suyo, que la Rl Justizia a<u>ia. Castigado Por diferentes delictos, Cooperando, en pazes. Con dhos enemigos. Dando Y Consintiendo, DiFerentes tlatoles. que sobre Re<u>elarze. Contralos españoles Hazian; Cuya Causa."

83. Joseph de Neira y Quiroga, June 14, 1687, "Criminal contra y Yndio llamado Canito por haber sido tridor á la Real Corona, 1686." Archivo Histórico de Hidalgo de Parral, Chihuahua, México. Microfilm copy in the University of Arizona Main Library, film 0318, Reel 1686B, fr. 758–803, Tucson.

84. One of the conspirators had claimed that they wished to form an alliance with the Apache in the hopes that they would "become their comrades" and help them kill the priests and Spaniards, take their horses and cattle, and take from the merchants their "shirts and trousers and clothing." AGI Escribanía 400 C, Cuaderno 2, 133. Quoted in Yetman, *Conflict in Colonial Sonora*, 85.

85. Pérez de Ribas, *Triumphs of the Holy Faith*, 330.

86. Susan Deeds, *Defiance and Deference in Mexico's Colonial North: Indians Under Spanish Rule in Nueva Vizcaya* (Austin: University of Texas Press, 2003), 6.

87. See Florián Paucke, *Hacia allá y para acá (una estada entre los indios mocobíes, 1749–1767)*, 3 vols., ed. and trans. Edmundo Wernicke (Tucumán: Universidad Nacional de Tucumán, 1942). Quoted in Weber, *Bárbaros*, 84.

88. Cañeque, "Emotions of Power," 98.

Chapter Five

A version of this chapter was previously published as "The Paradox of Friendship: Loyalty and Betrayal on the Sonoran Frontier," *Journal of the Southwest* 56, no. 2 (2014): 319–44.

1. For an in-depth analysis of the Pima Revolt, see Russell C. Ewing, "The Pima Uprising, 1751–1752: A Study in Spain's Indian Policy" (PhD diss., University of California, Berkeley, 1934); Russell C. Ewing, "The Pima Outbreak in November, 1751," *New Mexico Historical Review* 8 (1938): 337–46; Russell C. Ewing, "The Pima Uprising of 1751," in *Greater America: Essays in Honor of Herbert E. Bolton*, ed. Adele Ogden and Engel Sluiter (Berkeley: University of California Press, 1945), 259–80; Russell C. Ewing, "Investigations into the Causes of the Pima Uprisings of 1751," *Mid-America* 23 (April 1941): 138–51; and Roberto Mario Solmón, "A Marginal Man: Luis of Sáric and the Pima Revolt of 1751," *Americas* 45, no.1 (July 1988): 61–77.

2. Bernard Fontana, *Before Rebellion: Letters & Reports of Jacobo Sedelmayr, S. J.*, trans. Daniel S. Matson, (Tucson: Arizona Historical Society, 1996), x.

3. See David Yetman, *Conflict in Colonial Sonora: Indians, Priests, and Settlers* (Albuquerque: University of New Mexico Press, 2012), 36–49.

4. Christian Perez notes, "Pimas were ritually required to undergo a sixteen day period of fasting and cleansing after killing an enemy. The rebels knew that they

would be on the offensive for weeks. Perhaps the strategy of burning the Spaniards alive allowed one or two men to take responsibility for all the deaths and left the others free to continue the fight while he/they retired to purify themselves." See Robert Christian Perez, "Indian Rebellions in Northwestern New Spain: A Comparative Analysis, 1695–1750s" (PhD diss., University of California, Riverside, 2004), 290.

5.   Joseph de Utrera, S. J., Declaration of Don Juan Manuel Ortiz Cortés, October 23, 1754, AGI, Guadalajara, 419.

6.   Ewing, "Pima Outbreak in November, 1751," 340n17.

7.   John L. Kessell, *Mission of Sorrows: Jesuit Guevavi and the Pimas, 1691–1767* (Tucson: University of Arizona Press, 1970), 108.

8.   Ewing, "Pima Outbreak in November, 1751," 346. A military contingent consisted of twenty-five or fifty men.

9.   The presidio of Fronteras was established in the early 1690s in response to Indian raids in the area, mostly from Apache, Jano, Jocome, and Suma Indians, and was the only professional military company on the Sonoran frontier until the establishment of Terrenate in 1742. Fronteras had a military garrison of about fifty men.

10.   For population figures, see Pedro Tamarón y Romeral, *Demostración del vastísimo obispado de la Nueva Vizcaya, 1765: Durango, Sinaloa, Sonora, Arizona, Nuevo México, Chihuahua y porciones de Texas, Coahuila y Zacatecas,* ed. Bito Alessio Robles, (Antigua Librería Robledo, de J. Porrúa e hijos, 1937), 31. Sigüenza, *Libra astronómica y filosófica,* ed. José Goas (Mexico, 1954), 176, 363.

11.   Roberto Mario Solmón, "A Marginal Man: Luis of Sáric and the Pima Revolt of 1751," *Americas* 45, no. 1 (July 1988): 64. The six presidos in Sonora were San Carlos de Buenavista, San Miguel de Horcasitas, Santa Gertrudis de Altar, San Ignacio de Tubac, Terrenate, and Fronteras.

12.   Diego Ortiz Parrilla, declaration of Luis Oacpicagigua, March 24, 1752[a], AGI, Guadalajara, 419.

13.   Ortiz Parrilla's official title in 1751 was Lieutenant Colonel of the Royal Armies, Proprietary Captain of the Dragoons of Vera Cruz, Commandant of the detachments in the city of [Puebla] de los Ángeles, Governor and Captain General of this kingdom of Nueva Andalucía, Provinces of Sinaloa, Sonora, and the others adjoining, their presidios, frontiers, and the coasts of the Southern Sea. Ortiz Parrilla was governor of Sinaloa and Sonora until 1753. In 1756, he assumed command of the presidio of San Sabá in south-central Texas. And from June 1764 to December 1765, he served as governor of Coahuila.

14.   John Kessell, *Mission of Sorrows: Jesuit Guevavi and the Pimas, 1691–1767* (Tucson: University of Arizona Press, 1970), 109. For official policy, see *Recopilación de leyes de los Reynos de las Indias,* 4 Tomos (Madrid, 1681), http://fondosdigitales.us.es/media/books/752/recopilacion-de-leyes-de-los-reynos-de-las-indias.pdf.

15.   There is no consensus among scholars as to the actual number of dead. Most agree that the number of dead Spaniards was more than 100, but are less sure as to the number of dead Indians. Ewing places that total number of dead at about 150.

16. These concerns did not fall on deaf ears, for in the following year the presidios at Tubac and Altar were constructed, each garrisoned by at least fifty men. At the time of its establishment Tubac was a Pima *ranchería*. In time it became Arizona's first Spanish-speaking settlement.

17. Solmón, "Marginal Man," 71. For a discussion of "first generation" nativist movements, see Susan Deeds, *Defiance and Deference in Colonial Mexico: Indians Under Spanish Rule in Nueva Vizcaya* (Austin: University of Texas Press, 2003); Charlotte Grady, *The Tepehuán Revolt of 1616* (Salt Lake City: University of Utah Press, 2000).

18. See Patricia Escandón, "Economía y sociedad en Sonora: 1767–1821," in *Historia general de Sonora, Vol. 2: De la conquista al estado libre y soberano de Sonora*, ed. Sergio Ortega Noriega (Hermosillo, Mexico: Gobierno del Estado de Sonora, 1996), 275–98; José Refugio de la Torre Curiel, *Twilight of the Mission Frontier: Shifting Interethnic Alliances and Social Organization in Sonora, 1768–1855* (Palo Alto, Calif.: Stanford University Press, 2012).

19. Cynthia Radding, *Landscapes of Power and Identity: Comparative Histories in the Sonoran Desert and the Forests of Amazonia from Colony to Republic* (Durham, N.C.: Duke University Press, 2005), 166, 181.

20. Robert H. Jackson, *Race, Caste, and Status: Indians in Colonial Spanish America* (Albuquerque: University of New Mexico Press, 1999), 91.

21. Solmón, "Marginal Man," 70.

22. Solmón, for instance, writes that "Indian rebellions on the northern frontier were tribal responses to increased pressure from missionaries, mixed blood frontiersmen, Indian colonists, merchants, miners, free and slave blacks, and even from Spaniards themselves." See Solmón, "Marginal Man," 61.

23. Laura Matthew, *Memories of Conquest: Becoming Mexican in Colonial Guatemala* (Chapel Hill: University of North Carolina Press, 2012), 6. See also Laura Matthew and Michael Oudijk, eds., *Indian Conquistadors: Indigenous Allies in the Conquest of Mesoamerica* (Norman: University of Oklahoma Press, 2007).

24. David Weber, *Bárbaros: Spaniards and Their Savages in the Age of Enlightenment* (New Haven, Conn.: Yale University Press, 2006), 16.

25. John G. Douglas and William M. Graves, "The Colonial Period in the American Southwest," in *New Mexico and the Pimería Alta*, ed. John G. Douglas and William M. Graves (Boulder: University Press of Colorado, 2017), 5.

26. Raphael Brewster Folsom, *The Yaquis and the Empire: Violence, Spanish Imperial Power, and Native Resilience in Colonial Mexico* (New Haven, Conn.: Yale University Press, 2014), 1–12.

27. "The dance of historical change," writes David Harvey, "becomes as vulnerable to the sexual whims and fantasies of aging dictators, for example, as it does to coherent mass movements. And even when mass movements are at work, the determination of what contradictions are seen as primary is always up for grabs. Politics must engage with all moments of the social process simultaneously, establishing its own counter-coherences within and correspondence rules between discourses, institutions, social relations, power politics, and the imaginary and material prac-

tices." See David Harvey, *Justice, Nature, and the Geography of Difference* (Hoboken, N.J.: Blackwell Publishers, 1996), 107.

28. Ivy Schweitzer, *Perfecting Friendship: Politics and Affiliation in Early American Literature* (Chapel Hill: University of North Carolina Press, 2006), 16.

29. James Rodney Hastings, "People of Reason and Others: The Colonization of Sonora to 1767," *Arizona and the West* 3, no. 4 (Winter 1961): 321–40.

30. Diego Ortiz Parrilla, letter to Viceroy Juan Francisco de Güemes y Horcasitas, December 1751, BANC, Reel 1:3 M-15–3 M-16. "Los extragos executados por los q.ᵉ empuñaron las Armas fueron (señor) irremediables por q.ᵉ no haviendose penetrado ô llegado a mi noticia ni a la de âquellos Padres Missioneros la mas minima presumpta ni el menor rumor, ô indicio de la conspiraz.ᵒⁿ . . . y lo confiesan todas estas Gentes, de modo q.ᵉ las q.ᵉ perecieron y escaparon con la fuga se hallaban en los Pueblos revelados vajo la satisfaccion, y confianza q.ᵉ dictaba la imbariable amistad, y buena correspondencia de âquellos Naturales."

31. Joseph Utrera, S. J., Declaration of Don Juan Manuel Ortiz Cortés, October 2, 1754, AGI, Guadalajara, 419.

32. According to Oacpicagigua's testimony he reduced the pueblos of "Tucubavi and Bochuruni to the pueblo of Busani; those of Horcam and Yuubupac to the pueblo of Sario; those of Conteupac and Vecababia to the pueblo of Alquimuri; those of Comari, Bapac, and Quiquimicuc, Tojababa, and Aquitum—in the Papago nation—to the pueblo of Tubutama; the ranchería of Chiuctiut to the pueblo of Santa Theresa; the large ranchería of Guboc and that of Aquituni to the pueblo of Ati; the ranchería of Bamori and that of Camaquibutoca to the pueblo of Oquitoa; the ranchería of Tucson to the pueblo of Pitic; and that of Quitatac to the pueblo of Caborca . . . he gathered [at Tubutama] the ranchería of Pipian and the pueblo of Ymuris. He reduced many other unsettled and insolent Indians to the [pueblo] of Santa Maria Soanca. Likewise, he subdued the ranchería of Bapcomari to the pueblo of Cocospera, gathered the [ranchería] of Tuburisac in Guevavi, and reduced the [rancherías] of Upiatuban and Concuc, and the pueblo of Arivaca, which were composed of very few Indians. He also united the two rancherías of Toamuc and Suctuni. And in addition to this, he set in motion the reduction to the pueblo of various families that inhabited the wilderness and uplands, dispersed and distant from each other." See Diego Ortiz Parrilla, letter to Viceroy Juan Francisco de Güemes y Horcasitas, December 1751, BANC, Reel 1:3 M-15–3 M-16; and Diego Ortiz Parrila, declaration of Luis Oacpicagigua, March 24, 1752a, AGI, Guadalajara, 419.

33. Diego Ortiz Parrilla, letter to Viceroy Juan Francisco de Güemes y Horcasitas, December 1751, BANC, Reel 1:3 M-15–3 M-16. "Êra, y ha sido Amado, y querido tanto de los suios como de la Gente de razón con quien se manejaba muy sosiable afectuoso, Político, y tan demasiadamente liberal q.ᵉ caia en el exceso de Prodigo, y desperdiciador de sus Vienes . . . cuias circunstancias conocidas de todos han hecho commober â Grâl lastima por la repentina novedad, y perdición de un Yndio q.ᵉ sin cultivo havia descollado, y distinguidose con tantas prendas naturales dignas de recomendacion . . . Y por ultimo puedo asegurar â V. Êxa. Que en su Linea, y

naturaleza era el Vasallo mas Vil, y leal q.ᵉ tenia su Mag.ᵈ en todas estas Naciones reducidas."

34. The original document reads "De confianza," which I translated in the text as "trusted."

35. Ortiz Parrilla states that as a boy Oacpicagigua had gone with his father, who was then also governor of Sáric, on campaigns against the Seris.

36. Diego Ortiz Parrilla, letter to Viceroy Juan Francisco de Güemes y Horcasitas, December 1751, BANC, Reel 1:3 M-15–3 M-16. ". . . se portó como pudiera hacerlo el mas Zeloso Capitan, en servicio de su soberano, constaronme de Vista las fatigas q.ᵉ padeciò en la empresa el ardiente Êspiritu con q.ᵉ alentò a los suyos a los travajos, y el Generoso corazon con q.ᵉ alegre se exponia el primero â los riesgos, y assi mismo la Ovediencia, y subordinacion q.ᵉ manifestó en su proceder hasta q.ᵉ se concluiò la empresa."

37. On go-betweens, see Alida Metcalf, *Go-Betweens and the Colonization of Brazil, 1500–1600* (Austin: University of Texas Press, 2005), 1–15. See also Nancy Hagerdorn, "'A Friend to Go Between Them': The Interpreter as Cultual Broker during Anglo-Iroquois Councils, 1740–70," *Ethnohistory* 35, no. 1 (Winter 1988): 60–80.

38. See, for instance, Karen Spalding, *Huarochirí: An Andean Society Under Inca and Spanish Rule* (Palo Alto, Calif.: Stanford University Press, 1984).

39. Yanna Yannakakis, *The Art of Being In-Between: Native Intermediaries, Indian Identity, and Local Rule in Colonial Oaxaca* (Durham, N.C.: Duke University Press, 2008), 63.

40. Solmón, "Marginal Man," 75.

41. Diego Ortiz Parrilla, declaration of Luis Oacpicagigua, March 24, 1752a, AGI, Guadalajara, 419. The document does not say what the additional title was. The process of asking each new administrator to confirm one's title was a common practice throughout the Americas. In Peru, Viceroy Mendoza complained about the proclivity of Indians to litigate everything and of their insistence to have each new corregidor confirm in writing their titles of authority. See Colin M. MacLachlan, *Spain's Empire in the New World: The Role of Ideas in Institutional and Social Change* (Berkeley: University of California Press, 1988), 48.

42. Henry F. Dobyns, *The Papago People* (Indian Tribal Series, 1972), 23.

43. Kessell, *Mission of Sorrows*, 116.

44. Juan Pablo Gil-Osle, "Early Modern Illusions of Perfect Male Friendship: The Case of Cervantes's 'El curioso impertenente,'" *Bulletin of the Cervantes Society of America* 29, no. 1 (Spring 2009): 85–115.

45. Christian Perez, "Indian Rebellions," 297.

46. Kessell, *Mission of Sorrows*, 103.

47. Diego Oritz Parrilla, letter to Viceroy Juan Francisco de Güemes y Horcasitas, December 1751, BANC, Reel 1:3 M-15–3 M-16. "Se me ofrecen motivos para admirar, y aun saca lagrimas a mis ojos el suseso contemplado la honrradez, fidelidad, y exfuerso, con que este famoso Yndio se hà manejado en muchos Lances q.ᵉ hà podido dar evidentes muestras de su summa lealtad."

48. Anthony Rotundo has suggested that emotionally charged friendships among middle-class men in nineteenth-century U.S. society were extremely common even among the most masculine of men. An early nineteenth-century journal entry by a young engineer, Wyck Vanderhoof, reads: "We retired early, but long was the time before our eyes were closed in slumber, for this was the last night that we will be together for the present, and our hearts were full of that true friendship which could not find utterances in words, we laid our heads upon each other's bosoms and wept, it may be unmanly to weep, but I do not care, the spirit was touched." This entry shows that while Vanderhoof was concerned with his masculinity, his concern did not interfere with his display of emotion. It should also be noted that he was not homosexual, and he soon married. See Anthony Rotundo, "Romantic Friendship: Male Intimacy and Middle-Class Youth in the Northern United States, 1800–1900," *Journal of Social History* 23, no. 1 (1989): 5. See also Peter Robb, *Unequal Friendship: Europeans and Indians in Early Calcutta* (Oxford: Oxford University Press, 2014).

49. Catherine Lutz and Geoffrey White, "The Anthropology of Emotions," *Annual Review of Anthropology* 15 (1986): 413. See also Angel Rama, *The Lettered City*, trans. and ed. John Charles Chasteen (Durham, N.C.: Duke University Press, 1996).

50. Rebecca Earle, "Letters and Love in Colonial Latin America," *Americas* 62, no. 1 (July 2005): 40; Weber, *Bárbaros*, 101.

51. Andrea Noble, "The Politics of Emotion in the Mexican Revolution: The Tears of Pancho Villa," in *Latin American Popular Culture: Politics, Media, Affect*, ed. Geoffrey Kantaris and Roy O'Bryen (Woodbridge, UK: Tamesis, 2013), 251.

52. Diego Oritz Parrilla, letter to Viceroy Juan Francisco de Güemes y Horcasitas, December 1751, BANC, Reel 1:3 M-15–3 M-16. See also Weber, *Bárbaros*, 8.

53. "Great Cortes is far away, the man who discovered all these huge kingdoms of the New World. He rules beyond the equator as far as the star of Capricorn, and though so far away, he does not forget me." Quoted in J. H. Elliot, "The Mental World of Hernan Cortés," in *Spain and its World, 1500–1700* (New Haven, Conn.: Yale University Press, 1989), 27–41. Johannes Dantiscus (1485–1548) was the German-born prince-bishop of Wamia and bishop of Chelmno.

54. See Thomas Sheridan, ed., *Empire of Sand: The Seri Indians and the Struggle for Spanish Sonora, 1645–1803* (Tucson: University of Arizona Press, 1999), 17–19, 139–42.

55. Letter written by Father Gaspar Estiger, San Ignacio, April 22, 1750. BANC MSS C-B 840, item 216. The 1749 Seri Revolt highlighted some of the most disturbing realities of colonial rule. When Seris violently protested the unjust redistribution of their land to Spanish settlers, their women were deported to Guatemala and Yucatán as punishment. This gross abuse of power stepped over the invisible line of what was an acceptable level of exploitaton, forcing the men, who allied with Pima, Piatos, and Apaches, to rise in rebellion against Spanish rule. Seri hostilities continued off and on for the next several years, making and unmaking peace treaties with Ortiz Parrilla's successor Pablo Arce y Arroyo for the return of their lands and their women.

56. Ignacio Pfefferkorn, *Descripción de la provincia de Sonora*, trans. Armando Hopkins Durazo (Hermosillo, Mexico: Gobierno del Estado de Sonora, 1983), 123. During this raid Oacpicagigua and his Pima soldiers managed to kill twenty-two Seris and capture twenty-eight more as prisoners. See Father Gaspar Estiger, San Ignacio, April 22, 1750. BANC MSS C-B 840, item 216.

57. Roberto Mario Solmón, *Indian Revolts in Northern New Spain* (Lanham, Md.: University Press of America, 1991), 8. See also Lance Blyth, *Chiricahuas and Janos: Communities of Violence in the Southwestern Borderlands, 1680–1880* (Lincoln: University of Nebraska Press, 2012), chap. 3.

58. Fontana, *Before Rebellion*, xii; Perez, "Indian Rebellions," 307.

59. Diego Oritz Parrilla, letter to Viceroy Juan Francisco de Güemes y Horcasitas, December 1751, BANC, Reel 1:3 M-15–3 M-16.

60. On the Reglamento of 1772, see Sidney Brinckerhoff and Odie Faulk, *Lances for the King: A Study of Frontier Military System of Northern New Spain*, with a translation of the Royal Regulations of 1772 (Phoenix: Arizona Historical Foundation, 1965), 32–33.

61. Diego Ortiz Parrilla, declaration of Luis Oacpicagigua, March 24, 1752a, AGI, Guadalajara, 419.

62. The *alférez* was generally the next highest-ranking official after the *mayordomo*.

63. Diego Ortiz Parrilla, declaration of Luis Oacpicagigua, March 24, 1752a, AGI, Guadalajara, 419.

64. James C. Scott, *The Moral Economy of the Peasant: Subsistence and Rebellion in Southeast Asia* (New Haven, Conn.: Yale University Press, 1976); James C. Scott, *Domination and the Arts of Resistance: Hidden Transcripts* (New Haven, Conn.: Yale University Press, 1990).

65. According to Roberto Marío Solmón *capitanes de guerra* were often granted this privilege in addition to the right to wear Spanish clothing and use Spanish titles. See Robert Solmón, "Tarahumara Resistance to Mission Congregation in Northern New Spain, 1580–1710," *Ethnohistory* 24, no. 4 (Autumn 1977): 385.

66. Solmón, "Marginal Man," 75.

67. George Mosse, "Friendship and Nationhood: About the Promise and Failure of German Nationalism," *Journal of Contemporary History* 17, no. 2 (April 1982): 351–67. Mosse also argues that prior to the First World War, friendship between men, which had come to "symbolize the autonomy of personal relationships . . . as part of a highly self-conscious cult based upon the free interplay of personalities and the acceptance of individual difference," had become incompatible with the demands of modern nationalism, and thus friendship of this kind declined. The First World War helped re-create a unique and intimate bond between men who shared a similar experience of war.

68. Folsom, *Yaquis and the Empire*, 45.

69. Blyth, *Chiricahua and Janos*, 7.

70. *Calidad* essentially refers to the quality of the individual in relation to their society. *Calidad* can be affected by a host of factors such as race, ethnicity, gender, wealth, legitimacy, honor, or behavior. For a discussion of private and public space, see Ann

Twinam, *Public Lives, Private Secrets: Gender, Honor, Sexuality and Illegitimacy in Colonial Spanish America* (Palo Alto, Calif.: Stanford University Press, 1999).

71. Diego Ortiz Parrilla, letter to Viceroy Juan Francisco de Güemes y Horcasitas, December, 1751, BANC, Reel 1:3 M-15–3 M-16.

72. Pekka Hämäläinen, *The Comanche Empire* (New Haven, Conn.: Yale University Press, 2008), 8.

73. Anya Jabour, "Male Friendship and Masculinity in the Early National South: William Wirt and His Friends," *Journal of the Early Republic* 20, no. 1 (Spring 2000); Donald Yacovone, "Abolitionists and the 'Language of Fraternal Love,'" in *Meanings for Manhood: Constructions of Masculinity in Victorian America*, ed. Mark C. Cames and Clyde Griffen (Chicago: University of Chicago Press, 1990), 85–95; Samuel J. Watson, "Flexible Gender Roles During the Market Revolution: Family, Friendship, Marriage, and Masculinity Among U.S. Army Officers, 1815–1846," *Journal of Social History* 29 (Fall 1995): 81–106.

74. Jabour, "Male Friendship and Masculinity," 85.

75. Just like Ortiz Parrilla, the two previous governors of this region, Huydobro and Vildósola, had similarly contentious interactions with the Jesuits. Ewing argues that Huydobro encouraged his Indian charges to purposely oppose the Jesuits.

76. See John Leddy Phelan, *The Millennial Kingdom of the Franciscans in The New World* (Berkeley: University of California, 1970).

77. Weber, *Bárbaros*, 102.

78. Stuart Voss, *On the Periphery of Nineteenth-Century Mexico: Sonora and Sinaloa, 1810–1877* (Tucson: University of Arizona Press, 1982), 11.

79. Brandon Bayne, "A Passionate Pacification: Sacrifice and Suffering in the Jesuit Missions of Northwestern New Spain, 1594–1767" (PhD diss., Harvard Theological Seminary, 2012), 65.

80. As José Refugio de la Torre Curiel notes, the mission institution had many purposes, which included "congregating dispersed populations, reorganizing Indian communities along the lines of the corporate structures of the Spanish *pueblo*, promoting religious conversion, facilitating cultural exchanges, securing new territories, settling formerly transient groups, warding off the territorial ambitions of other nations, producing foodstuffs for internal consumption and local markets, activating local economies, and supplying labor." Torre Curiel, *Twilight of the Mission Frontier*, xxiv.

81. Voss, *On the Periphery of Nineteenth-Century Mexico*, 9.

82. Yetman, *Conflict in Colonial Sonora*, 1–3.

83. Kessell, *Mission of Sorrows*, 108. Taking children from indigenous families was a common practice. Often children were given to missionaries as gifts in order to solidify alliances. See Folsom, *Yaquis and the Empire*, 61; James Brooks, *Captives and Cousins: Slavery, Kinship and Community in the Southwest Borderlands* (Chapel Hill: University of North Carolina Press, 2002); Blyth, *Chiricahua and Janos*; and Hämäläinen, *The Comanche Empire*.

84. Carlos de Rojas, letter to Governor Pablo de Arce y Arroyo, Arizpe, January 18, 1754, AGI, Guadalajara, 419. See also Fontana, *Before Rebellion*, xxiv.

85. Carlos de Rojas, letter to Governor Pablo de Arce y Arroyo, Arizpe, January 18, 1754, AGI, Guadalajara, 419.

86. Gaspar Stiger, quoted in Carlos de Rojas, letter to Governor Pablo de Arce y Arroyo, Arizpe, January 18, 1754, AGI, Guadalajara, 419.

87. Diego Ortiz Parrilla, declaration of Luis Oacpicagigua, March 24, 1752a, AGI, Guadalajara, 419.

88. Joseph de Utrera, declaration of Ignacio Romero, 1752, AGI, Guadalajara, 419.

89. Kessell, *Mission of Sorrows*, 116.

90. Diego Ortiz Parrilla, declaration of Luis Oacpicagigua, 1752a, March 24, AGI, Guadalajara, 419. "He benido yo a cumplir con lo que me manda mi Governador a lo qual le dijo el P͆. Yo no quiero ver esa carta del Governador pues otras que me ha escrito las he tirado en la Lumbre."

91. Carlos de Rojas, letter to Governor Pablo de Arce y Arroyo, January, 18, 1754, AGI, Guadalajara, 419.

92. Kessell, *Mission of Sorrows*, 103.

93. Juan Nentvig, S. J., *Rudo Ensayo: A Description of Sonora and Arizona in 1764*, trans. and annot. Alberto Francisco Pradeau and Robert R. Rasmussen (Tucson: University of Arizona Press, 1980), 55.

94. Kessell, *Mission of Sorrows*, 103.

95. Kessell, *Mission of Sorrows*, 116.

96. Diego Ortiz Parrilla, declaration of Luis Oacpicagigua, March 24, 1752a, AGI, Guadalajara, 419.

97. Nathan Wachtel, *Los vencidos: Los indios del Perú frente a la conquista española (1530–1570)* (Madrid: Alianza, 1976), 224.

98. As quoted in Dana Velasco Murillo, *Urban Indians in a Silver City: Zacatecas, Mexico, 1546–1810* (Palo Alto, Calif.: Stanford University Press, 2016), 9.

99. Diego Ortiz Parrilla, declaration of Luis Oacpicagigua, March 24, 1752a, AGI, Guadalajara, 419. "Que bestuario es ese que traes no sabes que eso cor[r]esponde solamente a los Españoles? Anda y tira todo eso y tapa un Taparrabo y lebantandose enojado de la Silla le señalo unos Cargages que estaban arrimados a la Pared y le dijo estas son tus armas y las que debes cargar, haciendo lo que los demas Yndios que es mantenerse com Burras, Conejos, Liebres, Benados, Ratones, Y carneros Sinbarrones, y tampoco debes tu tener Bestias Caballos, Mulas, Manadas, Bacas, ni Cabras."

100. Spanish Ordinances of 1573. Quoted in David Weber, *The Spanish Frontier in North America* (New Haven, Conn.: Yale University Press, 2009), 106.

101. Diego Ortiz Parrilla, declaration of Luis Oacpicagigua, March 24, 1752a, AGI, Guadalajara, 419. See also Bernard Fontana, *Before Rebellion: Letters & Reports of Jacobo Sedelmayr, S. J.* (Tucson: Arizona Historical Society, 1996), xii; Kessell, *Mission of Sorrows*, 103.

102. Cheryl English Martin, "Popular Speech and Social Order in Northern Mexico, 1650–1830," *Comparative Studies in Society and History* 32, no. 2 (April 1990): 305–24. See also William Taylor, *Drinking, Homicide and Rebellion in Colonial Mexican Villages* (Palo Alto, Calif.: Stanford University Press, 1986).

103. Diego Ortiz Parrilla, declaration of Luis Oacpicagigua, March 24, 1752a, AGI, Guadalajara, 419.

104. Diego Ortiz Parrilla, declaration of Luis Oacpicagigua, March 24, 1752a, AGI, Guadalajara, 419.

105. Diego Ortiz Parrilla, declaration of Luis Oacpicagigua, March 24, 1752a, AGI, Guadalajara, 419. "Te habras detenido, y aquerenciado, con el S^r. Gov^or."

106. In Joseph de Utrera, declaration of Manuel Ortiz Cortéz, October 1754, AGI, Gudalajara, 419, Cortéz argues the complete opposite. In his testimony, given to a Jesuit father two years after the uprising, he states that he had heard him say that the fathers always treated him "with intimacy and trust" and that "that Lord Governor Parrilla had taught and instructed [Oacpicagigua] how to respond." Ortiz Cortés's testimony is typical of the contradictory nature of many of these reports. It is also possible that Ortiz Cortés was simply trying to please his interrogator with proper responses.

107. Diego Ortiz Parrilla, declaration of Joaquin de Rahum, January 8, 1752b, AGI, Guadalajara 419.

108. Kessell, *Mission of Sorrows*, 103. Keller's vituperative demeanor was not universal among all the Jesuits and may have, according to Kessell, been a symptom of his heavy drinking.

109. Diego Oritz Parrilla, letter to Viceroy Juan Francisco de Güemes y Horcasitas, December 1751, BANC, reel 1:3 M-15–3 M16.

110. Sophie Woodward, "Looking Good, Feeling Right—Aesthetics of the Self," in *Clothing as Material Culture*, ed. Susanne Küchler and Daniel Miller (Oxford: Berg, 2005), 21. See also Arnold J. Bauer, *Goods, Power, History: Latin America's Material Culture* (Cambridge: Cambridge University Press, 2001); Rebecca Earle, "Nationalism and National Costume in Spanish America" in *The Politics of Dress in Asia and the Americas*, ed. Mina Roces and Louise Edwards (Sussex: Sussex Academic Press, 2007).

111. Rebecca Earle, *The Body of the Conquistador: Food, Race and the Colonial Experience in Spanish America, 1492–1700* (New York: Cambridge University Press, 2012), 7.

112. Diego Ortiz Parrilla, declaration of Luis Oacpicagigua, March 24, 1752a, AGI, Guadalajara, 419.

113. Letter from Father Juan Nentvig to father visitor General Joseph de Utrera, AGI, Guadalajara, 419; BANC Reel 1, 3M-8.

114. Joseph Utrera, Declaration of Don Juan Manuel Ortiz Cortés, October 23, 1754, AGI, Guadalajara, 419.

115. *Informe* to his excellency by Father Miguel Quijano, BANC MSS C-B 840, item 216.

116. Kessell, *Mission of Sorrows*, 109. The concept of a "just war" was different for Spaniards than it was for the Indians. It implied that the Spanish had the absolute right to conquer and rule over them. Should the Indians resist, it was the right of the Spanish to wage war on them. This attitude was a carryover from the *reconquesta*.

117. Diego Oritz Parrilla, letter to ViceroyJuan Francisco de Güemes y Horcasitas, December 1751, BANC, Reel 1:3 M-15–3 M-16.

118. Joseph Utrera, Declaration of Don Juan Manuel Ortiz Cortés, October 23, 1754, AGI, Guadalajara, 419. In this testimony Father Nentvig summarily denies that any of this accusations were true.

119. Gregorio Antonio Romero, Soamca, October 16, 1754. Quoted in Kessell, *Misson of Sorrows*, 109.

120. Joseph Utrera, Declaration of Don Juan Manuel Ortiz Cortés, October 23, 1754a, AGI, Guadalajara, 419.

121. Joseph Utrera, Declaration of Manuel, Governor of Tubutama, October 29, 1754b, AGI, Guadalajara, 419.

122. Kessell, *Mission of Sorrows*, 111.

123. Solmón, "Marginal Man," 73.

124. Solmón, "Marginal Man," 64.

Conclusion

1. Inga Clendinnen, *Ambivalent Conquests: Maya and Spaniard in Yucatan, 1517–1570*, 2nd ed. (Cambridge: Cambridge University Press, 2003), 7.

2. Clendinnen, *Ambivalent Conquests*, 7.

3. Clendinnen, *Ambivalent Conquests*, 7.

4. For an excellent study of the role of frontiers, see Tom Sheridan and Donna Guy, eds., *Contested Ground: Comparative Frontiers on the Northern and Southern Edges of the Spanish Empire* (Tucson: University of Arizona Press, 1989).

5. David Weber, *The Spanish Frontier in North America* (New Haven, Conn.: Yale University Press, 2009), 7.

INDEX

ABOUT THE AUTHOR

Ignacio Martínez is an assistant professor at the University of Texas at El Paso. His scholarly interests include the Atlantic World, the social and intellectual history of colonial Mexico, the Spanish borderlands, and the history of emotions.